# THE DEVELOPING CHILD

Bringing together and illuminating the remarkable recent research on development from infancy to adolescence, for students of developmental psychology, policy makers, parents, and all others concerned with the future of the next generation.

**Series Editors**

Jerome Bruner
New York University

Michael Cole
University of California, San Diego

Annette Karmiloff-Smith
Neurocognitive Development Unit,
Institute of Child Health, London

# PATHWAYS TO LANGUAGE

## FROM FETUS TO ADOLESCENT

Kyra Karmiloff
Annette Karmiloff-Smith

HARVARD UNIVERSITY PRESS
*Cambridge, Massachusetts, and London, England*

First Harvard University Press paperback edition, 2002

*Library of Congress Cataloging-in-Publication Data*
Karmiloff, Kyra.
    Pathways to language : from fetus to adolescent / Kyra Karmiloff and Annette
Karmiloff-Smith.
      p.    cm. — (The developing child)
Includes bibliographical references and index.
ISBN 0-674-00476-0 (cloth)
ISBN 0-674-00835-9 (pbk.)
1. Language acquisition.  I. Karmiloff-Smith, Annette.  II. Title.  III. Series.
P118 .K29 2001
401'.93—dc21        00-050583

# CONTENTS

It might seem strange for a book about language acquisition to have the word "fetus" in its title. Of course we do not mean to imply that the unborn baby already knows and understands language. But the fascinating journey of language acquisition does indeed begin during intrauterine life and continues through to adolescence and beyond. Starting with the fetus's growing sensitivity during its last months in the uterus to the particularities of its mother's voice and rhythms of its native language, linguistic capacities emerge far earlier than researchers had previously thought. Then, from the moment of birth onward, the infant is continually processing the speech that fills his world. New and exciting research techniques have allowed us to probe the multileveled processes of learning language. Well before the child produces his first words, we now know that he has been actively processing the sounds, rhythms, and basic building blocks of the words and grammar of his mother tongue.

Even once language production is well under way, there is still much to learn. The child does not simply reproduce what he hears, but actively creates language, experimenting with the rules that he has extracted from the input. Parents have listened with wonder to the innovative productions of these budding linguists and marveled at the nature of children's inventiveness. Who can fail to admire the little two-year-old who gazes at a firework display and exclaims, "Look, Mommy, light-bubbles!" or the three-year-old who announces that "Daddy's brooming the kitchen"? But language acquisition goes well beyond learning to produce words, grammar, conversation, and stories. Children become socialized through interpersonal interaction, and here language plays a central role.

In writing our book, we refer to the fetus as "it" and, to avoid using a single gender throughout, we refer to the infant and child as "he" or "she," alternating the pronouns from chapter to chapter. We provide rough guidelines as to the ages at which children reach various developmental milestones in their language acquisition. It is crucial for the reader to bear in mind, however, that the pathways to language can vary depending on individual differences. One child may produce his first words at nine months, whereas another may not say anything recognizable until sixteen months or beyond. The same applies to the later onset of grammar: it differs considerably from child to child.

Throughout the book, our aim is to provide the reader with an exciting yet accessible introduction to all of these intricacies of developmental psycholinguistics—the study of how language develops in children. The book gives a broad overview of the field, and at the end of the book we provide a list of further readings for each chapter.

This is our second daughter-mother book venture. The research and writing often took place over electronic mail well into the small hours of the night between London and Cambridge, England, after one of us had finished changing diapers ("nappies" in our version of English) and telling bedtime stories, and the other had dragged home from her research lab. After each draft chapter was completed over e-mail, we met during weekends to discuss each other's contributions. So it is with special gratitude that we extend thanks to our families: to little Misha, our son/grandson, who played happily on the carpet when we got together (and who posed for the brain imaging illustration in Chapter 2); to Dylan, who eavesdropped on our discussions about the book while still in utero; and to our respective partners, Gideon and Mark, for their patience when we disappeared into our studies every weekend and most evenings. We also express particular thanks to Julia Grant and Elena Longhi for chasing missing references; to Elena Lieven, Steven Pinker, and Daniel Slobin for reading relevant sections of Chapter 5; and to two anonymous re-viewers for their useful comments on the whole book. Last but not least, our thanks to Elizabeth Knoll, Kirsten Giebutowski, and Julie Carlson of Harvard University Press for their encouragement and editorial help.

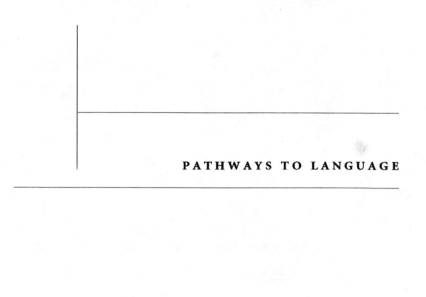

PATHWAYS TO LANGUAGE

# 1

## WHAT IS LANGUAGE ACQUISITION?

Language acquisition is a journey that begins in the fluid world of the womb and continues throughout childhood, adolescence, and even beyond. During this long period of acquisition, the learner faces a vast array of challenges. From the young infant's clumsy attempts to get the articulatory system in his mouth, throat, and larynx to produce the specific sounds of his native tongue, through to the much later complexities of producing and understanding long narratives, the child's language capacities undergo numerous changes. Innovative research techniques now allow us to follow this amazing journey closer than ever before.

In the past, the acquisition literature situated the onset of language at about twelve months, when children produce their first recognizable words. We have now come to realize that acquisition gets under way long before this, even prior to birth. From as early as twenty weeks gestation, the hearing system of the fetus is sufficiently developed to enable it to begin processing some of the sounds that filter through the amniotic liquid. The fetus's world is filled with a cacophony of gurgles and grumbles from the mother's body, along with the constant rhythm of her heartbeats. These noises provide early auditory stimulation. But most stimulating of all are the filtered sounds of language.

From the sixth month of gestation onward, the fetus spends most of its waking time processing these very special linguistic sounds, growing familiar with the unique qualities of its mother's voice and of the language or languages that she speaks. It also becomes sensitive to the prosody—the intonation of sentences and rhythm patterns within words—that structures her speech. In its last three months in the womb, the fetus is busy eavesdropping on its mother's conversations—an important preparation for life in the outside world. Already equipped with some experience of what language sounds like, the newborn comes into the world prepared to pay special attention to human speech, and specifically to his mother's voice. These earliest intrauterine experiences prime the newborn for linguistic input and can therefore be viewed as playing an important role in the overall process of language development.

Just as the fetus is capable of listening in on its mother's conversations, so have new research methods allowed scientists to eavesdrop on the sounds that fill its intrauterine world. Minute microphones, placed outside the wall of the uterus, can measure the noises that filter through to the womb, and ultrasound techniques record fetal responses to what it is hearing. We can now determine not only what the fetus hears, but also whether it distinguishes between different sounds. Experiments carried out only moments after birth then provide us with vital clues about the effects of the prenatal auditory experiences on newborn behavior. With such data, scientists are now able to raise questions about the extent to which the neonate remembers what he heard in utero. Can he recognize his mother's voice even though it is no longer filtered through liquid? Can he distinguish between his mother tongue and other hitherto unheard human languages? And what has he learned about the sound structure of speech? Answers to these and other questions provide valuable insights into the earliest moments of language acquisition.

These are truly fascinating times for students of developmental psycholinguistics. Until recently, acquisition research focused almost exclusively on language production. Nonverbal communicative behavior and vocalizations before the age of twelve to fifteen months were considered to add little to our knowledge of language acquisition—the focus was on production of recognizable words. Now, by contrast, the vital role of early babbling in tuning the articulatory system to the particularities of the infant's native tongue is the subject of numerous in-depth studies. Over the last two decades, novel infancy research techniques have been developed that shed light on these much earlier stages of language learning. Along with a new understanding of fetal and neonatal speech processing, the importance of early mother-infant nonlinguistic dialogue has been recognized. The amount and nature of early adult-infant interaction may of course vary from culture to culture, and such differences help researchers decide which aspects of the social environment are crucial to language acquisition.

We now have at our disposal a whole range of innovative methods for discovering what infants understand prior to their own first words. There is therefore no longer a need to rely solely on what children say in order to gauge their level of linguistic knowledge. Researchers can now explore, better than ever before, how speech perception and language comprehension develop during the crucial period preceding the first production of recognizable words. Modern research techniques have allowed us to discover hitherto unsuspected infant capacities for speech segmentation. They have also pointed to the much earlier emergence of the infant's realization that words refer to objects, people, places, and actions. We now know that well before two years, infants already understand that word order, for instance, conveys crucial information about meaning. Scientifically controlled experiments with prelinguistic infants are now commonly used to further our knowledge of the roots of language acquisition.

Although by the age of five most children speak fluently and with ease, language acquisition is far from complete. Children continue to acquire complex grammar and new linguistic meanings during their school years. Other aspects of language learning persist into adolescence and even through adult life. And because language is dynamic, even as adults we have to continually adapt to changes that occur in our native tongue throughout our lives. The constant updating of dictionaries is clear evidence of the changing nature of language, with new entries of modern terms like "e-mail," "modem," and "internet" posing a threat to words like "typewriter" that may one day become obsolete.

The field of psycholinguistics was created as a meeting ground for psychology (which is concerned among other things with the processes of language comprehension, production, and memory) and linguistics (which analyzes the structure of language). Developmental psycholinguistics, in particular, addresses how these two aspects of language are progressively acquired by children. A detailed account of all the different psychological and linguistic approaches in the field is beyond the scope of this book. So we will refer to the theories that pertain specifically to the issues concerning *how* language is acquired—our central focus here. At the heart of this debate is the issue of innateness. Does the newborn come into the world prewired for language acquisition as a result of our human evolutionary history? Are there specialized mechanisms in the brain just for language learning? Or does the infant learn language in much the same way as he learns about the physical and social worlds? Opinions are deeply divided. Arguments revolve around the dichotomy between nature (our biological endowment) and nurture (the world we experience). No theory denies that *both* nature and nurture play some role in language learning. Rather, theories differ fundamentally as to the importance of each. It is true that we are the only species to develop full-fledged grammatical languages. Something, therefore, must be specific to human biology to have enabled us to do this. But nurture must also play an important role. There are some six thousand different languages in the world, and it is obvious that no child is born already knowing English, Swahili, or Russian. Experiencing input as part of everyday life from a particular language (or more than one language) is thus essential for acquiring native tongues. The argument among theorists of language acquisition ultimately revolves around whether nature or nurture plays the leading role.

Nativist theories of language acquisition, which argue for the existence in the infant brain of innate or prewired linguistic structure, have been particularly influential since the 1960s. This is when the famous American linguist Noam Chomsky demonstrated that behaviorism (which holds that the newborn brain is a tabula rasa, or blank slate on which experience simply imprints its structure) could not alone account for language acquisition. Chomsky argued that for complex grammar to be acquired, input simply does not provide sufficient examples to allow the child's brain to build grammatical structures from scratch and to know, for instance, which words are nouns or verbs and which parts of sentences can and cannot be moved. If the child based his hypotheses about linguistic structure simply on what he heard, he would draw a large number of erroneous conclusions about the grammatical structure of his native tongue. Hence behaviorism cannot account for language acquisition.

There are several versions of the nativist approach, but the central tenet is that infants are born with a so-called Universal Grammar (or UG) and specialized language-learning mechanisms for acquiring their native tongue. From this viewpoint, a common set of universal principles underlie every one of the world's languages, despite the very different surface characteristics of each language. Nativist theorists tend to argue that children are born prewired with these linguistic principles and set of parameters, which are simply triggered by the specific linguistic input. The nativist view claims that linguistic experience is needed only to allow the child to discover the local realization of universally specified principles and parameters. The brain mechanisms by which the child learns language are considered to be not only innate, but also entirely domain specific—that is, dedicated only to language learning. We will deal with this in detail in Chapter 5.

At the opposite theoretical extreme is the cognitive view of language learning propounded, in particular, by the famous Swiss psychologist Jean Piaget. For Piaget and his followers, language acquisition calls on the same general learning mechanisms that the child uses to learn about physics, number concepts, space, social conventions, and so forth. According to this approach, there is nothing unique about the way in which children learn language. Cognitive development is deemed to be a prerequisite and foundation for language learning. Thus for Piaget, concepts like "object permanence" are seen to underlie the onset of early word use. One of Piaget's disciples, Hermine Sinclair, also argued that the child's ability to nest a set of Russian dolls (one inside the other) lays the foundations for the child's subsequent capacity to understand how sentences can be embedded within one another. The cognitive view, then, claims that general learning mechanisms are simply applied to linguistic input once they have become established in general cognitive development.

Other theorists place social interaction at the center of their claims about the processes of language acquisition. Jerome Bruner, for instance, has stressed the importance of the principles of interaction for language learning. Beginning within the mother-infant relationship, and subsequently expanding to the rest of the child's social environment, conversational conventions help children become sensitive to the rules for dialogue and turn-taking. Such theories may explain how children enter the world of dialogue, but say little about how the intricacies of grammar are acquired. They seem to assume that there is enough information in the day-to-day linguistic input for the child to discover the structure of his native tongue. For both the cognitive and social views, the mechanisms by which the child learns language are therefore domain general: they are the same as those used for learning about other aspects of the world.

The debates that separate these different theoretical positions will arise throughout the book because they influence both the kinds of hypotheses constructed and how the research data are ultimately interpreted. We argue, however, that the nature versus nurture dichotomy is not a useful one, and that we should focus instead on the dynamic interaction between the two. Our view is that language is indeed special, but we hypothesize that evolution's solution has not been to prewire complex linguistic representations into the neonate mind. Rather, we believe that evolution has done two interesting things. First, evolution has made the period of postnatal brain development in humans extremely long, so that environmental input can shape the structure of the developing brain. But the brain is not in our view a blank homogenous slate, as behaviorists would hold. Our second argument is that evolution has provided us with a number of different learning mechanisms that, although not domain specific, are what we would call "domain relevant." It is by interacting with various environmental inputs that each mechanism becomes progressively more domain specific. By this we mean that prior to and at birth, the infant possesses some minimal predispositions that make him pay particular attention to certain parts of the environment like, say, faces and voices. From the start, different brain mechanisms will be more attuned to processing one type of input over another. Thus a mechanism that is sensitive to sequential, fast-fading input might pay particular attention to oral or signed language but not to faces, and as it becomes increasingly specialized at processing language, it will become more devoted to that specific domain. This is why we end up in adulthood with such specialized language areas in the brain. In other words, the infant brain does not start out with circuits dedicated only for processing language, but it does end up with specialized circuits as a function of experience. So, our view considers language knowledge to be the complex product of the interaction between some initial, domain-relevant (not domain-specific) predispositions and the rich structure of the linguistic input. Thus it is not a question of nature *or* nurture; rather it is about the intricate interaction between the two. An understanding of this interaction will ultimately explain how the dynamic process of language acquisition takes place from fetus to adolescent.

Our book aims to guide the reader through the exciting pathways to language. Throughout, we will necessarily have to be selective in our choice of theoretical issues and empirical studies, because the area of developmental psycholinguistics is now extraordinarily vast. We do, however, discuss the most prominent issues as a way of introducing the reader to this fascinating field. Chapter 2 offers an informative guide to the experimental paradigms that have been designed to tease out information about speech perception and language acquisition. It may be hard for the reader to imagine how we can carry out language-related experiments on very young infants who cannot yet speak. Yet we will see just how inventive researchers have been in devising carefully controlled methods that shed light on both fetal sensitivity to speech input as well as language processing in the early postnatal months. Other methods can now probe the linguistic knowledge of toddlers and older children in greater depth than ever before. These provide vital insights into how the mental representations of speech built up during the first few months form the foundations of subsequent language development. In particular, we will consider the difference between so-called off-line approaches, which always involve a degree of metalinguistic awareness, and "on-line" techniques that tap into real-time language processing. We will also describe some of the revolutionary non-invasive brain imaging techniques. These reveal minute changes in blood flow and electrical activity in the brains of infants and young children as they actively process linguistic input. Such images show us how the brain becomes progressively specialized and localized for language during postnatal development.

With a clear understanding of the basic experimental paradigms, the reader will then be ready to explore the pathways to language. In Chapter 3, we examine the role of the fetus's intrauterine auditory experiences in preparing the infant to attend to and process speech during the first few months in the outside world. We will particularly stress the difference between speech and language, and warn against automatically generalizing from one to the other, as sometimes happens in the literature. Early *speech* processing of the sounds of language cannot be equated with knowledge of the meaning and structure of *language*. Our main focus in Chapter 3 is therefore sensitivity to speech input, as demonstrated by current research into fetal, newborn, and infant behavior.

Chapters 4 to 6 explore language at three different levels: word, grammar, and narrative discourse. Most studies of language acquisition have concentrated on middle- to lower-middle-class families and on the English language, and these represent the main sources of data on which theories are based. But the total picture of how language is acquired must also include examination of the world's many different languages whose structures differ from English. Sociocultural variables will also affect a child's patterns of linguistic interaction, and these will in turn influence language acquisition. Wherever possible, we will bring the sociocultural dimension and non-English data into our discussions throughout the book.

In Chapter 7 we turn to atypical language development in children with focal brain damage and genetic disorders, focusing on Specific Language Impairment, Down syndrome, and Williams syndrome. Here we challenge the automatic assumption, often made in the literature on atypicality, that the study of abnormality is necessarily a window on normal language acquisition. We will stress that it is wrong to think of the atypical brain as a normal brain with parts intact and parts impaired. Rather, we argue that the brains of children with genetic disorders show an overall pattern of developmental differences from the outset. Finally, Chapter 8 reexamines the crucial nature-nurture debate against the backdrop of the extensive research data presented in the book. We consider the role of evolution in enabling humans to develop language, how human language differs from the communication systems of other species, and what it ultimately means to have language.

All over the world children learn their native tongues effortlessly. If they cannot hear, they readily acquire the intricacies of sign language. Unlike the development of reading skills, learning a spoken or signed language does not require lessons; it simply happens as a function of development and experience. Yet the complex patterns of linguistic output that children ultimately produce are breathtaking. They can talk or sign about the present, the past, and the future. They can refer to imaginary events and to abstract concepts. They can use language to pass on information, or to trick and deceive. They can play with language, making up new words or new meanings for old words. Language is a system that allows for dynamic change and flexibility. It is vital to human life both as a powerful vehicle for social interaction and as an infinitely creative tool for representing real and hypothetical experiences and feelings. The intricate trajectory that children take in learning the manifold aspects of their native tongue is one of the most fascinating areas of human psychology—and is a journey that the reader is now invited to follow.

# 2 | EXPERIMENTAL PARADIGMS FOR STUDYING LANGUAGE ACQUISITION

Paradigms for the study of language acquisition can be classified into three broad areas: speech perception, language production, and language comprehension. Speech perception investigates how individuals, from the fetus to the adult, process the *sounds* of language. Research into language production focuses on what children *say*, and studies of language comprehension are concerned with what children *understand*. While speech perception can occur without involving meaning, both language comprehension and language production concern how words, grammar, and discourse contribute to meaning. Together, data from these three approaches provide an overall picture of the challenges that children face when learning their native tongue.

For many years, language research focused almost exclusively on language production. How did this bias develop? First, studies were strongly influenced by the predominant psychological theories of the first half of the twentieth century. And second, there was at the time a lack of appropriate experimental methods for studying language comprehension. The theoretical bias came primarily from Burrhus Skinner's behaviorist theory, which encouraged language researchers to focus on children's overt production. The underlying linguistic competence that might be revealed through children's understanding of language was not appreciated. Central to the behaviorist view was the belief that before a child actually began speaking, we could learn little about her knowledge of language. This premise failed to account for the fact that, particularly in the early stages of language acquisition, what a child understands may be much more indicative of her knowledge of language than is what she can say. For instance, we pointed out earlier that infants are sensitive to differences in the word order of short sentences as they begin their second year of life, which is well before they produce anything more than a few recognizable, single words. Infants, then, actually have a knowledge of language that is not displayed in their utterances. The same is true for adults learning a foreign language. They tend to understand considerably more than they are able to say.

Although theoretical considerations were in part responsible for the focus on production, psycholinguistic research was also restricted by a lack of sophisticated experimental methods for studying early language comprehension. In the 1960s, Chomsky's devastatingly critical review of Skinner's behaviorism revolutionized psycholinguistic thought and led researchers to seek new methods for uncovering linguistic competence. The emphasis shifted away from production and toward devising ways to investigate language comprehension. This presented linguistic scientists with a difficult challenge. After all, in a naturalistic setting such as day-to-day interactions between a parent and infant, it is feasible and straightforward to write down and analyze what the child says during each exchange. But it is far more difficult to determine whether the child understands particular sentences in their entirety, or whether she gleans their meaning merely on the basis of a selection of words and redundant cues. Natural speech contains a multitude of levels that go well beyond lexical items. Picture the following situation. A mother instructs her child to "put the spoon in the cup," and the infant performs the action correctly. But can we really take this as evidence that the infant fully comprehended the sentence on the basis of its words and structure? Joint attention (mother and infant attending to the same object or event) and gestures such as the mother pointing may have contributed to directing the infant's attention. Past experience of spoons and cups may then have guided her actions to place the spoon inside the cup, without the child necessarily understanding the preposition "in." Physical constraints—you cannot put cups in spoons—might also play a role. It is quite feasible that, in this case, word order is not vital in determining the successful outcome of the exchange. So how much of the sentence (that is, the strictly linguistic context) did the infant really understand? The only way to answer such questions is to devise controlled experiments to gauge the precise level of the infant's language comprehension.

Theoretical attitudes and methodological paradigms have undergone vast changes in the last twenty years, allowing researchers to focus on the earliest moments of speech and language processing—those crucial months preceding not only the child's first words, but even her first breath. Studies of speech processing now begin by focusing on the fetus in the uterus to discover what role, if any, prenatal experience plays in language acquisition. This, together with the growing interest in language comprehension, which also begins surprisingly early in an infant's life, represent some of the principal areas of research taking center stage in the study of early language. The resulting infant methodologies have now also been adapted for use with older children. In general, experimental approaches have become increasingly sophisticated, making use of the most up-to-date technology. Researchers can now investigate all the different dimensions of language, from the stimulation it provides to the growing fetus in the last months of gestation, to the meta-linguistic judgments of middle childhood and the subtle complexities of the adolescent speaker. Furthermore, exciting brain-imaging techniques have recently been adapted for safe use with babies and children. These provide the means to chart the structural and temporal changes taking place in the brain's real-time processing of language.

## Methods for Studying Speech Perception

### FETAL STUDIES

In recent years innovative methodologies have been developed for studying speech perception during fetal development. New research techniques have provided evidence that the roots of language acquisition can be traced to the fetus's processing of auditory stimuli during the final three months of gestation. This is the time when the fetus becomes familiar with some of the sounds and rhythms of its mother tongue.

Thanks to a few pregnant psycholinguistic researchers who offered to have a small microphone inserted and placed on the outside wall of the uterus, we now have a good idea of what the fetus can hear inside its mother's body. This led to the development of a number of methods for studying fetal sensitivity to language. The principal method used to assess what the fetus processes in the womb involves measuring modifications in fetal movements (usually kicking rate) and fetal heart rate in response to changing stimuli. In order to analyze the nature of this responsiveness, the researcher must habituate the fetus to an auditory stimulus. This is done by repeatedly playing the same sound through specially adapted speakers placed on the mother's abdomen until the fetus has become used to that sound. Then a new, different sound is presented. The fetus's behavior is monitored throughout with ultrasound or heart-monitoring equipment. Of course, there is no presumption that the fetus understands anything that it is hearing. The question is whether, after having heard the same stimulus many times, the fetus will show sensitivity to a change. Sentences or even short stories have been used, where one set of words might be repeated with changes in word order. Alternatively, if the mother is bilingual, she could be asked to speak one language and then switch to the other language. If the fetus starts to kick more vigorously or quickens its heartbeat when any such changes are introduced, we can infer that it is already able to process certain aspects of linguistic stimuli while still in the uterus.

The logic behind this method is that initially, upon hearing a speech stimulus, a resting fetus will become active and its heart rate and / or kicking will increase. After hearing this same sound repeatedly, however, it will gradually habituate (become "bored" with the stimulus), and quiet down. When a new stimulus is introduced, it is expected that the fetus will again increase its kicking rate, or its heartbeat will quicken, if it is able to detect the difference between the stimuli. This is called the recovery rate. If the change is not detected by the fetus, its movement and heart rate are predicted to remain stable. This monitoring method is sensitive to very small changes in fetal responsiveness and thus provides a good means of discovering which aspects of its mother's speech the fetus may already be processing.

## POSTNATAL STUDIES

### High-Amplitude Sucking Technique

The high-amplitude sucking technique can be used with the youngest of infants because it capitalizes on the reflex action of sucking, which is what they do best. Peter Eimas and his collaborators were among the first to use this technique. In a typical experiment, the infant is placed in a reclining baby chair, facing a blank wall or screen about three feet away. To capture the baby's attention, an attractive image is projected onto the wall or screen, just above a loudspeaker through which test stimuli will be played. To avoid influencing the infant's behavior by their reactions, parents and observers are prevented from hearing the experimental stimuli. Adults present have to wear tightly fitting headphones through which music is played. Before the trials begin, the experimenter places a non-nutritive nipple (like a pacifier) in the baby's mouth. This is attached to a computer that records every suck the baby makes (see Figure 1). The auditory stimulus is programmed to respond to changes in sucking rate: the baby's behavior actually influences what she will hear. Once a baseline rate of normal sucking has been established at the start of the experiment, the trials can begin.

There are several versions of this technique. In one experiment, the baby has to suck at a high rate to activate the playing of her mother's voice, but if she slows her sucking rate a stranger's voice is played. Data show that infants of only a few days old can learn to control their behavior in order to produce the stimulus they prefer to listen to. So the newborn will actually suck harder in order to hear her mother's voice. In other versions of the high-amplitude sucking technique, the stimuli might be syllables or words from both the

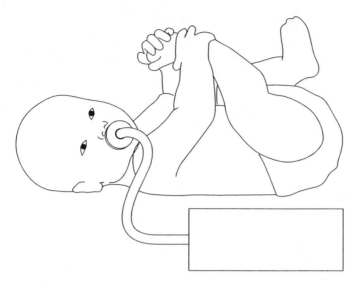

*Figure 1*   High-amplitude sucking technique

child's native tongue and another unknown language. Again, the infant's differential sucking rates can be analyzed to see not only whether the baby is sensitive to such cross-linguistic differences, but also which of the two stimuli the baby prefers to hear.

*Head-Turn Preference Procedure*
The head-turn preference procedure (HPP) is used to test infants' abilities to discriminate between contrasting types of auditory stimuli. This technique is only suitable for testing infants who already have good control over their head movements, that is, those who are four months old or older. During these experiments, the infant is seated either in a special baby chair or on the parent's lap, in a three-sided testing booth. The panels to the right and left of the baby each contain a red light in front of a loudspeaker. A green light is mounted on the center panel, behind which are hidden a computer terminal and a response box operated by the researcher (see Figure 2). A camera, linked to the computer, records the infant's head movements. The researcher can monitor what is taking place

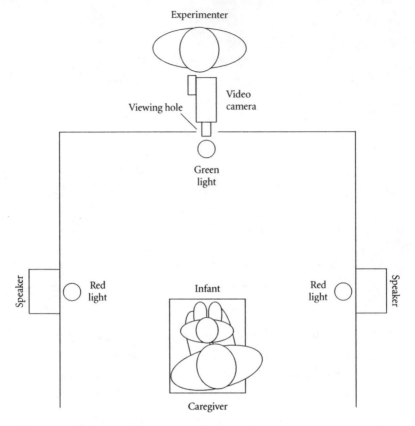

*Figure 2*    Head-turn preference procedure

inside the booth by looking through little holes in the screen. Every time the infant turns her head (left, center, or right), the experimenter presses the corresponding button on the response box. The computer calculates and records the duration and the direction of the infant's head turns. It also controls the flashing of the light and the presentation of the auditory stimuli. As with previously described techniques, by wearing tight-fitting headphones neither the mother nor the researcher can hear the stimuli that the infant hears; in this way they are prevented from influencing her head turns.

Each experiment is made up of a familiarization phase and a test phase. The aim is to discover whether the infant is capable of discriminating between two types of contrasting language stimuli. For example, this approach might be used to test infant sensitivity to sounds like "ba" versus "da," or words in French versus words in Russian. The technique is versatile and can be adapted for use with many lexical or grammatical contrasts. During the familiarization phase, the baby hears stimuli related to only one of the two classes of test stimuli (say, French utterances). The trial phase, in contrast, involves the random presentation of both types (French or Russian utterances). At the beginning of the procedure, the green light on the center panel starts flashing to capture the infant's attention. When the baby is focused on this center light, one of the red lights (left or right) begins to flash. The infant should instinctively turn her head to look at the new light. At this moment, the French familiarization stimuli are played on the loudspeaker behind this red light. These continue to be played either for a set number of presentations (familiarization), or until the infant looks away for more than two seconds indicating that she has become bored. This is the point at which the infant is said to have habituated to the stimuli she has been hearing. It is postulated that she will also have related the turning of her head to the emission of stimuli on the loudspeakers. The experimental phase begins immediately, with random presentations of both types of stimuli (French or Russian utterances) from either the right or left loudspeaker. Switches from French to Russian are randomly assigned to the left or right loudspeakers throughout the test phase, so the infant does not associate one particular side with one particular class of stimuli. The rationale is that if the infant is able to discriminate between the French and Russian utterances, she will turn her head for a longer time to hear the French sentences. This is because, if the habituation phase was successful, the infant will be attracted to the test stimuli that are familiar to her. In other words, the baby has already been primed to prefer this type of stimuli over the other, completely unfamiliar type (the Russian utterances). This approach has been used extensively in infancy studies by research teams such as those led by Richard Aslin, Anne Fernald, and Peter Jusczyk, and has led to many interesting discoveries about early infant sensitivities to speech stimuli.

## Methods for Studying Language Production

### OBSERVING AND TRANSCRIBING SPONTANEOUS LANGUAGE OUTPUT

The earliest method for collecting data on child language was the written diary kept by psychologists and linguists who had become parents. These meticulously kept journals provided extensive records of the language-related utterances produced by a child within the naturalistic setting of the home. By the 1960s, written record-keeping was gradually replaced by audio recordings of children's language production. The most influential studies using this approach were by Lois Bloom, the late Roger Brown, and their respective students. Brown's research provided detailed, longitudinal accounts of the language development of three children, nicknamed Adam, Eve, and Sarah. Researchers visited the homes of these children on a regular weekly or bimonthly basis, from the time they uttered their first words to the end of their third year.

Brown's students were all trained psycholinguists, and their data went well beyond the earlier diary studies. Records contained not only what the children said, but also vital accounts of the contexts in which the children's utterances were produced, together with general information about intonation patterns, pauses, errors, self-corrections, and any other relevant details that might assist in the subsequent linguistic analysis of the rich database. The Brown records charted the order in which a number of linguistic categories appeared: the order of single words (for example, "dog," "teddy," "allgone," "no"); the order of production of different grammatical morphemes such as the present progressive "ing" ("running"), prepositions ("in" and "on"), plural marker on nouns (as in "dogs"), irregular past tense ("came"), possessive marker ("Mummy's"); articles ("a" and "the"), regular past tense "ed" ("walked"), and third-person regular verb ("walks"); the types and timing of two- and three-word combinations (for example, "Daddy gone," "where

Mummy shoe?"); and the gradual elimination of errors in speech as each child became a more fluent speaker.

Following Brown's audiotaped work, the use of videotaping became increasingly popular. The addition of visual images to the data was recognized as offering even more insight into the overall context of language production. But the process of collecting, transcribing, and analyzing observation data is extremely time consuming and labor intensive. An hour-long videotaped session of child language production can take twenty hours or more to transcribe. The task entails not only noting every language utterance made by the child subject; the contexts in which each utterance appears must also be described in full, including the people and objects present, any events occurring during the recording, where the child was looking or pointing when she spoke, how others reacted to her speech, and how parental input influenced the interactions. Details about changes in the child's intonation must also be noted.

A common and serious problem that arose in the reporting of such observational studies was the relatively idiosyncratic way in which individual researchers encoded their data. Many devised their own systems to represent different aspects of the collected information, often rendering their material unusable by others in the field. The ever-growing interest in developmental psycholinguistics called for a more standard way of recording and analyzing data on child language production. The heavy emphasis on English data was also challenged, leading to a new consideration of the many other rich and interesting languages of the world.

## CHILDES

At the beginning of the 1980s, two well-known child language researchers, Brian MacWhinney and Catherine Snow, proposed setting up a computerized database on child language production that would be made available to the entire academic community. Their ideas culminated in the creation of CHILDES—the Child Language Data Exchange System. This is a database that can be accessed worldwide and to which any relevant research material can be contributed in a standard format. It thus overcomes the previous difficulties caused by individualized coding systems. Today, the system contains data from some twenty-two different languages, easily accessed via the internet (we provide the American, European, and Japanese website addresses in the reading list for this chapter at the end of the book). Well over a thousand researchers have already consulted the database, and approximately eight hundred published articles cite CHILDES as their main research resource. Brown's longitudinal data on Adam, Eve, and Sarah were the first to have been fully transcribed onto the CHILDES system, with each child's data covering over one hundred files.

Contributions from the world's researchers include material on both first language acquisition and second language learning. The data provide detailed transcripts ranging from early mother-child dialogues to lengthy narrative monologues produced by children. The CHILDES database can be used in conjunction with various transcription and statistical analysis software packages compatible with both PCs and Apple Macintosh computers. It provides an extraordinarily rich source of information for those interested in child language development, offering details of the words, grammar, and errors produced by children learning to speak, as well as descriptions of the contexts in which speaking occurs. There is also vital information about prosody, stress, and pause patterns that give each speaker's language its own identity. Thus, CHILDES provides everything that one would expect to find in original published sources of well-executed observational studies. But unlike any other source of data, it also gives far more details than could ever be included in published works. It is thus the closest a researcher can come to observing real child data.

CHILDES has transformed the study of child language development. It has provided inspiration and new directions to research in the entire field of developmental psycholinguistics. Now rather than proceeding straight from hypothesis to experimental investigation, researchers can perform an initial assessment of their hypotheses on real child data prior to controlled testing of their own subjects. This can save time, money, and heartache by providing early validation of new research proposals as well as vital clues for improvements. Subsequently, once a study is carried out, the newly gathered data can in turn be registered onto the CHILDES database. The system is therefore continuously being updated and enriched by new material and novel methods of analysis.

While the value of a database like CHILDES cannot be overestimated, it is worth raising a word of caution to new researchers. With such an extensive source of data available at the click of a button, it becomes tempting for students of child language to use CHILDES as their exclusive source of evidence and forgo carrying out data collection of their own. As a result, they may work entirely from written transcripts and never actually hear for themselves the fascinating discourse of child subjects. But experiencing some child language first-hand through observation and / or experimentation is vital to any student of language acquisition. To make the CHILDES written transcripts richer, contributors have recently been encouraged to make available on the network the original videotaped data from which transcripts were derived. Nonetheless, students in the field of linguistics are strongly advised to complement CHILDES data with original data.

## LANGUAGE PRODUCTION EXPERIMENTS

Spontaneous interactions between children and adults, as well as between children and siblings or peers, are regarded as an ideal source of data in language production studies. But observation of spontaneous speech is increasingly accompanied by semi-structured and / or structured experimentation. Pioneers in child language research, like Daniel Slobin, Lois Bloom, and Susan Ervin-Tripp, recognized that a combination of research methods can significantly enrich the data—and not only research carried out in a strictly experimental setting of the laboratory. Even in the naturalistic setting of the home, a researcher who associates a number of different approaches can more fully assess new language developments. For instance, the use of semistructured, ad hoc experiments can help ascertain whether the appearance of a new linguistic structure produced by the child in one context will generalize to other language contexts. Take the following example. During an observational session, a child who has until now only ever used the singular word "car" suddenly says "cars." Does this represent the application of a newly acquired grammatical rule for forming the plural of nouns? In other words, did she purposely apply the rule "add s" to the singular "car"? Or was the infant simply repeating a new word she has heard for a collection of cars? Does she even realize, at this stage, that there is a relationship between the words "car" and "cars"? Simple on-the-spot experimentation allows the researcher to capitalize on this important moment of language observation. For instance, by presenting the child with pairs of other objects that the child is able to name in the singular (such as perhaps cups or dolls), the researcher can determine whether the novel utterance of the plural "s" generalizes across different linguistic contexts.

### Elicited Production Using Nonce Words

Different children have different linguistic experiences. For instance, some may know words that others of a similar age do not know. How, then, can the researcher avoid confounding individual experience and linguistic knowledge? One solution has been to use nonce terms, which are invented words that obey the phonotactics of the language (what combinations of sounds are legal in the language being studied). So, for example, "lopet" is a possible English word, whereas "lpote" is not, because English never combines the phonemes "l" and "p" at the beginning of a word. In a sense, then, nonce terms are words that could have existed in the language (say, a noun like "wug" or a verb like "gorp") and to which we would quite spontaneously add an "s" for the plural "wugs" or an "ing" or "ed" for tense marking ("gorping" or "gorped") if we learned them as new words. Such nonce terms can be used in conjunction with the elicited production approach, whereby young subjects are prompted to produce the missing part of a sentence in which a critical grammatical rule is called for.

Jean Berko-Gleason pioneered this approach with the Wug Test in the 1950s. The technique has been used extensively and forms part of developmental psycholinguistic research to this day. Berko-Gleason invented a series of nonce terms, including "wug," and encouraged children to use such terms in different linguistic contexts within carefully planned experiments. The general idea is that when prompted by the linguistic context in which the terms appear, children will transform these when necessary to obey obligatory grammatical markings like plural "s" on "wugs" or past tense "ed" on "wugged." During the Wug Test, the child is shown a picture of, for instance, a bird-like creature and told that it is called "a wug." She is then shown another "wug" and told: "So now there are two of them," and finally asked, "now I have two . . .?" (rising intonation). At this point the child is expected to produce the plural "wugs."

The use of nonce terms enables researchers to find out whether, in new situations, young children are capable of generalizing to new words obligatory grammatical markers relevant to their native tongue. With nonce terms, the child's response cannot be explained simply by past experience, because she had never heard the words "wug" or "wugs" before. In contrast, rote learning could explain the production of various real words containing such plural markers in children's spontaneous everyday language. For instance, if a child has only ever heard the plural of the word "clouds" when she looks up at the sky, she may use this plural "clouds" correctly in her speech, but not actually know the word "cloud" in the singular. In this case, therefore, the correct usage of the word "clouds" cannot be taken as evidence that the child is correctly applying a plural marker. Rather, she may simply be using a familiar lexical item that, to her, refers to a fluffy white mass in the sky. To this young child, therefore, the word "clouds" is not formed by adding an "s" to "cloud" but is a lexical term in its own right. It is through the use of nonce terms that researchers can overcome these confounding factors and discover the true status of the grammatical markers present in the child's output.

From our knowledge of written language we conceptualize the plural rule as simply "add an 's'" to singular words. In spoken language, however, the sounds we actually produce when pluralizing are influenced by the rest of the linguistic context of the word. So the plural of "dog" is pronounced "dogz", whereas "cat" becomes "cats", and "dish" becomes "dishez." The Wug Test allows the researcher to ascertain not only whether children can add the plural marker in general, but also whether they are sensitive to the different allomorphs (varying forms of the same addition) on the endings of the nonce terms to be pluralized. So an experiment might examine whether a child correctly transforms "sich" into "sichez," "fap" into "faps," and "gog" into "gogz."

The nonce word approach can also be adapted to investigate a range of other grammatical structures such as tense marking on verbs. For instance, the experimenter may tell the child:

Every day I gorp. (Pause)
Just like every day, yesterday I . . . (rising intonation)

At this point the child should produce the past tense "gorped." Again, although we think of past tense as the addition of "ed," there are in fact several allomorphs, so the actual pronunciation changes as a function of the sounds that precede the marker. Thus, we pronounce "worked" as "workt," in contrast to the past tense of the verbs "to end" and "to plan," which are pronounced "ended" and "plannd." The Wug Test can be adapted to examine these allomorphs as well as to test both regular and irregular tense markings. Most verbs in English are regular (walked, speeded, planned). But some frequently used verbs like "come," "go," "sing," and "eat" have irregular endings: we say "came," not "comed"; "went," not "goed"; "sang," not "singed"; and "ate," not "eated." Such exceptions to language represent further challenges to children. To test children's knowledge of such variations, we can present them with nonce verbs whose endings differ to make them sound either like regular or irregular verbs. An example would be comparing nonce terms like "ting" and "gick" to see if children transform them to "tang" and "gicked."

Children seem to be particularly receptive to invented words if they "sound right," and they will spontaneously treat them as if they were real words. The experiments are designed to be fun and creative. So the elicited production approach with nonce terms can be both gratifying for the child and informative to the researcher. The data are unique in uncovering how children integrate their growing knowledge of grammar as well as new words (also known as lexical items).

*Elicited Imitation with Spontaneous Correction*
Elicited imitation is a useful and much used tool for probing language development. This method involves placing the child within an experimental context that elicits repetition of different types of model utterances and examines the child's ability to repeat them. Some of the utterances to be repeated are constructed with correct grammar, whereas others contain mistakes that the child is expected to correct spontaneously. The experiments are presented in the form of a game, to encourage the child's active cooperation. For instance, the child may be shown puppets that "speak" and that make language errors. At the onset of a trial, the child is prompted to "repeat what the puppet says." It is assumed that if the child is sensitive to violations of particular grammatical rules, she will correct them spontaneously in her repetitions. For example, the child might be asked to repeat the incorrect sentence:

(1) I've got two foots.

If she possesses the knowledge that there are certain exceptions to the "add s" rule for plural transformation, she will actually change what she heard and repeat it in the right way as in (2) below:

(2) I've got two feet.

Alternatively, the puppet may make a syntactic error:

(3) This is my blue big tractor.

A child who is sensitive to word order rules should spontaneously imitate this utterance as:

(4) This is my big blue tractor.

The manner in which children correct sentences provides us with vital clues to their levels of language knowledge.

This method has shown that children not only spontaneously modify incorrect language; they also drop certain repeated words in sentences if these are extraneous to meaning. But they do not leave out repeated words if they can find a grammatically valid justification for the repetition. For example, if the child hears:

(5) David runs runs up the hill.

she is likely to repeat it with a correction as:

(6) David runs up the hill.

The repetition of the verb is treated as an error and spontaneously dropped from the imitation. By contrast, if the word repetition can in any way be interpreted as a valid lexical item, then it will be preserved:

(7) Model: David runs up the hill hill.
(8) Child's imitation: David runs up the hill hill.

Here, the noun "hill" is repeated by the child. In this case, she will imitate the model sentence completely because she has interpreted "hill-hill" as a possible compound noun.

Elicited imitation is particularly versatile because most grammatical structures of language lend themselves to this sort of manipulation. Another way to test early knowledge of language through this approach is to make the model sentences far too long for the child to repeat in full. In this way, the researcher can analyze which parts of the sentence are processed in short-term memory and which are not. LouAnn Gerken used this method to find out why toddlers leave out articles like "a" and "the" from their early spontaneous productions, like "Look! Big dog garden." By analyzing what the children reproduce or what they leave out when you give them a full sentence to imitate, the researcher can ascertain whether they are sensitive to grammatical structures and whether these cause extra processing demands. We give concrete examples of these imitation studies in Chapter 5.

Elicited imitation can also be used to test other levels of production, as well as combinations of levels. One dimension of natural speech that has been examined through this approach is the linguistic use of stress and intonation. To investigate this aspect of language, researchers systematically alter prosodic patterns across model sentences to see how they affect a child's ability to imitate utterances. A common finding is that if a child hears a prominent but unexpected stress in a model sentence, she will preserve the stress but transfer it to a more appropriate position in the sentence. For example:

(9) *The* ball is on the floor.

is more likely to be repeated as:

(10) The *ball* is on the floor.

The child's ability to correct inappropriate grammar or prosody provides vital information about his or her level of linguistic development. But the mistakes that children make when imitating language are equally telling. This approach has therefore been molded to examine other linguistic dimensions that are likely to cause the child to produce errors. For instance, complexity of sentence (structure) may be pitted against sentence length (number of words) in model sentences. By making a grammatically easier sentence considerably longer than a grammatically complex one, we see whether sentence length or complex grammatical structure plays a greater role in the child's ability to process and correctly repeat an utterance. For example, sentence (11) below contains a complicated left-branching, embedded relative clause, whereas sentence (12) is six words longer but contains a simple structure using the conjunction "and":

(11) The boy the girl kicked went home.
(12) The girl kicked the boy very hard and then he went straight home.

Both sentences have similar lexical items and are similar in meaning. But sentence (12) provides extra details ("very hard" and "straight"), making it considerably longer than (11). So one might expect (12) to be more difficult for children to repeat than (11). If that were the case, we would conclude that sentence length was a greater obstacle to the child than structural constraints. If, however, children actually produced more errors when imitating shorter sentences like (11), then the researcher can conclude that it is complexity of grammatical structure and not number of words that affects children's ability to repeat. In fact, data show the latter to be the case for young speakers. Five-year-olds repeat longer sentences like (12) well, but a typical error that they make when imitating sentences like (11) often changes both structure and meaning, as we see in (13) below:

(13) The boy kicked the girl, then he went home.

Researchers can draw valuable conclusions from such results. These suggest that it is the embeddedness of clauses (that is, the extent to which the main clause of the sentence is interrupted by subordinate clauses) that poses a problem for children of this age. Clearly, at this stage of language development, complexity of syntactic structure affects performance to a greater extent than does sentence length. These issues are discussed at length in Chapter 5.

The types of errors and modifications that children make when imitating speech provide us with vital insight into the child's level of linguistic knowledge. Most importantly, they furnish us with a better understanding of the types of hurdles that children need to overcome when learning their native tongue. A wide range of different grammatical structures can be studied using variations of the elicited imitation approach. But most psycholinguists agree that the data resulting from such experiments are far more valuable if they are also supported by similar, spontaneous speech data. This is because failures to demonstrate certain language abilities in rigidly controlled settings may be due to the demands of the experimental task. It is therefore also necessary to verify whether these are present in the child's natural speech.

*Elicited Transformation*
Elicited transformation is another means by which researchers can test the developmental level of language production in children. It allows the researcher to discover whether the child can correctly apply various grammatical rules in *changing* linguistic contexts. The

method is similar to elicited imitation, although in this case the child's task requires complex linguistic transformations as opposed to accurate repetition. The tests take the form of a turn-taking game. Before the experimental phase begins, the child is primed with a number of practice trials that provide a series of model transformations and allow the child to rehearse the task until she clearly understands what is required of her. During testing, the child is expected to provide the transformations automatically and without further assistance. In certain instances where the task proves too demanding, however, some further prompting may be necessary.

This method can be adapted to test a large number of different grammatical structures. For example, if the researcher wishes to find out whether a child correctly uses the grammar of tags in English, the following exchanges might take place during the experimental phase:

(14) *Experimenter:* He's going home . . .
    Child: isn't he?

(15) *Experimenter:* They'll take a long time . . .
    *Child:* won't they?

(16) *Experimenter:* She can't stay with us . . .
    *Child:* can she?

This type of sentence completion involves a complicated structural transformation. First the child needs to recognize the experimenter's utterance as an incomplete statement; then she must turn it into a question by identifying the subject noun and the verb and reversing the polarity (for example, "will" becomes "won't they"; "can't" becomes "can she"). Many languages only use a single form for all tag questions (for instance, "n'est-ce pas?" in French and "nicht wahr?" in German), so English is particularly complex for children in this respect.

The elicited transformation method can also be used to test a child's ability to convert direct speech into indirect or reported speech. Although as adults we take this ability very much for granted, it actually involves a transformation of major parts of the sentence, as can be seen in the following examples:

(17) *Experimenter:* "I want an ice cream," said Lucy.

(18) *Child:* Lucy said that she wanted an ice cream.

(19) *Experimenter:* "You must put the toys in the basket," Mom said to me.

(20) *Child:* Mom said that I had to put the toys in the basket.

In such sentences, the child not only has to identify the verb and pronoun, but also has to transform the present tense of the verb into the past tense. It is also necessary for her to change the pronoun into the one appropriate for reported speech, while at the same time accurately maintaining the meaning of the original sentence. The ability to create reported speech from direct speech clearly involves complex linguistic abilities. The method of elicited transformation lends itself particularly well to experimental testing of more advanced aspects of language acquisition.

Another version of elicited transformation involves prompting the child to produce passive sentences with the same meaning as corresponding active sentences. For instance, the active sentence "The boy hit the girl" can be transformed into the corresponding passive structure "The girl was hit by the boy." Again, success at such a task requires a sophisticated knowledge of language and an ability to significantly alter sentence structure. The child has to take the agent of the action out of the subject position of the sentence and replace it with the patient of the action (whomever or whatever is acted on). The following pairs of examples provide further illustrations of this type of transformation:

(21) *Experimenter:* The man cleaned the bath.

(22) *Child:* The bath was cleaned by the man.

(23) *Experimenter:* The boy kissed the girl.

(24) *Child:* The girl was kissed by the boy.

(25) *Experimenter:* The tree hit the car.

(26) *Child:* The car was hit by the tree.

The first pair of sentences (21 and 22) are what is called "irreversible" because clearly baths cannot clean men. This makes the transformation easier for the child. Sentence pairs 23–24 and 25–26, however, are "reversible": boys can kiss girls and vice versa, and trees can come down in storms and hit cars, just as cars can hit a tree in an accident. Young speakers, up to about age six, find transformations of reversible sentences particularly difficult. Clearly, the structure of a sentence is crucial to its meaning, and children's errors in making elicited transformations help the researcher ascertain where their challenges lie.

*Methods for Eliciting Narrative*
Researchers use a variety of methods for getting children to produce sequences of sentences by reporting past events or telling imaginary stories. As of about three years of age, children can be encouraged to do so with the following types of prompts:

- asking the child what happened at school, at the party, on vacation, and so on
- asking the child to recount a well-known fairy tale
- telling the child a novel story and asking the child to repeat it
- providing the stem of a story (a couple of sentences introducing the characters and the setting) and asking the child to continue
- asking the child to tell a story based on a sequence of pictures

Analyses of the child's resulting narratives are based on identifying either story structure (whether the narrative has a beginning, development, and end), or on examining the linguistic devices used in the story (pronouns, full noun phrases, different verb tenses, and so forth). We deal with this in detail in Chapter 6.

## Methods for Studying Language Comprehension

The array of language tasks described in the previous sections provides researchers with a rich source of information concerning the processes of language production. But as we stressed in the introduction to this chapter, children's comprehension often reveals greater language competence than their production abilities would suggest. So several research methods have been developed specifically to delve into what children understand. Unlike production methodologies that can only be used with children who are already producing words, comprehension methods can be applied to pre-linguistic infants.

### THE PREFERENTIAL LOOKING TECHNIQUE

Like the head-turn preference procedure, the preferential looking technique capitalizes on a natural infant behavior. Rather than assessing the direction and length of head turns, this method focuses on children's differential looking behavior when given a choice of two visual displays. This approach is used in studies of early language comprehension. It has also been adapted to explore various other aspects of infant cognition such as number judgments and discrimination by shape, size, and color.

Until fairly recently, computerized testing was unavailable. The preferential looking procedure was initially carried out using what is known as the Fagan Box (see Figure 3) to study word comprehension. It is still used today because it is portable and easily manipulated to suit different types of visual stimuli. These might include, for instance, pictures of different objects or animals for testing vocabulary, as well as faces or other more abstract displays. The apparatus is a viewing box that has a hinged panel or lid across the front and contains two compartments into which visual stimulus cards are slotted. A light concealed in the viewing box illuminates the displays and the baby's face when the panel is lowered. The two compartments are usually about 25 to 30 centimeters apart, far enough apart for the experimenter to be able to determine easily which of the two displays the infant is looking at. There are usually at least two experimenters, one who manipulates the stimuli and the lid, and the other, the observer, who monitors the infant's reactions through a peephole centered between the two compartments. The infant cannot see the observer.

At the start of a trial, a rattle is used to draw the infant's attention to a central point in the area where the two displays will appear. Once she is focused, the lid is lowered to reveal a pair of stimuli for a fixed amount of time, say 10 to 20 seconds. During the presentation period, the experimenter says: "Look, look at the X," where X is the

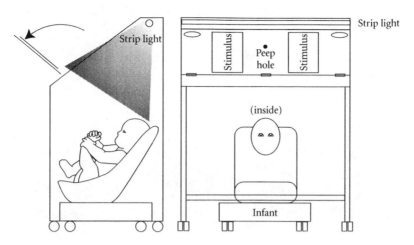

*Figure 3*   The Fagan Box

name of the right-hand object, the left-hand object, or neither. The infant is expected to look longer in the direction of the named object if she understands that word. If neither object corresponds to the experimenter's label, then the infant should look at both stimuli for equivalent periods of time. The same holds if the baby does not know the word. Once the set time has expired, the lid is raised, the next set of stimulus cards is slotted in, and the procedure is repeated.

The observer is able to see the direction of the infant's gaze in the corneal reflection of the infant's eyes. This allows the observer to measure on two stopwatches (one for the left card, one for the right) the cumulative visual looking time for each stimulus as the baby moves back and forth between the displays.

The computerized version of the preferential looking technique is very similar, but more flexible and precise. In this case, the pairs of visual stimuli are displayed on two monitors, while the auditory prompt is played on a central loudspeaker (see Figure 4). In its most up-to-date form, the stimuli are presented on a single wide screen to avoid the possible confounding effect of different onset times from two monitors. The observer views the child's direction of looking through a hidden lens above the monitor(s). To record how long the infant looks at each display, the observer presses one of two buttons

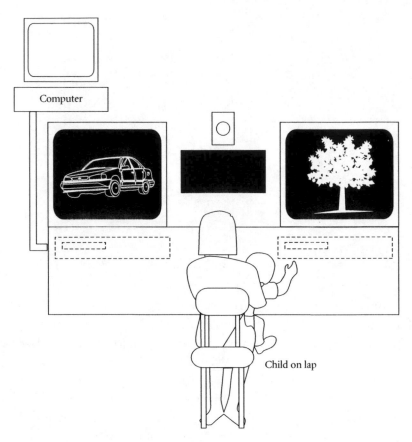

*Figure 4*   Preferential looking procedure (adapted from Kathy Hirsh-Pasek and Roberta Michnick Golinkoff, *The Origins of Grammar: Evidence from Early Language Comprehension,* Cambridge, Mass.: MIT Press, 1996, fig. 3.1, p. 60; used by permission)

corresponding to each display. The buttons are connected to a computer that registers the precise looking times to each of the stimuli and presents the data in a form ready for statistical analysis. The observer is blind to the position on each trial (left or right) of the stimulus corresponding to the auditory prompt.

In the computerized version, the infant's looking behavior is also videotaped to allow for subsequent observer reliability tests. Apart from obvious advantage of more precise stimulus presentation and measurement of responses, one of the major benefits of the computerized presentation is that both static and animated displays can be used. This means that the infant can be tested for her comprehension not only of isolated words, but also of simple grammatical structures. For example, the infant's sensitivity to simple word order might be tested by using two subtly different animated displays: on one side, a girl pushing a boy, and on the other, a boy pushing a girl. The baby's looking response to the auditory prompt "the girl is pushing the boy" is then measured. The words "girl," "push," and "boy" apply to both displays. Only the word order itself indicates which display is being referred to, so the infant's looking behavior will tell us whether or not she is sensitive to different meanings conveyed by word order. Studies using the preferential looking technique will be discussed in Chapters 4 and 5.

### OFF-LINE TECHNIQUES

Research with older children can be divided into off-line and on-line procedures. Off-line techniques measure comprehension by getting children to perform an action or produce language after hearing a linguistic stimulus. They therefore involve conscious decisions or reflections by the child. On-line techniques, by contrast, measure language processing as it occurs in real time.

The acting out technique is one of the most common off-line methods of testing children's language comprehension. In this case, the child is provided with a group of props (dolls, animals, or objects) and asked to act out the experimenter's utterance. For example, if the researcher is interested in whether children understand the difference between active and passive sentences, the child might be asked to use toy animals to show the experimenter "the dog pushes the cow" versus "the cow is pushed by the dog."

Another technique uses picture pointing. In this case, the child is presented with four pictures to choose from, and asked to point to the one that depicts the action in the experimenter's utterance (for example, "the cow is pushed by the dog"). The three other pictures to choose from might show a cow pushing a dog (the child's answer if she only took word order into account), a cow feeding a dog (the child's answer if she ignored the verb), and perhaps a horse pushing a cat (the child's answer if she did not pay attention to or understand the nouns).

While the techniques of picture pointing and acting out offer some advantages for guessing what aspects of language the child understands, they have several shortcomings. In the picture pointing task, it is the experimenter who decides which erroneous answers the child might give, and the group of pictures presented may thus actually influence the child's responses. In the acting out technique, young children often have problems simply coping with manipulating two dolls or objects simultaneously. A third problem is that both techniques are off-line. The child's task is not like normal language understanding, which takes place in real time. Rather, the child first hears a sentence and then, post factum, acts out or points to the meaning contained in the sentence. This involves some degree of conscious reflection or a metalinguistic component that may be beyond the capacity of young children. So despite having possibly understood the experimenter's utterance, they may not actually be able to display that knowledge in an off-line task.

### ON-LINE TECHNIQUES

On-line techniques tap into the actual processes of language comprehension as they occur in real time. For instance, we can use this approach to test whether the child is sensitive to the difference between transitive and intransitive verbs. On-line experiments are designed around the following procedure. The child is instructed to monitor (or listen) for a particular word, say "dog" or "lion," in sentences played on a loudspeaker or through headphones. Everything is carefully standardized in advance, and all words are counterbalanced for their length and their frequency in normal, everyday language. The target word is positioned immediately after the grammatical form being tested for. For instance, in the following examples, "dog" occurs in one case after a correctly used transitive verb, and in another immediately after an ungrammatical transitive example. Similarly, "lion" appears after a correctly used intransitive verb and directly after an ungrammatical intransitive example. The text prior to the target word must be neutral so that the child cannot anticipate the target "dog," for example, from a verb like "stroked." Examples 27–30 illustrate this on-line technique:

(27) The boy was out on a walk and he watched a DOG passing by.
(28) The boy was out on a walk and he watched to a DOG passing by.
(29) The girl was sitting at the pool and she shouted at a LION passing by.
(30) The girl was sitting at the pool and she shouted a LION passing by.

The child is asked to press a response button as quickly as possible when she hears the target word. The button box is attached to a computer that records the child's reaction time from the onset of the first sound in the target word to the moment, milliseconds later, when the child presses the response button. The prediction is that if she is sensitive to the difference between transitive and intransitive verbs, she will take longer to react to the target words in the ungrammatical sentences. This is because the processing of ungrammatical structures will take longer if the child has already acquired the correct grammatical use of transitive and intransitive verbs. This kind of technique picks up very fine-grained differences in reaction times that reflect the child's processing load when faced by grammatical versus ungrammatical linguistic structures. Furthermore, it does not require the child to reflect on her actions before responding, nor consciously reformulate what she has heard. Because they tap into unconscious processes, on-line techniques are particularly suitable for children who cannot easily perform acting out and pointing tasks that require some metalinguistic awareness. While on-line methods often reveal competence that off-line techniques miss, they are more difficult to design and can be tedious for children because of the large number of trials required for statistical analyses.

## Questionnaire Studies

The parental questionnaire represents yet another approach available to researchers for examining young children's language comprehension and production. There are some advantages to using this method if resources (time and funds) are limited. Questionnaires are particularly good for reaching a wide and varied sample quickly. One of the most commonly used language questionnaires—the MacArthur Communicative Development Inventory (CDI), developed by Larry Fenson and his colleagues—has now been validated in laboratory settings. A large group of parents was asked to first complete the questionnaires at home, then bring their children to be tested in an experimental setting to verify whether the words and structures reported by the parent to exist in the child's repertoire were the same as those produced and understood in the laboratory. The correlations between the questionnaires and the experimental setting were excellent.

The CDI has been used successfully in many studies throughout the world. The American version has been adapted to cover numerous other languages, thus making it a useful tool for cross-linguistic comparisons. Parents are required to record the words that their children can understand (or both say and understand) at specific developmental stages. They are given clear instructions as to how to recognize signs of comprehension. For instance, parents are asked to record the very first signs that their infant recognizes his or her own name (for example, when the child looks up when called), or when their child shows comprehension of words like "no" (noting whether the child momentarily stops what she is doing when hearing the word). Comprehension of expressions such as "Where's daddy?" or "Where's the truck?" can also be detected by the child's actions, in this instance the child looking around for the parent or toy on hearing such questions.

Parents of slightly older infants are asked to note whether their child understands a series of simple phrases like "Are you sleepy?" "Throw the ball," "Open your mouth," and so forth. This is accompanied by a vocabulary checklist of animal sounds (for example, quack quack, woof woof), animal names (bird, donkey), vehicle names (airplane, car), toys (balloon, book), food and drink (carrots, juice), clothing (button, coat), body parts (finger, tooth), furniture and rooms (chair, bedroom), small household items (clock, towel), outside things and places (rain, park), people (brother, teacher), games and routines (bath, peekaboo), action words (push, wipe), words about time (later, now), descriptive words (broken, soft), pronouns (she, mine), question words (where, why), prepositions and locations (down, in), and quantifiers (some, more). Parents are also asked about the appearance of communicative gestures like pointing, and the onset of joint games, social routines such waving bye-bye, actions with objects, pretend play, and imitation of adult actions.

Filling in this type of parental questionnaire requires no formal training, so it is an excellent way of making use of the family context as a surrogate experimental setting. Once a child's language becomes more complex, however, parental questionnaires are less reliable. Controlled experiments conducted by trained researchers are then necessary for testing the child's understanding of more subtle linguistic markers and grammatical structures. In addition, the results of questionnaire studies are dependent on response rates. Middle-class educated parents tend to fill in questionnaires more readily than other, less privileged groups, so at times the results risk not being representative of children in general. Yet questionnaire studies have yielded some very valuable and interesting data by cataloguing individual children's language development in the natural context of the home.

Parental questionnaires have also been developed to record children's early language production. The CDI contains one column for understanding and another for production to document whether children actually say all the words or phrases that they understand. In general, the questionnaire approach can be a very valuable instrument in longitudinal research. In such studies, parents are sent questionnaires to fill in at different stages of their infant's and toddler's development. Together, these data provide detailed information about the order and rate at which children acquire different words over time, much in the same way as the diaries we mentioned at the beginning of the chapter. If used correctly, the home-based parental questionnaire is a reliable indicator of a child's level of language acquisition at particular moments in development.

## Brain Imaging Techniques

One of the most exciting advances of recent years is the development of imaging technology for studying the brain circuits that process language. There are a number of imaging techniques suitable for use with adults—structural and functional Magnetic Resonance Imaging (MRI and fMRI), Magnetic Encephalography (MEG), Event Related Potentials (ERP), and Positron Emission Tomography (PET). These various methods measure changes in either blood flow, glucose uptake, or electrical activity in the brain while the child or adult processes an auditory (or visual) stimulus. Generally, only ERPs are used with infants and children because they are completely noninvasive. High-density ERPs, or HD-ERPs, are measured by placing on the child's head a very lightweight hair net composed of sixty-four tiny damp sponges attached to sensors (see Figure 5). These record the natural electrical activity occurring inside the child's brain as she listens, for instance, to a word, a sentence, or a nonlinguistic sound. Nothing goes *into* the head, and the net is so light that the child rapidly forgets it is there.

During an ERP experiment, researchers place the child in a seat in a soundproofed testing booth, next to the parent. The sensors that make up the ERP net are positioned on the child's scalp over specific areas of the brain. There are no actions or responses required of the child apart from listening to changing linguistic stimuli while wearing the net. While the sounds are played, a computer records the natural electrical activity generated in the child's brain. Unlike many brain imaging techniques that chart only the *location* of brain activity, ERP recordings generate information in real time about both location and the timing of changing waves of brain activity. The researcher can thus identify where electrical impulses are being fired in response to different linguistic inputs, as well as the latency and amplitude of the peaks of activity in the brain across milliseconds of time, from the onset of the stimulus through the full time course of the brain's response. This method allows the researcher to chart how the child's brain becomes progressively specialized and localized for various kinds of language input over the course of development.

*Figure 5* Infant in HD-ERP net

## Conclusion

The development of innovative experimental techniques has opened new doors to the field of developmental psycholinguistics, surmounting a number of the limitations of purely observational research. Nonetheless, the continued use of diary records and questionnaires is vital and should never be entirely replaced by laboratory-based experiments. Through careful observation, the researcher and / or parent can discover many subtle and sometimes surprising capacities in the language-learning child. They can also chart on an hourly and daily basis not only what the child produces, but also what the child does not produce. These are important clues to the child's current level of language development that more formal visits or experimental studies, conducted weekly or monthly, cannot observe. But observation must always, in our view, be followed by carefully controlled experimentation to further validate the observational data and to test precise hypotheses about acquisition. The wide array of methodologies available today makes developmental psycholinguistics a fascinating and challenging field of study. Their use has vastly increased our knowledge of the extraordinary journey to language acquisition from the eavesdropping fetus to the fluent adolescent.

# 3

# SPEECH PERCEPTION
# IN AND OUT OF THE WOMB

In this chapter we focus on an important question: When does language acquisition begin? Is it in the first year when the infant looks around for her mother as her father asks "where's Mommy?" Or is it the first time that the infant herself says "Mama"? In fact, speech perception begins far earlier—in the final months of life in the uterus. During the last trimester of intrauterine development, the fetus is known to be actively processing the sound of its mother's speech and extracting invariant patterns across the complex auditory input that is filtered through the amniotic fluid. This blurs phonetic information but leaves intact the rhythmic properties of speech. Of course, the fetus does not understand anything that it is hearing. Rather, it is learning to recognize the melody and rhythms of language, that is, the intonation contours and the stress patterns that constitute the particularities of both its mother's voice and the sounds that will become its native tongue.

In Chapter 2, we outlined the principal techniques that have allowed researchers to assess the fetus's sensitivities to auditory inputs during the last three months of intrauterine life. This research has shown that the presentation of auditory stimuli consistently elicits changes in the fetus's heart rate and in motor responses like kicking. The data are so reliable that Peter Hepper and his collaborators have shown that it is now possible to detect congenital deafness while a baby is still in the uterus.

But what, precisely, does the fetus discriminate in the muffled auditory input that filters through the amniotic liquid? Data show that fetuses clearly differentiate between language and other sounds, like music or white noise. But their processing goes beyond such broad discriminations. The fetus is also sensitive to certain features within language and music. For instance, it reacts to changes in musical styles (classical to pop; Mozart to Beethoven). In terms of linguistic input, the fetus can be even more discriminating. It seems that the fetal brain is already becoming attuned to dimensions of speech that will be useful for subsequent life in the outside world. For example, the mother's voice heard through the amniotic fluid sounds very different from her voice heard after birth. Nonetheless, experiments show that the newborn infant recognizes his mother's voice at birth, indicating that recognition of the maternal voice is actually learned prenatally. If given the choice, newborns do prefer to listen to their mother's muffled voice as it sounded in utero compared with its sound outside the womb. But if the choice is between the latter and another female voice, they prefer their mother's ex-utero voice. This strong preference exists prior to any real language experience outside the womb, which implies that, while in the uterus, the fetus is able to extract information about some of the invariant, abstract features of its mother's voice that transcend the muffling effect of the amniotic liquid. Obviously this has strong survival value because it encourages the newborn to attend to his mother's voice. It also plays a vital role in the early bonding process.

## Recognizing the Native Tongue

Recognition of the maternal voice is not our only clue to the presence of fetal speech processing. Early studies of infant language discrimination have shown that at four days and even earlier, newborns prefer to listen to their mother tongue over certain other languages, although they do not yet discriminate between different unknown languages. By using the non-nutritive sucking technique, Jacques Mehler and his collaborators in Paris have demonstrated that babies born to French-speaking mothers will suck harder to hear French over Russian. They do not change their sucking rate in response to a change from Russian to English, however, which suggests that they cannot yet tell them apart. It is not, of course, the meaning of the words or the grammar of French to which these newborns are sensitive. Rather, it is something about the rhythmic characteristics of prosody (intonation and stress patterns) that differentiates French from other languages. Again, these are characteristics of speech that can be detected even when a voice is muffled to make it sound as it would in the uterus. Such abstract features of speech, isolated from words and discourse, may seem far removed from meaningful language. Yet, as we shall see, these are precisely the characteristics of speech that will enable growing infants to become progressively sensitive to the phrase structure and word boundaries of their native tongue.

For the newborn, the rhythm of his mother tongue is one of the most salient features of speech input. Building on Mehler's seminal findings, a group of researchers in Paris set out to discover precisely what it is about the rhythmic nature of human languages that helps the infant differentiate some languages and not others. They analyzed a range of different languages and identified three broad rhythmic groups: stress-timed languages, syllable-timed languages, and mora-timed languages. Languages like English, German and Dutch are classified as stress-timed, because their rhythm is determined by the way that stress falls on different parts of words. Stressed syllables can occur in various positions within words, although each language tends to have a predominant stress pattern. In English, for example, the predominant pattern is strong-weak, as in "MAtheMAtics" "BIcycle," and "PENcil." Stress is also used to make important distinctions between some nouns and verbs if the word is the same in both cases ("a CONtrast" versus "to conTRAST").

Languages like French, Spanish, and Italian are called syllable-timed, because all the syllables in words are stressed equally. Whereas stress-timed languages have varying rhythm across words, these languages have a constant rhythm. In French, for instance, when producing the words "mathematique" and "bicyclette," the speaker places equal stress on all syllables, so they sound very different from their English equivalents.

The third rhythmic group is composed of mora-timed languages, which include, for example, Japanese and Tamil. These languages have "light" and "heavy" syllables within words. A light syllable counts as a single mora, as in a sound like "da," because it has a very short acoustic realization. A heavy syllable is counted as two morae, as in a sound like "hon," because its heavier stress results in a longer acoustic realization. So, although the word "Honda" has two syllables ("Hon-da"), with respect to the rhythm of the Japanese language it has three morae: "Ho-n-da."

Based on these rhythmic groupings, Thierry Nazzi, Anne Christophe, and collaborators in Paris joined forces with John Morton and his team in London to test French and English babies' sensitivity to this difference between language families. Using the preferential sucking technique, they showed that both French and English two-month olds could differentiate their own language from a mora-timed language, Japanese. When the babies were tested with a language from the same rhythmic group as their own, however, they showed no change in sucking rate, indicating that they could not tell the difference between, say, English and Dutch. This finding led the researchers to develop the "rhythmic class hypothesis," which claims that one of the first things that very young infants discover is how rhythm organizes their native language. This is what enables them, in the very first months of life, to differentiate and show a preference for their mother tongue from languages belonging to another rhythmic group. It is not until five months that infants discover more subtle, language-specific information, which enables them to make distinctions between languages within the same rhythmic class. In summary, between birth and two months infants process basic rhythmic characteristics of languages. From five months onward, they begin focusing on the specifics of their native tongue.

## Motherese

The rhythm of the input that the infant hears is not only determined by the native tongue. It is also affected by the special way in which people talk to young children. Once the infant is born, in many cultures he is usually addressed with what is called motherese (also referred to as parentese). Motherese is infant-directed speech. It possesses special characteristics in prosody and content that differentiate it from adult-directed speech. Stress patterns within words and sentences are exaggerated, as are intonation contours around phrases. Many repetitions and vocatives (ways of attracting the infant's attention) are used, and questions with rising intonation often replace statements that would normally be used in adult-directed interactions. Here are a few examples of typical motherese (showing the stressed syllables in capitals):

- Aren't YOU a nice BAby? Good GIRL, drinking all your MILK.
- Look, look, that's a giRAFFE. Isn't that a NICE giRAFFE?
- DOGgie, there's the DOGgie. Ooh, did you see the lovely DOGgie?

Clearly, it is neither the grammar nor the meaning of motherese that initially holds the attention of infants. The words and meanings are really irrelevant at this stage. Rather, it is the melodic features of the acoustic signal itself, with its exaggerated prosodic contours. Early on, as we stressed above, it is prosody in particular that helps very young infants organize and remember speech-related information.

But motherese also shows that the dynamics of social interaction play a role in encouraging the infant's attention to language. In some cultures, mothers often set up "dialogues" with their babies, even when they are still in the womb. They will frequently speak to the fetus, feel it move in response, and then respond to those movements with further speech. Once the infant is born, such parents already treat their babies as a valid interlocutor, as if he understands what they are saying. They know, of course, that the newborn does not comprehend the words themselves. But, as Jerome Bruner has argued, these mothers behave as if their babies do understand and thereby actively involve them in these dialogic exchanges. Quite unconsciously, parents ensure that they have eye contact with the infant and then use the exaggerated devices of motherese to maintain joint attention. Very quickly, as parents realize that the infant is responding to their voices with increased kicking, arm movements, wriggles, coos, and gurgles, the two gradually begin taking turns in the interactions: the parent speaks, pauses for the infant to kick or coo, responds to the baby's action, and so on. Throughout, the parent acts as if the infant is understanding the content of speech. Here is a typical example of mother-infant interaction:

> *Mother:* Oh, so you're HUNgry, are you?
> *(Baby kicks.)*
> *Mother:* YES, you ARE hungry. WELL, we'll have to give you some MILK, then, won't we.
> *(Baby coos.)*
> *Mother:* Ah, so Mommy was RIGHT. It's MILK you want. Shall we change your DIaper first?
> *(Baby kicks.)*
> *Mother:* RIGHT! A clean diaper. THAT's what you want. GOOD girl.

Note how the mother speaks as if her baby is understanding and truly responding to the content of her questions. She treats the baby as an intentional being, capable of social interaction. This type of precocious turn-taking lays the foundations for later linguistic interaction. These "conversations" that are initially one-sided linguistically may actually constitute an important preparation for taking part in later dialogue when the toddler will be capable of using language to replace the primitive kicks and gurgles.

Not all cultures respond to prelinguistic infants in this way. As Bambi Schieffelin has shown in exciting cross-cultural work, in some cultures parents barely speak to their infants until the infants themselves are producing speech. In such cultures the early development of motor skills such as sitting and walking is valued far more than language learning. When these infants do begin to speak, they are addressed with adult-like language. Motherese is simply not part of such infants' experiences in their social world. Nonetheless, all such children end up with a full command of their mother tongue. So we need to be careful when generalizing from Western cultures. There is no denying that, where available, infant-directed speech makes language particularly attractive to the baby. But since children in all cultures become fluent speakers, motherese may not be crucial to actual language acquisition. There are many different pathways to the end state.

## Segmenting the Speech Stream

### THE SOUNDS OF WORDS

For older children and adults, speech is not processed as an uninter-
rupted string of phonemes. We segment the speech we hear into
units such as clauses, phrases, and individual words. The young infant, however, faces the task of segmenting the speech stream without knowing any words in advance. So how does the baby learn to
break speech down into units that will enable him to eventually acquire words and grammar? How does the child learn to distinguish
the sounds of closely related words like "pat" and "bat"? It is argued
that infants begin by building up a representation of possible candi-
date words based on sound patterns. It is only later that they learn to
map these patterns onto meaning. That is to say, for the very young
infant, units of speech are not yet "language." They are represented
as groups of sounds as yet independent of meaning and grammar.

Grouping individual sounds into larger units allows the baby to
start structuring the speech stream into more manageable chunks.
But what sources of information might the young infant use to segment the input in this way? There are, in fact, several different types
of clues in the input itself. First, the infant may learn to recognize
the sound sequences that occur most frequently in his native language, and become sensitive to how these occur together in different
linguistic contexts. This might help the infant discover the distributional regularities of sounds in the language. Patricia Kuhl, James
Morgan, Jennifer Saffran, and Janet Werker have devised ingenious
experiments that demonstrate that very young infants are sensitive
to such regularities as they process speech. In one experiment, for
instance, it was shown that even in early infancy babies are very
good at processing three-syllable strings like "gakoti" and "tigako" as
similar. This is only true, however, if the pairs of strings can be represented with only two, rather than three, common units. In this
case, both strings are made up of "gako" and "ti" but in different orders. Babies are far less successful at this task when the three syllables
making up the strings all vary in their positions, as in the pair
"gakoti" and "tikoga." The latter requires breaking down and storing

in short-term memory each string as three separate units ("ga," "ti," "ko"). So we see that being able to group frequently *co*-occurring sounds in the input reduces the processing load, and thus may in turn help the infant recognize and represent possible word candidates.

As the infant brain gradually learns to detect which sound combinations are the most frequent in his language, he also becomes sensitive to which combinations of sounds are legal and which are not. This is called the phonotactics of a language, and it provides important clues to speech segmentation. Phonotactics determine the constraints on possible sound combinations occurring inside words, as well as at the beginning and end of words. In every language, some sound combinations are illegal. Because the sounds themselves vary between languages, so the phonotactic constraints can differ from language to language. In English, for instance, the consonant cluster "sp" is legal at the end ("lisp"), in the middle ("unspoken"), and at the beginning of a word ("special"). In Spanish, however, an "e" always precedes the combination "sp" at the start of a word ("especial"). In segmenting the speech stream into units, the infant's task involves computing how legal sound combinations are distributed in the input of his native tongue.

Becoming sensitive to phonotactics is not only important for learning how sounds occur together; it is also crucial for discovering word boundaries. In English, for instance, the sound combination "tb" is not legal at the start of a word. So if the child hears "t" and "b" next to each other in the speech stream, he will come to realize that this must mark a boundary between two words (like "sit back"). There are also certain sound combinations that are legal both within words and at word boundaries. For example, the sound string "rimen" is common to both "expe*rimen*tal" and "ve*ry men*acing." In the different linguistic contexts, this sound combination has subtly different phonological realizations. The baby is able to use such differences in the acoustic signal as a clue to word segmentation. Anne Christophe and her colleagues in Paris devised an experiment to test the sensitivities of French newborns to such phonological subtleties. They extracted, from recordings of adult speech, the common sound combination "mati" as it occurred both in the middle of the French word "math*émati*cien" and at the boundary of two words "panora*ma ty*pique." Using the high-amplitude sucking procedure, they then played these two extracted segments to newborns. Data showed that the infants' sucking rates changed when the within-word string "mati" was switched to the between-words string "ma_ty," even though both strings contained the same combination of sounds. Thus, it appears that such young infants are already sensitive to very subtle differences in the phonological realization of identical sound combinations as they appear within and between words. This sensitivity, along with the ability to group sounds into regularly occurring patterns, will form the basis of the infant's capacity to segment the speech stream into wordlike units.

Stress patterns within words may also provide important clues to help the baby discover word boundaries in the speech stream. In English, a strong-weak pattern of syllable stress is far more common ("TAble," "CARpet," "TRACtor") than a weak-strong pattern ("ciGAR," "giRAFFE"). In other languages, the predominant stress pattern may be different. Infants therefore have to identify the stress pattern most common in their mother tongue and use that to hypothesize, in English for instance, that a word is more likely to begin at the onset of the stressed syllable. Peter Jusczyk and his collaborators showed that six- to nine-month-old English infants prefer to listen to lists of bisyllabic words that exemplify the predominant strong-weak pattern of English, rather than lists containing words with the weak-strong pattern. It is only later, around ten to eleven months, that they can identify the less dominant weak-strong stress pattern within words like "girAFFE." So stress patterns may be yet another source of information to help the infant segment the flow of speech into linguistically relevant units.

Sound frequency may also play an important role in early segmentation. Well before they understand what words mean, infants have been shown to be sensitive to familiar word patterns. As early as seven months, they can extract a word that recurs in a variety of sentence contexts. This is an important achievement because, like individual syllables or syllable strings, the phonological realization of individual words is affected by the words that surround them. This early capacity for word recognition has been confirmed in a number of experiments where infants were tested for their ability to extract a common word from a series of different utterances. In these studies, babies were played a number of different sentences that had one word in common (a word like "pot," for instance). This shared word appeared in different positions in the sentences. During the familiarization phase, the infant might hear, for instance, a group of sentences like:

I'll give you a pot of sugar.
Put some tea in the pot.
His pot is full of water.
Pot of tea or coffee?
Put the red pot on the table.

Note how the target word "pot" appears in various positions within the sentences, and how the sounds preceding or following this word differ. Once the familiarization phase is complete, the auditory stimulus is switched to a single word uttered many times. This is either the word that had been common to the sentences ("pot" in this case), or another word like "car." Infants show a clear preference for the word that had appeared in the sentences played during the familiarization phase. This implies that they had processed "pot" as a common, recurring part of the complex strings of different phonemes in the stimulus sentences. That is to say, even though they were too young to understand any of the sentences or words they heard, they were still able to extract and remember a common sound pattern. This again shows how, prior to any language comprehension, infants' sophisticated speech perception abilities help them segment the input into what will later become the meaningful words of their language.

In sum, there are at least four different clues in the speech stream that can assist the young infant in segmenting the complex sequence of sounds that make up speech. These are (1) distributional regularities, (2) phonotactics, (3) frequency of sound patterns across words, and (4) subtle differences at prosodic boundaries. Together, these clues help the infant discover the word units of his mother tongue.

## GROUPING SOUNDS INTO GRAMMATICAL UNITS

The fact that motherese exaggerates prosodic contours means not only that word boundaries are highlighted in the speech stream, but also that grammatically relevant segments are made available to the infant. Take the following sentences, which show two different ways of grouping words:

> [It was the boy] [not the girl] [who took the ball].
> [It] [was the] [boy not] [the girl who] [took the] [ball].

Clearly, the grouping in the first example provides information about the constituent structure of English grammar that the unnatural pause patterns in the second example do not. Motherese is known to exaggerate these natural clause boundaries. Unwittingly, therefore, parents who use motherese provide their infant with clues to the way that grammar structures their native tongue. This may again facilitate the subsequent development of grammar.

Experiments demonstrate that around four to six months, babies use prosodic cues to begin structuring the stream of incoming input into grammatically relevant chunks. They display different responses to speech where pauses are inserted correctly, compared to speech containing pauses at incorrect positions. Infants first become sensitive to this type of grammatical segmentation at the level of clause boundaries ("the big boy hit the little dog" has two clauses: "the big boy" and "hit the little dog"). It is only subsequently, as they approach the end of their first year, that they begin using prosody to determine subclausal units at the phrase level ("the," "big boy," "hit," "the," "little dog"). This ability demonstrates that very early on in life, long before the onset of grammatical production, infants can capitalize on the exaggerated prosodic organization of motherese to learn to segment speech into grammatically relevant units. Although these units are not yet meaningful to the baby at this age, this type of early segmentation is vital to the later acquisition of grammar.

Children in cultures that do not use motherese must obtain segmentation information from adult-directed speech, which may not be as transparent. Experimental comparisons of speech segmentation in infants across different cultures have yet to be carried out.

## Conclusion

As we have seen, the abilities of young infants to discriminate among speech sounds and group these sounds are neither all present at birth nor all learned through experience. Rather, the fetus and young infant use language-relevant mechanisms to actively process auditory stimuli well before they understand words or grammar, thereby becoming increasingly sensitive to certain important features of the speech stream. These early sensitivities then help to channel the processing of all subsequent input in linguistically relevant ways.

A common assumption about language acquisition is that it progresses slowly, starting with sensitivity to phonetic contrasts, then moving to syllabic contrasts, then to words, and subsequently to sentences, before finally reaching the level of extended discourse. But the research discussed in this chapter suggests that language perception actually develops at many levels simultaneously. In addition, throughout development the knowledge acquired at each level constrains learning at all other levels. Infants do not move unidirectionally from smaller to larger linguistic units. Rather, they often start by storing the larger prosodic units that they subsequently break down into linguistically relevant parts.

Throughout the entire period prior to producing recognizable words, infants' brains have been actively processing the language in their environment, using a mixture of clues from prosody, clausal and phrasal structure, and distributional patterns of sounds, syllables, and words. These constitute the structure particular to their native tongue. The capacity for speech perception enables infants to construct their first truly linguistic representations of what they hear. As these are gradually built up, the infant's articulatory system is maturing, leading to the production of language-like sounds, initially in the form of cooing and babbling, and later, first words—the subject of our next chapter.

The fetus's, newborn's, and young infant's capacities for speech perception are impressive. But it is vital for the reader not to confuse speech perception with language. Some theorists have used the fact of speech discrimination capacities in newborns to jump to the conclusion that we are born with "language." But in the developing child, processing speech and understanding language are not the same. This chapter has shown how sensitivities to speech can become quite sophisticated prior to any understanding of words or grammar. As the story of language acquisition unfolds throughout the book, the reader will see that there is much more to language learning than being able to appropriately segment the speech stream.

# 4

## LEARNING ABOUT THE MEANING OF WORDS

Parents impatiently await their infant's first words and regard this as one of the most exciting milestones in development. Whereas in Chapter 3 we considered speech perception in terms of units of sounds, in this chapter we are concerned with the acquisition of words as symbolic and meaningful: the emergence of the infant's first productions and the development of the lexicon (the words that form a language). The very earliest stage of vocal output between two and three months is referred to as cooing (vocalizations that are interactional but nonlinguistic). The baby is learning to create sounds at varying pitches and exploring what her voice can do. Between four and six months, the variety of vocalizations she makes increases significantly. The infant now produces raspberry noises, interrupted by vowel-like sounds. This clumsy transition between vowel and consonant-type utterances is called marginal babbling. At first, infants may produce sounds outside those in her native tongue that may belong to a variety of world languages. With time, however, the sounds that she does not hear often are produced increasingly rarely.

From about seven months onward, vowel-consonant transitions become smoother. Productions now take the form of repeated syllabic strings such as "da-da-da-da." This stage is referred to as canonical babbling, and toward the end of the first year it becomes quite complex, involving variegated sequences such as "babi-babi," "biba-biba." Research into the structure of babbling suggests that it is not until about ten months of age, when speech processing is becoming increasingly specialized, that the child's native tongue begins to affect the kinds of sounds the baby utters.

Some time around the beginning of the second year, babbling and word production tend to coexist in the infant's vocal repertoire: each features similar syllables, intonation, and timing. It can be rather difficult, then, to distinguish early words from complex canonical babbles. When do the repeated syllables "ma-ma-ma" become a symbol for "mother"? Is the utterance "ahhr" still merely a babble if the baby is pointing to a car at the same time, or is it the child's idiosyncratic yet consistent sound for "car" that now has real referential status? Even experienced researchers can, at times, find it difficult to determine the nature of these sounds, because the transition from canonical babbling to first words is neither clear-cut nor abrupt.

As we saw in Chapter 3, well before uttering her first word, the infant has been busy segmenting the incoming speech stream at word boundaries. As adults we take this ability for granted. In fact, it is no easy task, because the acoustic signal itself does not provide obvious clues as to where one word ends and the next begins. In spoken language, unlike written language, there are no helpful, consistent gaps between words. But early on in language development the infant discovers the phonotactics of her language and learns which sound combinations are legal and which are not. As we saw, she is also particularly sensitive to stress patterns. Such clues help the infant learn to segment the stream of sounds into separate words. They also assist her in recognizing the presence of the same word when it appears in different linguistic contexts, or when it is pronounced by different speakers, both of which dramatically alter the acoustic signal of individual words.

Although segmentation is vital for preparing the infant for speech, learning the lexicon of one's language involves far more than simply distinguishing word boundaries. What is a "word" anyway? If you try to define this term, you will see just how difficult it is. The *Oxford English Dictionary* defines a "word" as "a sound or combination of sounds forming a meaningful element of speech." But this is inadequate because words also break down into even smaller units of meaning known as morphemes. These include parts of words such as "ed," which conveys past tense ("walked," "painted," "cleaned") or "er," which conveys the concept of agent ("butcher," "dancer," "teacher"). Although morphemes convey meaning, they are not referential in isolation: they have to be attached to the stem of a word. A word, on the other hand, can on its own refer to or symbolize an object, action, event, person, abstract thought, and so forth.

So how does the infant learn that words are actually meaningful, referential symbols? There are few clues in the words themselves (apart from onomatopoeic words such as "sizzle," "crack," or "moo"). On the whole, however, the sounds that form individual words are completely arbitrary. For instance, why is the sound "car" used to represent a type of vehicle? A car could just as easily have been called a "bip" or a "toma." Indeed, across different languages the speech sounds chosen to represent the same meaning are completely different ("car" becomes "voiture" in French, for instance, or "coche" in Spanish). None of these sounds convey the shape, purpose, or even the sound of a car.

Not only are words arbitrary, they are also conventional. By this we mean that people learning English accept that "car" refers to that kind of vehicle, rather than each person choosing his own word to represent this meaning. We would find it very difficult to communicate with one another if we did not have such a tacit agreement with respect to the convention of naming. Over time, some words may be altered by slang, replaced by new ones, or even borrowed from other languages. But such changes are only accepted as part of a language when enough people adopt them.

Having considered the arbitrariness and the conventionality of words, we can see that in order to build up her receptive lexicon, an infant needs to recognize that a word like "car" refers to the whole category *car*, not simply to an individual car. To determine the correct meaning of words, infants must use clues other than the sounds of which the words are composed. For adults, this is a relatively easy task. But the prelinguistic infant cannot ask for definitions, examples, or clarifications. If you point to a picture of a brown dog in a book and say to the infant: "DOG! That's a DOG," how is she to know that you are referring to the four-legged animal on the page, rather than, perhaps, the page, the entire book, or the finger you are using to point? Even if her attention is correctly drawn to the dog it-self, how does she come to realize that it is the animal as a whole that the word "dog" refers to, and not its tail, its furry coat, its long ears, or the fact that it is standing? Pointing alone is clearly too vague to convey the precise meaning of a new word. And there are no phonetic clues to meaning either. Even if, in this case, the toddler successfully learns that the word "dog" refers to the canine in the picture, how does she then come to know that the same sound refers to the whole category *dog* including pictures of other dogs and real dogs walking past her in the street? Furthermore, once she has learned the meaning of the new word spoken by others, what is the process that allows her to produce the sequence of sounds that makes up the word "d-o-g"? All of these steps must be taken into consideration if we are to understand how infants progress from early speech perception to understanding and producing words themselves.

## Biological and Environmental Influences on Vocabulary Development

Overall, the general pattern of language development is relatively similar across children. Though most of the research has centered on English and other Western languages, the cross-cultural work that has been carried out suggests that most children go through roughly the same sequence of stages on their way to becoming fluent speakers. While the sequence may be similar, however, individual *rates* of language development vary considerably. This is particu-larly true for word learning. There is considerable variation in the size and content of children's lexicons, not only from child to child, but also between the sexes. It is therefore important to take account of the influences—-both biological, environmental, and socio-cultural—-that directly and indirectly contribute to individual dif-ferences in language production.

Research has shown that girls tend to produce language earlier than boys. This turns out to be a biological influence. Extensive investigation into the linguistic environments of infants has revealed that this gender difference is not a result of linguistic experience. Studies of Western cultures show that parents talk as much and in a similar way to baby girls as they do to baby boys. It is thought, therefore, that differences between the sexes must be due to certain physiological factors that result in girls' brains maturing somewhat faster than boys. As a result, girls are able to gain control over their articulatory apparatus slightly earlier than boys. A further biological influence is suggested by the link that has been found to exist between maternal verbal intelligence (also referred to as verbal IQ) and infant language production. Verbal IQ refers to the mother's score on items of standardized intelligence tests that measure her language abilities as compared to those that measure her spatial and numerical reasoning. The children of mothers with high verbal IQ tend to display more advanced language skills than do children of mothers with lower verbal IQ. This finding has been further corroborated by studies of language development in adopted children. Robert Plomin and his collaborators have shown that child vocabulary competence is not simply related to adoptive mothers' verbal behavior (an environmental influence), but is also correlated with biological mothers' intelligence (a genetic effect). General biophysiological factors, such as genetic make-up, can therefore clearly affect language development even at the level of word production.

Researchers have identified the presence of a number of general, nonlinguistic influences that play an indirect, although significant, role in word learning. Rather than being specific to language development, these general factors affect the overall environment within which the child grows. Maternal socioeconomic status (SES) is one such factor. In Western societies, mothers of high SES have been shown to address their children more frequently, and with a greater variety of words in longer utterances, than those of lower SES. Other parental characteristics such as education, social competence, knowledge of child development, and attitudes toward parenting can also contribute to the way that parents interact with their infants, thereby affecting the contexts within which words are acquired.

In terms of more direct influences, the role of parental input (the actual speech that the child hears on a day-to-day basis) has been shown to be an important influence on word learning. Specifically, the language that the child experiences affects the onset and progress of word production. By contrast, as we saw in the last chapter, linguistic input does not seem to have a significant impact on the onset of babbling. Because the infant never hears babbling, she has no model to copy. So all infants tend to enter the canonical babbling stage at around seven months, regardless of how much or how little verbal stimulus they receive.

In order to begin building up her vocabulary, however, the toddler has to rely almost completely on the speech she hears. Here, the input model is crucial, whatever the cultural or socioeconomic environments. But what precisely is it about parental speech input that facilitates or hampers word learning? In Chapter 3, we discussed the importance of the special features that characterize motherese found in many, although not all, cultures. Caregivers who tailor their infant-directed speech by emphasizing intonation and stress, and by repeating words, make language more salient to the young listener. But it is both the *way* words are delivered as well as the *content* of adult speech that are important.

In their studies of American families, developmental psycholinguists Letitia Naigles and Erika Hoff-Ginsberg have shown that when children acquire new verbs, for instance, the frequency with which each verb occurs in parental input has the greatest effect on speed of acquisition of that verb. Interestingly, verb acquisition is also affected by the position of the target word within parents' utterances. When verbs regularly appear at the end of speech segments, as in questions like, "where's Daddy *going?*" they are actually easier for infants to learn than when they appear at the start of sentences or mid-sentence, such as "Daddy's *going* to work." A second factor that contributes to the rate at which a verb is acquired is the diversity of grammatical structures in which the verb appears. So it is beneficial for the toddler to hear the same verb used in a number of different ways: in questions, in commands, in exclamations, or in declarative statements. In each case, the verb will be surrounded by different types of words, and the word order, as well as intonation and stress patterns, will vary. The verb itself will take different forms according to tense ("run," "ran," "running") and / or person ("I run," "she runs"). All of these factors make the verb more noticeable, encouraging the child to try to understand its meanings. The effects of linguistic contexts also hold for the learning of nouns, adjectives, and the like.

Even when parents are supplying such supportive models, clearly the child's own capacities for processing linguistic input and discovering meaning and structure continue to play a crucial role. This is exemplified by the cross-cultural work of Eleanor Ochs, Bambi Schieffelin, and Shirley Heath. These researchers have shown that in some cultures the simplified register of child-directed speech is not used, so it cannot be essential to language acquisition. But of course such children do participate in the everyday activities of their culture, which provide a basis for socialization and language development.

In sum, even though infants do not understand everything in the speech that they hear during the first eighteen to twenty-four months, what parents actually say to them, and how they say it, can affect the nature of their subsequent word production. The variety of words used, the manner in which they are presented, and how often a child is addressed and drawn into speech-based interaction may all influence individual differences in word learning rates.

## First Words

Infants begin producing their first recognizable words between roughly twelve and twenty months. This, however, does not mean that they have no receptive lexicon before they can speak. The child's receptive lexicon refers to the words she can understand, as opposed to her productive lexicon, the words she can produce. Research shows that infants begin to recognize and understand a number of words common to their daily routines long before they utter their first words. Using parental diaries, Paula Menyuk and her colleagues found that at around twelve months mothers estimated that their infants understood on average at least ten words. Infants' language comprehension increased to fifty words by fourteen months, and to over one hundred by eighteen months. As far as the productive lexicon is concerned, by twenty-four months most toddlers can produce some fifty different words. These first words tend to be similar across cultures and languages and include the names of familiar people, objects, animals, food, body functions, and social routines or commands. Word comprehension and production thus progress at separate rates. This difference is further supported by the finding that while girls usually produce words earlier than boys, comprehension rates turn out to be far more equal between the sexes throughout development.

It has long been presumed that when toddlers initially begin speaking, they produce nouns (like "dog," "car," "bath," "shoe," or "bottle") before verbs (such as "go," "run," "drink," or "jump"). Understanding the meaning of nouns (which usually refer to relatively clear, tangible whole objects) might seem easier than learning the meaning of verbs. Perhaps this is because it is more difficult to point to an action than to an object or a person. It is true that the earliest words produced by infants are indeed often nouns. Nonetheless, Alison Gopnik has shown that verbs, adverbs, and the like appear early too. Words like "gone" (used by infants to denote that something is finished or someone has disappeared), "bye-bye" (to refer to someone or something about to disappear), "done" or "there" (denoting successful goal achievement), "uh-no" (denoting failure to achieve a goal), and "more" (requesting recurrence of food, a game, or an event) are also very common first words.

Rather than simply identifying first words, what is more revealing is discovering the function these words have for the child. This provides clues as to why some words might develop before others. While infants may copy their caregivers in simply naming things, the very earliest words produced are often termed proto-imperatives because they refer to something that the infant wants. These are not real imperatives in the adult sense (a command like "give me a cookie now"). They are called proto-imperatives because they fulfill the same function but are not expressed in the same linguistically formal way. So, for instance, the toddler might say "juice" or "bottle" to indicate that she is thirsty and wants a drink, or "door" to signal that she wants the door opened so that she can go out. Such instrumental uses of words are designed to lead to a desired outcome, rather than simply refer to an object. But as soon as the child discovers that words are more powerful than actions in controlling other people's attention, many of her words become proto-declaratives—words used to establish joint attention and make a statement about the world. Unlike proto-imperatives, proto-declaratives are not expressions of need or wanting, but rather represent a sharing of information. So, for instance, the toddler might look at her mother and say "bird" while pointing up to the sky, to convey the equivalent of "Look, there's a bird flying past in the sky." Using language simply to share a common experience with the listener is particular to human communication. Animals tend only to use communication in a proto-imperative way.

Early uses of words to make demands and share experiences exemplify what Katherine Nelson deems to be the first function of word production: learning what words *do*. So the toddler's first task in lexical development is to work out how words are used in regulating social interaction, thereby affecting the behavior of others. She also needs to understand that the same word may be used both proto-imperatively and proto-declaratively. So the toddler learns that she can use the single word "juice" to express a number of different things: to ask for a drink, to refer to an image of a carton of juice on television, or to signal that the little boy who just walked past is drinking juice.

While early words may be used to convey different meanings in different contexts, we can see that one of their most notable features is that they rarely refer to a single thing, be it an object, a person, or an action. Throughout the first months of word production, infants usually select a single word to convey a whole event, a wish, or to highlight their own achievements or failures in order to gain appropriate attention, praise, or assistance. So the child may use the word "dog" to signify "the dog is scratching himself," "the dog's leash is hanging on the hook," or "I want the dog to come in." It might even be used to point to a past event, that is, a toy that the toddler saw the dog chewing earlier. The complex meanings that the infant may wish to convey will be limited linguistically at this stage because of the constraints of single word production.

Since the meanings of toddlers' single word utterances change scope according to context, being aware of the situation within which the infant's utterance is produced is often the only way that caregivers can understand her intentions. The importance of both shared experience and shared linguistic context was beautifully illustrated many years ago by Catherine Snow, who documented this conversation between an experimenter and an eighteen-month-old infant while the mother was out of the room.

*Child:* Bandaid.
*Experimenter:* Where's your bandaid?
*Child:* Bandaid.
*Experimenter:* Do you have a bandaid?
*Child:* Bandaid.
*Experimenter:* Did you fall and hurt yourself?
*(Mother enters the room.)*
*Child:* Bandaid.
*Mother:* Who gave you the bandaid?
*Child:* Nurse.
*Mother:* Where did she put it?
*Child:* Arm.

The child and her mother continued for several more turns a conversation composed of extensive conversational exchanges about their shared visit to the doctor. It is important to note that they had not merely shared the experience of making the visit, but above all had previously shared the linguistic experience of discussing the visit together. Unlike the experimenter, the mother therefore knew what kinds of questions would elicit the child's broader word knowledge. As Jerome Bruner and his collaborators showed, this kind of interaction between mother and child provides a kind of "support system" that serves as a scaffold for early lexical development.

## Undergeneralizations and Overgeneralizations

Until recently, research into word use focused mainly on children's initial tendency to under- and overgeneralize the meaning of words. Apart from using single words to embody entire events or desires, it was noted that toddlers use them to refer to overly narrow or overly broad categories of referents. Thus, in certain contexts the word for a whole category might be used like a proper name (undergeneralization) to signify one particular referent, while at other times a single word may be produced to refer to several categories (overgeneralization). An example of undergeneralization would be the child's use the word "train" to refer only to his own wooden engine, not to real trains or to cartoon trains on television. Undergeneralization tends to occur very early in lexical development. In contrast, overgeneralization happens somewhat later and is exemplified by a child's tendency to refer to any four-legged animal—cat, dog, horse, sheep—as "doggy."

Early theories postulated that under- and overgeneralizations resulted from toddlers' tendencies to attach word meaning only to the most noticeable properties of objects. So, in our example, the word "doggy" would, to the child, refer to "animal *with four legs*" rather than represent a specific category of animal. The argument was that the toddler's interpretation of words was restricted by the most salient perceptual features of their referents. In consequence, it was further argued that a child's lexicon only increased once she added a greater variety of features to the meaning of words. Recent studies of perceptual development, however, have shown that very young infants can and do perceive even the most subtle differences between and across category members. One study showed that three-month-olds could not only differentiate between cats and dogs (a between-category distinction), but also distinguish among different kinds of cat (a within-category distinction). Thus perceptual limitations alone cannot explain the existence of under- and over-generalization in language.

Current theories acknowledge that there are a number of different constraints on the development of word meaning. Clearly, the way in which the toddler perceives different categories will contribute to her interpretation of new words. But generalizations seem actually to result from a combination of the toddler's conception of categories and the limitations of her productive vocabulary, which in its early stage amounts to only a handful of words. With such a restricted vocabulary, the infant does not necessarily have enough words to name all the categories she has conceptualized. In some instances, she may well have correctly processed the perceptual and conceptual differences that demarcate categories of animals or objects, but not yet possess the words to express these differences. She is forced to generalize the use of the few words she does possess in order to extend the function of her limited vocabulary. So she may know that cats and horses are different from dogs, but only have the word "dog" to refer to the different four-legged animals she has so far encountered. Note that she does not call horses "truck." In using the word "dog," she has chosen the best word in her limited vocabulary for the job at hand. In other instances, however, the child may not yet have made the required conceptual distinctions, and so the correct vocabulary terms cannot yet be learned.

## The Effect of Vocabulary on Categorization

It is not only cognition that constrains vocabulary growth; a child's vocabulary level can also enhance or hamper her understanding of the world. Sandra Waxman and her collaborators have shown that the use of words can direct infants' attention to what is common among objects and thereby encourage them to form new conceptual categories. Waxman tested thirteen-month-old infants with a simple method in order to ascertain whether the presence or absence of a label affects whether or not a new conceptual category is formed. She divided her infants into two groups. One group was presented with a number of interestingly novel objects of varying shapes and colors that could be grouped as belonging to different classes based on these perceptual properties. The researcher then picked up one of the objects and, without labelling, said: "Look at this, look at this, find me another one." This group of infants was not very successful at forming the new category: they had difficulty in selecting an appropriate "other one." By contrast, the second group of infants was shown the same novel objects, but this time the experimenter labelled the selected item: "Look at this blick, look a blick, find me another blick." In this case, the thirteen-month-olds were successful in selecting an object from the same class. Labeling an object signified to the child that a category was involved, because children of this age are sensitive to the fact that nouns refer to categories. Those in the second group were thus more successful in searching for objects from the same class than those in the first group. So there is a dynamic feedback between developing cognitive skills and growing vocabulary, and words can act as an invitation to form a category.

Adjectives seem to play a similar role in focusing the infant's attention. They serve to highlight common features among objects (for example, color and texture) rather than categories. To test this observation, Waxman devised another set of experiments using a similar paradigm to teach children a nonce adjective like "blickish." They were shown, for instance, four purple horses. One was selected and the experimenter said: "Look, this one is blickish, find me another blickish one," giving the infant then the choice of a purple horse or a blue horse. If toddlers took adjectives as category labels, then they would be as likely to choose the blue horse as the purple horse. If, however, they knew that nouns denote categories whereas adjectives denote properties, then they should select the one with the same "blickish" property (the purple horse). It was found that indeed, as young as thirteen months, toddlers could differentiate between the functions of nouns and adjectives. These linguistic forms help young children categorize the objects in their world.

## Constraints on Word Learning

As the child's conceptual and lexical competence increases, she learns to process new words more efficiently. At the start of this chapter, we gave the example of pointing to a picture of a dog in a book to illustrate just how difficult the word learning task might be. So what is it that helps children pinpoint the precise meaning of words? There are three broad theoretical approaches that seek to answer this question. The first, technically called the lexical constraints hypothesis, is concerned with cognitive processes that constrain the meaning of different lexical items. The second approach concerns social constraints on word learning, and the third theory focuses on strictly linguistic constraints provided by the grammar of language itself. Although many researchers seem to consider only one of the three hypotheses to be explanatory, we argue that cognitive, social, and strictly linguistic constraints all help children narrow down the meaning of words.

## LEXICAL CONSTRAINTS HYPOTHESIS

Despite its label, the lexical constraints framework is a general cognitive approach to word learning. It has been investigated by a number of developmental psycholinguists and looks at how various cognitive factors influence the way in which children map new words onto the objects to which they refer. Four main cognitive constraints have been identified that help children narrow down the meaning of words: mutual exclusivity, fast mapping, whole object constraint, and taxonomic constraint. These limit the number of possible interpretations of new words that the child might have. The mutual exclusivity constraint stipulates that in a given language an object cannot have more than one name, so if the child already knows the word "car," he will not think a new word refers to cars. In other words, in the early stages of word learning, the child does not expect synonyms. The second constraint, fast mapping, stipulates that novel words map onto objects for which the child does not already have a name. These two constraints are fairly similar in scope and are not differentiated by some researchers. Of course, children being brought up bilingually will apply the constraint to each one of their languages. For these children, there will be two words for one referent, but they will be stored separately for each language.

The following example illustrates the mutual exclusivity and fast mapping constraints. A mother says "Look! That's a CUSHION" when her child is looking at a chair with a cushion on it. If the toddler already knows the English word "chair," she will automatically map the new English word "cushion" onto the unknown object, rather than onto the chair. It is only after their use of language is well established that children accept that one object might have two or more names. This is when they accept that the three words "animal," "dog," and "poodle" might refer to one and the same referent. The important aspect of these initial constraints is that they can operate even in the case of a single presentation of a word and therefore do not necessarily rely on the repeated use of novel words.

Closely linked to these two constraints is the whole object constraint, which stipulates that a novel word heard in the presence of a novel object refers to the whole object rather than to its component parts or to its features such as color, shape, or texture. So if the child sees a novel animal and hears for the first time "giraffe," she will not think the word refers to its long neck but to the whole animal. By contrast, once she knows the word "giraffe" and hears "look at the long NECK," she will search for the most salient part of the animal to attach meaning to the new word. So the child progresses from labeling whole objects to hypothesizing that new words refer to the parts, shape, or color of objects. Interestingly, color is usually the last attribute to be considered as the possible meaning of a new word, because it is far less informative about the function of an object. In sum, the whole object constraint specifies that novel words refer to whole objects, unless the name for the whole object is already known, in which case the child maps the word to a part or a feature.

Finally, the taxonomic constraint stipulates that when taught the name of a new object, children restrict their interpretation to a specific taxonomic category. For example, if a child is taught the new word "bus" and is asked to find another bus, she will choose an object from the vehicle category (truck, car, train) if there is no other bus, rather than simply selecting a non-vehicle object with the same color or texture as the original bus.

As we can see, the four different constraints on word learning allow the child to process and acquire new words without having to run through endless possibilities about meanings upon first hearing them. And as her vocabulary grows, the constraints on word processing become increasingly efficient. But it is important to note that these constraints are not applied rigidly in all contexts. They operate probabilistically as default strategies in the absence of more salient cues. So, for instance, if a parent very pointedly taps on the eyes of a teddy bear and repeatedly says "Eyes, these are the eyes," then even if the child does not know the word for the whole teddy bear, she may consider the part as a possible meaning, because the parent is so obviously emphasizing it. But in the absence of very strong alternative cues, the four lexical constraints are used as the best default strategy for guessing the meaning of new words.

Several studies have shown that lexical constraints develop early. Fast mapping, for instance, operates in children as young as two to three years of age. Furthermore, data from Carolyn Mervis and her collaborators suggest that the earlier the child begins to employ fast mapping, the quicker the rate of vocabulary growth. It seems probable, then, that fast mapping may be a prerequisite to the rapid word learning phase that occurs at around two years (see later section on vocabulary spurt). The mutual exclusivity and the whole object constraints are commonly used by children as young as three years when identifying the referent of a new word. Developmental psychologists disagree about whether all the lexical principles are available simultaneously to children at this young age, or whether each one becomes operational at different ages. For instance, one psycholinguist, Ellen Markman, has argued that the constraints are all available at the same developmental time, but that they are selected probabilistically according to the different contexts in which new words are learned. She believes that it is the context of word learning rather than the age of the child that will call for one or several constraints to operate. By contrast, other researchers, such as Roberta Golinkoff and Kathy Hirsh-Pasek, claim that the lexical principles become operative at different stages in development, with the taxonomic constraint being the last to be displayed in normal development.

Along with the lexical constraints framework, researchers have proposed other, more general cognitive explanations to account for the order of acquisition of lexical terms. For instance, it has been argued that the learning of spatial terms like "in," "on," "under," "in front of," and "behind" is constrained by the child's progressive understanding of the concepts underlying these terms. From this viewpoint, the child would not be able to acquire the meaning of, say, "under" until she had grasped that objects can be positioned one on top of the other. But of course learning can go in the other direction too, from linguistic terms to conceptual understanding. In fact, cross-linguistic research shows that the way in which a particular language expresses spatial relations, like containment and support (how objects can fit into one another and be placed upon one another), can significantly influence the way in which children think about spatial concepts.

In sum, learning the meaning of words does not occur in isolation from the child's cognitive development. The child makes use of a wide range of constraints in her attempts to interpret each new word that she encounters.

## SOCIAL CONSTRAINTS

Aspects of the child's social environment can also provide valuable clues to the meaning of novel words. An obvious example is the tendency many parents have of providing labels for those objects to which the child is already paying attention (as in our earlier "cushion" example). But there are other, more subtle aspects of parent-child interaction that can help to constrain the infant's interpretation of a new word. Very early in life, infants pay attention to where adults are looking and pointing. A parent will say: "Look at the dog" and will point and look back and forth between the child and the animal to direct the child's focus of attention toward the correct target. Establishing joint attention and gaze alternation in this way is a partial but vital clue to conveying meaning in such interactions. Interestingly, toddlers make sure that they know where their parent is looking, even while they themselves are engaged in another activity. In one study, it was found that if parents named an object while the child was focused on another, the child would look up, establish where the adult was looking, and map the new word just heard onto the adult's focus of attention (the target object), rather than onto the object she was focused on. This shows how important social clues may be in helping to establish word meaning.

## LINGUISTIC CONSTRAINTS

While cognitive and social constraints both provide vital cues to meaning in the task of word learning, the structure of language itself also plays an important role. It is now known that from an early age children not only pay attention to nouns, verbs, adjectives, and adverbs—the so-called content words of language—but are also sensitive to function words such as articles (like "a" and "the"), demonstratives (like "this" and "that"), prepositions (like "in" and "onto"), and so forth. In fact, function words operate as useful constraints for processing the meanings of new content words. Take the example of the nonce term "gorp." The presence of an article "that's a gorp" tells us that "gorp" is a common noun. But if no article were present (for example, "that's Gorp"), we would guess that it was a proper name or that it refers to a substance, depending on the referent. Similarly, in "he's going to gorp," the word "to" indicates that gorp is a verb.

One of the very first experiments on infant understanding of function words was carried out by John MacNamara over twenty years ago. He showed that toddlers as young as seventeen months are sensitive to distinctions between common nouns and proper names. MacNamara invented a series of nonce words (zav, mef, roz, kiv, pex, jop, wug, zon, tiv, vit, neg, cak) to test this. Infants were shown a doll and told, "that's Zav." In this case, it was hypothesized that if they were sensitive to the grammatical distinction between the presence and absence of an article, then they should take Zav as the doll's proper name and only pick up that particular doll when the experimenter asked for "Zav." Conversely, when they heard "That's a zav" and were asked for "a zav," they should hand any one of the group of dolls to the experimenter. This is precisely what happened. Interestingly, the infants did not pay attention to the grammatical distinction between the presence and absence of an article when the same procedure was used to refer to blocks. This suggests that they also know that people or dolls have names, but blocks do not.

The presence or absence of an article also signals the mass-count distinction—the difference between individual objects that can be counted (such as dogs) and substances that cannot (such as water or sand, which form uncountable masses). Thus we say "a glass" but not "a water." Grammatical morphemes also help to distinguish nouns from verbs. Although nouns often take articles, they do not usually take the addition of the morphemes typical of verbs. So a verb can be identified by the presence of "ing" as in "running" or the presence of "to" as in "to run." If the child hears "the dog is running" she will know that "dog" and "running" are from different linguistic categories and map one onto the actor and the other onto the action. All of these linguistic clues, together with social and cognitive constraints, help children narrow down the possible meanings of new words.

Function words like articles and morphological markings on the ends of words not only help to make the distinction between different linguistic categories; they can also be clues to meaning. Daniel Slobin has hypothesized that children use an operating principle that stipulates, "Pay attention to the end of words." He suggests that this is one of the major constraints on early word learning. As we mentioned earlier, the marker "er" gives clues to the fact that referents like "singer" are animate agents. The presence of the sound "ed" on the ends of verbs points to past tense. Similarly, the marker "s" on dogs, tables, and glasses signals pluralization. Fascinating research using nonce verbs and nouns (for example, "to gorp" or "a wug"), has demonstrated that children as young as three employ such grammatical clues to guess the meaning of words they have never heard before. In sum, one good strategy for distinguishing words and word classes is to pay attention to the ends of words, as Slobin suggests.

Another form of linguistic constraint is the principle of contrast, identified by Eve Clark as yet another important aspect of word learning. It stipulates that speakers and listeners take every difference in form (for example, "run" versus "runs") to signal a difference in meaning. And it may also be a way that parents help their children understand distinctions in meaning. For instance, parents sometimes use words with opposite meanings in the same sentence to make the utterance clearer to their young children. So they may say, "That's not a BIG truck, it's a SMALL truck" or "The boy's not RUNNING, he's WALKING." Such contrasts may make meaning more transparent and help children store information that goes beyond one particular word to include close synonyms and opposite meanings. Sensitivity to contrast may also help children discover that such pairs of words as "big" and "small" or "running" and "walking" belong to the same word class. In this way, children can progressively build up a rich network of interconnected meanings.

Susan Carey invented a clever experiment using overtly contrasting terms to show how quickly children around three years of age can learn a new word. In the task, one of the terms was known to the child and the other was a new word that belonged to the same word class and conceptual category as the known term. The aim was for the children to learn a new adjective after minimal exposure. Using words that they would not have heard before, such as "chromium," she gave children instructions like "Don't take the red tray, take the chromium tray." Here the familiar word "red" provides a useful contrast to the unfamiliar word "chromium" and highlights the linguistic category of the new word (color adjective). Thus the child can use the principle of contrast as a shortcut to the correct meaning of "chromium." This type of research has shown that young children can learn new words very rapidly, even on a single presentation. In normal daily language experience, we can see that the young child has the benefit of a wide range of helpful, contrastive linguistic clues. These clues help her pinpoint the meaning of new words and work out the relationships between them.

## The Vocabulary Spurt

In a study of nearly two thousand American children, Larry Fenson and his colleagues charted the progress in word learning by infants

and toddlers between eight and thirty months. They found that children produced an average of ten words at thirteen months. But of
course, as we have stressed, there is considerable individual variation, with some children producing ten words at eight months and
others almost none until sixteen months. The fifty-word level was
reached, on average, around seventeen months (with a range of ten
to twenty-four months), and by twenty-four months the toddlers
produced between forty and six hundred or more words. At all of
these ages, infants were found to understand significantly more
words than they could produce, with most thirteen-month-olds understanding just over one hundred words and seventeen-month-
olds understanding on average 180 words. By around thirty to
thirty-six months, most toddlers in the study had acquired roughly
150 words in their productive lexicon.

When the child's vocabulary reaches the 150-word level, for most
(but not all) children there is a sudden increase in the rate at which
new words are learned. For some children, the spurt occurs earlier
when they are producing only 70–100 words, whereas for others it
happens when they can say about 200 words. Prior to the vocabulary
spurt, children learn on average about three words per week. But
when they enter the vocabulary spurt stage, their learning of new
words increases dramatically to about eight to ten words per day.

Researchers have differed in their interpretation of this sudden
explosion in labeling. Some have argued that the child experiences a
"naming insight"—a sudden realization that every object and action
has a name. Others have suggested that the spurt is due to a conceptual change in the child's overall cognitive development. This
has been linked to the fact that it is usually when children can
exhaustively sort objects into categories that their vocabularies start
to increase exponentially. Today, however, it is more generally accepted that the vocabulary spurt is simply a function of the child's
current state of learning—that is, the number of words already
learned. In sum, development does not proceed by equal incre-
ments, but is nonlinear. Note that individual differences can be more
readily accounted for by dint of this explanation. It is not therefore

claimed that children undergo the vocabulary spurt at any particular *age*. Rather, they do so at the point at which their vocabulary reaches a certain size. Virginia Marchman and Elizabeth Bates have called this the critical mass hypothesis. This stage of vocabulary development also coincides with the point at which grammar takes off—the subject of our next chapter. So from this point onward not only does vocabulary increase very rapidly, but we simultaneously witness the beginnings of grammar in the form of consistent word combinations and morphological marking. Interestingly, even children who are developmentally delayed and who start producing words much later than typically developing children usually also start to combine words grammatically once their productive vocabularies have reached at least 150–200 words.

## Representation and Storing of Words in the Brain

Although children use the whole array of clues available to them when deciphering the meaning of linguistic input, their early representations of the precise meaning of individual words are shallower than adults'. Frank Keil has shown that children tend to move from representing word meaning according to the characteristic features of objects to representing the defining features or core meaning. Thus "grandma" may initially mean a woman with gray hair and a walking stick who knits and brings presents at Christmas, and only later can a "grandma" be a young-looking, dynamic working woman who is crucially the mother of someone's parent. So the shift from characteristic to defining features is a critical aspect of how children change their mental representations of the words they have learned.

As children's vocabulary expands, so do the demands on the child's processing. In an earlier stage when the lexicon was very small, the sound of each word was relatively unique. Now that more words are known, there may be growing competition in the accessing of similar-sounding individual words. For example, when all the child knows is "dog," "cat," "bath," and "juice," then simply hearing the first sound of any of these words will enable the child to start guessing what word is coming. Most other clues to identifying the word can be ignored. But once the child's vocabulary is wider and includes words like "bathing," "baby," and "bake," as well as "dog," "doll," and "dolphin," she will need to hear more than the first couple of sounds to anticipate the whole word. So as the lexicon grows, different strategies for fast retrieval of word representations will be used. What was helpful at one stage may become less so as the child faces new challenges in the rapid and efficient processing of linguistic input in real time. Once new words are learned, they are stored in long-term memory. One might imagine that the inexperienced young mind can only store newly acquired words as one long list, with each new one added onto the end. In fact, from early on children store words in a highly organized hierarchical way. To demonstrate this, primed monitoring tasks have been designed to investigate the precise nature of long-term memory storage. Priming in psycholinguistic experiments involves listening for a target word (like "doctor"), preceded by either a closely related prime (like "nurse") or an unrelated word (like "bread"). Children are trained to listen carefully for a target word ("dog," for instance), which is also depicted in a picture. They then hear a list of many different words and are asked to push a response button as fast as possible after hearing the target word. In the list, "dog" may be preceded by a taxonomically related word such as "animal," by a word related in meaning such as "cat," by a thematically related word such as "bone," by a word that sounds similar such as "fog," or by a totally unrelated word such as "book." If, for memory storage, meaning relations (semantics) are more important than sound relations (phonology), then primes like "cat" should give rise to faster reaction times to "dog" than when the target is preceded by "fog." Differences in the speed with which subjects react to "dog" after each type of prime, versus the unrelated word, can tell researchers how the target word is stored in memory and, in general, how memory for the lexicon is organized. If, on the other hand, the reaction times for related and unrelated words were the same, then one could conclude that words are simply stored in long-term memory as unordered lists.

Lorraine Tyler and her collaborators have shown that from as young as five years of age, and perhaps before, children store words in memory much like adults do, with semantic relations being more important (that is, causing faster reaction times) than thematically and phonologically related cues. But although this finding indeed shows that children's memory is organized hierarchically, it does not mean that thematically and phonologically related information is irrelevant. We know from research on early reading ability, using both behavioral and brain imaging data, that young children rely on sound patterns such as onset and rhyme (phonological information) when they start learning to decipher words in written form. So the rhyme between "cat" and "mat" or "dog" and "fog" turn out to be important for reading, because they map the common sounds of two words to similar letter strings, helping the child represent written words. In terms of productive vocabulary and oral language comprehension, however, rapid auditory retrieval of word meaning is facilitated most by the semantic relations between words. So linking words in memory in terms of their related meanings is an important facet of development.

## Metalinguistic Awareness of the Concept "Word"

While language is an important tool for communication, it can also be treated metalinguistically—as an object of knowledge in its own right. Just as the child works out how physical objects work, so she spends a lot of time fathoming how language functions. The following dialogue between a mother and her four-year-old daughter illustrates beautifully children's metalinguistic curiosity. It dates back over twenty-five years, but remains one of the best examples of the analytic way in which even young children embrace language. From a very young age, they are clearly interested in how words work and not simply in what they refer to.

*Yara (four years old):* What's that?
*Mother:* It's a typewriter.
*Yara (frowning):* No, you're the typewriter, that's a typewrite.

Recently the four-year-old son of Yara, now thirty-two, was cooking with his mother and got very angry:

> *Alexander: I'm* not the cook, I'm the cooker, Mummy. I'm the cooker today.

Mother explained that the stove was the cooker.

> *Alexander (furious):* No, no, no, that's the cook, it's me the cooker.

In acquiring language, children go beyond simply learning the new labels that parents provide. They also analyze the words they hear to see how they function as part of the wider linguistic context. In these examples, the four-year-olds' spontaneous corrections imply that they have understood something about the morphological marker "er" and expect it to mean animate agent and not inanimate object. Metalinguistic awareness, therefore, involves processes functioning at a different level from those responsible for simply understanding or producing language. Since it might contribute to the child's growing competence, metalinguistic awareness is also of interest to developmental psycholinguists.

Much of the research on metalinguistic awareness has been concerned with overt explanations of individual aspects of language—looking, for instance, at children's explanations of grammatical errors. One approach is particularly relevant to this chapter, because it focuses on children's awareness of the concept "word." The principal aim of this type of research is to determine how children decide what is or is not a word. One of the most extensive developmental studies on the concept "word" was carried out by Ioanna Berthoud-Papandropoulou, a developmental psycholinguist from the Piagetian school of thought in Geneva. In a series of experiments, she endeavored to find out what counts as a word for children. So, for instance, she asked the following type of questions:

- Is "table" a word?
- Is "silence" a word?
- Is "when" a word?
- Is "the" a word?

In response to these questions, Berthoud-Papandropoulou found that five-year-olds think that only concrete nouns referring to objects are words. Although by about age seven children accept that abstract nouns are words, it is not until as late as ten years that they consistently accept articles like "a" as "real" words.

Using a different technique, this researcher also asked whether children would perform better if they were presented not with isolated words, but words embedded in whole sentences. She focused on children's capacity to ignore meaningful relations and attend solely to word boundaries. In one task, for example, she asked children to count the number of words in sentences like "six boys are playing." Interestingly, children around four to five years of age confused the number of protagonists (six) with the number of words (four). This points to young children's failure to appreciate consciously the arbitrary relationship between the linguistic sign and the object that it represents. Somewhat older children around six to seven years of age displayed quite different results. Rather than attending to the number of protagonists, they tended to confuse word boundaries with phrase boundaries. It was common, therefore, for these children to say that the sentence had "two words," reflecting the following sentence breakdown: [six boys][are playing]. Another tendency at this age was to count only the three content words, [six], [boys], and [playing], but not the auxiliary verb "are." For these young speakers, verbs like "to be" were not considered words. The same was found for other function words like the auxiliaries "has" or "was," and articles like "the" or "a." It was sometimes not until nine years of age that children counted these words as "real words."

The results of the research into children's concept of "word" suggest that prior to seven years of age children show a strong tendency to count only content words—also known as open class words (nouns, verbs, adjectives, adverbs)—as words. From the point of view of young children, who have limited metalinguistic awareness, function words—also known as closed class words (for example, articles, pronouns, prepositions, auxiliary verbs)—lack autonomous status as words. They do not count as words when isolated from nouns and verbs. This is why they are not considered words.

We already know from Chapter 3 that very young infants are capable of segmenting words in the speech stream, and obviously this ability does not disappear. But here we address the child's *conscious* awareness of word status, which is quite different from unconscious segmentation of speech stimuli. So while children are indeed able to represent all the words that they hear as individual words, they do not yet seem to consciously know what a "word" is. Of course, this all depends on what we mean by "know." It may well be that at some level the child realizes that "the" is a word, but in a task that requires her to consider this directly and consciously, she responds incorrectly. Asking children to count or define words involves reflective judgments in tasks where language is not being used normally. We seldom say a sentence and then ask the listener to tell us how many words we have used! Children may simply misunderstand what is expected of them in such off-line (unfamiliar) tasks.

What happens if one uses a more on-line approach, as defined in Chapter 2? In a series of experiments focusing on normal on-line language processing, Annette Karmiloff-Smith and her collaborators tried to ascertain if four- and five-year-olds could display more competence in knowing what a word is than earlier research had suggested. During these experiments, children were told a story. At key moments during the storytelling, the researcher stopped and asked the child to "repeat the last word I said." Unlike the metalinguistic tasks discussed above, in this situation normal, on-line language processing occurs but the construction of a full representation of the speech stream is interrupted. The metalinguistic part of the task comes into play at the moment that the child has to extract, from her representation of the speech input so far, a single unit (a word) and repeat it. This is a very different task than answering the reflective questions usually asked in other metalinguistic experiments—those experiments require children to consciously create and interpret representations of words and make judgments as to their status. By contrast, in the on-line approach, children can respond more automatically, which allows researchers to see more precisely how the child conceptualizes words.

The experiment was designed so that if children were unclear about what "word" meant, they could recall the "last word" as a combination of words ("on-the-floor" instead of "floor," "knock-over" instead of "over," "to-think" instead of "think"), or as a single syllable ("lence" instead of "silence," "thing" instead of "nothing"). Alternatively, they might respond with missegmentations ("isa" instead of "a," "norange" instead of "orange"), or with anticipation errors, guessing at the next word that the researcher would produce ("the cat" when the last word heard was actually "the"). Such responses were expected from younger subjects who may not yet have a clear idea of what a word is.

Below is an example of one of the stories used in these experiments (ellipses show the point at which the experimenter stops and asks, "What was the last word I said?"). Note how after the child is given the chance to respond, the experimenter always backtracks slightly so that the child will not lose the gist of the story:

> This is the story of a little girl called Jenny who lives in a lovely [. . .] who lives in a lovely house in the country. Jenny has a big [. . .] Jenny has a big dog who likes to sit under Jenny's bed when she's sleeping. Whenever Jenny tries to go to sleep, the naughty [. . .] the naughty dog starts to bark and keeps her awake. One day Jenny decides to have some silence [. . .] she must have some silence at night. So she puts the dog in [. . .] she puts the dog in the kitchen. But the dog is so naughty that he sits at the door whining and [. . .] he sits at the door whining and barking and scratching the floor. Jenny is not at all pleased. At night she tries to think of some way to keep the dog quiet. Suddenly she has a [. . .] she has a good idea. [. . .]

The story continues, stopping also on other function words like "the" and "to," and on other content words like "eat" and "carry."

Results showed that 54 percent of the four-year-olds, and 96 percent of the five-year-olds, considered both content and function words to be words. They correctly recalled content words like "lovely" and "silence," as well as function words like "and" and "the." So by the age of five, children no longer made the errors typical of seven-year-olds in the metalinguistic tasks that demand conscious reflection, discussed earlier. By contrast, four-year-olds failed to repeat most function words. Interestingly, the experiments demonstrated that when "the last word" was a function word with considerable semantic content (for example, the word "under" versus a word like "a"), even the youngest four-year-olds performed well. So it appears that children experience a transition between four and five in their more unconscious understanding of what "word" means.

The capacity to give the status of word to all words, regardless of their grammatical role, predates learning to read, which most children start sometime between ages four and six. In the past, some researchers have suggested that metalinguistic awareness of the concept "word" might result from the child perceiving the spaces between written words. Clearly, the data from the on-line experiment described here show that metalinguistic development begins earlier and may be an essential part of learning to produce and understand oral language rather than an optional extra. Indeed, we may one day find out that it is a prerequisite for rather than a product of reading.

## Changing Meanings of Words

One of the interesting characteristics of words is that their meanings do not remain static; they can change. This is another facet of word learning that the child will encounter as she becomes a fluent speaker. Adolescent language, which younger children are often exposed to in school and from siblings, is a particularly good illustration of this. The following examples include terms that traditionally (or "officially") have a negative connotation, but have been coined by adolescent groups and given a very positive meaning:

- Oh man, your new shoes are wicked!
- Wow, that's a real bad song! I love it.
- That jacket is sick, man. Can I borrow it?
- That new car is so ghetto. I'd sure like one.

The appropriation of words by adolescents is found in many different cultures and languages. In Quebecois French, for instance, "une soirée écoeurrante" (literally "a sickening party") is used to refer to "a great party." In Brazilian Portuguese, the word "irado" ("enraged") is now used by adolescents to mean "excellent" or "wonderful."

These amusing examples support a point that we made earlier in the chapter: words are both arbitrary and conventional, and if enough people (such as the powerful adolescent peer group) adopt a new meaning, this new meaning may eventually be accepted by members of the wider linguistic environment. Such changes are somewhat rarer with respect to grammar, although they do still occur. One well-known example is the expression "between you and I," which is increasingly replacing the grammatically correct "between you and me" in many English-speaking communities. Though of great interest, the history of language change is well beyond the scope of our book. But the examples given above attest that language is not static, but constantly evolving to enable us to expand our communicative powers.

Language is infinitely creative, yet this creativity does not really stem from the number of words we have in our vocabulary. Rather, it is how we combine words grammatically that allows us to share every new thought, feeling, or experience. But first, what is grammar? Defined most simply, grammar refers to the set of relationships that structure language. The term includes both morphology and syntax (and is therefore sometimes referred to as the morphosyntax of language). Morphology involves the analysis of structure at the word level. It focuses on how morphemes (the smallest units of meaning) are organized and combined to form words and alter meaning in different linguistic contexts. In English, for instance, morphemes include suffixes (for example, plural "s" as in "dogs," past-tense "ed" as in "walked"), and prefixes ("un" as in "undo," "para" as in "paramilitary"). These are called bound morphemes because they are attached to the words that they modify. Although these bound morphemes represent only very small parts of words, their addition or omission can completely transform the meaning of sentences. Some languages, like Tagalog, also have what are known as infixes. These morphemes occur within words, rather than at the beginning or end, and also alter meaning. Suffixes, prefixes, and infixes are collectively known as affixes. In contrast to bound morphemes, unbound morphemes stand alone within sentences. They are not parts of words, but rather whole words, and include not only nouns and verbs that have no extra morphemes attached to them (like "dog" and "go" without the addition of plural or tense markers), but also function words, which alter meaning in similar ways to the bound morphemes. Other examples in English of unbound morphemes are the articles "a" and "the," conjunctions such as "and," and prepositions like "in," "out," "on," and "under." To say "I found a dog," for example, means something very different from "I found the dog."

Languages differ as to how morphemes are organized. In Swedish, for instance, the indefinite article "en" (as in "en hus," a house) is unbound, whereas the definite article "et" (as in "huset," the house) is a bound morpheme added to the ends of nouns. Learning how morphological markers are manifest in a native language is a crucial part of grammar acquisition.

Apart from morphology, the other aspect of grammar—syntax— goes beyond the word level and focuses on structure at the clause and sentence level. The study of syntax aims to uncover the principles governing such grammatical structures as word order. For instance, "Dog bites man" means something quite different from "Man bites dog." Syntactic principles also regulate the movement of phrases both within sentences (the intrasentential level) and across sentences (the intersentential or discourse level). In English, for example, to form a question from a statement, certain (but not just any) parts are moved to the front of the sentence. So the statement "The girl who is on the swing is happy" can be transformed into a question by moving the verb in the main clause (the second "is") to the front of the sentence: "Is the girl who is on the swing happy?" The first "is" in the relative clause cannot be moved, however, because this would yield the ungrammatical "Is the girl who on the swing is happy?" Such movement rules are at the center of our implicit knowledge of syntax.

In order to get a handle on the complexities of grammar, the language-learning child needs to pay attention to multiple levels of language. Apart from learning the individual words that make up his language, it is crucial that he notices how bound morphemes and unbound morphemes function, as well as the ways in which words and phrases are put together to form grammatical sentences. Learning how the morphosyntax of his particular language manifests itself begins in the second year of life and progresses throughout childhood. The actual onset depends to some extent on the language being learned. In a language like Turkish (an agglutinative language in which many bound morphemes are added one after the other at the ends of words), morphosyntactic productivity seems to emerge relatively early—at around eighteen months. By contrast, English-speaking children, whose language is made up of more unbound morphemes, start to produce morphosyntax at around twenty-four months.

"Allgone drink," "Mummy shoe," "shoe Mummy," "many cars," "two mouses." These are typical examples of early grammatical productions in English-speaking toddlers. Word combination and morphological marking stand out among the most striking steps in early language production. Although these initial utterances sound ungrammatical to adults, early uses of morphosyntax allow the toddler to gain far more control over his communicative efforts. He now chooses not only which words to put together, but also their order. By using the same two words in different orders, the child may intend very different meanings. For instance, "Mummy shoe" might indicate possessive marking (Mummy's shoe), whereas "shoe Mummy" might describe an action (Mummy is putting on her shoe) or a request (Mummy, fetch my shoe). Context and intonation will usually be essential in helping the listener understand such early attempts at using grammar. The ability to alter meaning by applying rudimentary morphosyntax to words is often considered to be the first sign of becoming a grammatical being. But as we shall see next, sensitivity to grammar is present in much younger infants, and thus, like vocabulary knowledge, the acquisition of morphosyntax cannot be explored through children's productions alone.

So when and how is grammar acquired? This question lies at the very heart of competing psycholinguistic theories of language development. The debate hinges on fundamental issues about the innateness and uniqueness of human language, the extent to which the structures of language are built-in and specific only to humans. We know that other species have developed complex systems of communication. Birdsong, whale song, the dance of the bees, and the call repertoires of some primates all display remarkable communicative complexity. Research has even demonstrated that certain species are capable of mimicking some aspects of human language by learning lists of arbitrary symbols (manual signs, plastic geometric shapes, and the like). Chimpanzees have been trained to make requests for food, for instance, using manual signs. But as impressive as these achievements are, Laura Pettito and her collaborators have queried the extent to which such symbols really have true referential status for the animal itself. Does the sign for "banana" really refer to an internally represented concept of that fruit in the chimpanzee's mind, or does it simply embody the total situation of obtaining food from a trainer? We discuss this important issue in Chapter 8.

Even if it were conclusively shown that other species are capable of something homologous to arbitrary word usage, this would still be far removed from anything like human language: we seem to be the only species capable of using grammar to group arbitrary symbols (words) together and to subtly modify meaning in creating sentences. Take, for instance, the following two utterances: "the boy kissed the girl" versus "the girl kissed the boy." The three arbitrary symbols, "boy," "kiss," and "girl," could potentially be learned by other species. But although the words are identical in both sentences, the meanings are completely different because of the two different word orders. Meaning can also be transformed by the addition or omission of morphemes like the plural marker "s" as in "the boys kissed the girl" versus "the boy kissed the girls." Adding or omitting one tiny sound, "s," to one word in a sentence creates a very different image in our minds. These subtle yet crucial variations, made possible by grammar, set human language apart from the communication systems of all other species.

## Infant Sensitivity to Grammar

As we saw in Chapter 2, early research on language acquisition concentrated on analyzing child language production rather than comprehension. This was due to a lack of methodologies for studying prespeech capacities in infants. Thus, for a long time, psycholinguists were unaware of the true extent of very young infants' implicit knowledge of grammar. In the 1980s, however, researchers began using some of the new techniques available, such as the head-turn preference procedure, to investigate early sensitivities to grammatical form in far more detail and at a far earlier stage of language development than ever before. This work has led to significant advances in our understanding of grammar acquisition.

Sensitivity to word order was one of the first areas to be investigated. The goals of this research were twofold. The first was to see whether newborns and very young infants could even detect differences in the order of presentation of different sounds, irrespective of meaning. Second, researchers looked at older infants to identify the stage at which they become sensitive to the fact that variations in word order affect meaning.

One example of studies using the head-turn preference procedure showed that from as early as two months of age, infants can detect changes in the order of sounds. Actual words were used in the experiment but obviously, to such young infants, these were just meaningless language-like sounds. During trials, infants listened to the following string repeatedly, "cats-would-jump-benches." Once they habituated to (got bored of) that string of sounds and stopped turning to listen to it, it was changed to "cats-jump-wood-benches," a string whose words all sound the same as those in the previous sentence but occur in a different order. Amazingly, at just two months, the infants showed a differential response to the new stimulus, demonstrating that they had detected the subtle change in the order of the sound strings.

Another, more abstract approach to infant sensitivity to grammar was deployed by Gary Marcus and his colleagues. Rather than presenting the same string of sounds in two different orders, they manipulated a series of short syllable strings to represent two different types of order: same / same / different and same / different / same. The seven-month old subjects were first habituated to a particular three-syllable string, such as "ga-ga-ti" (same / same / different). Then for one group of infants the stimulus changed to a string like "wo-wo-fe" (completely different syllables, but obeying the "same / same / different" abstract structure), whereas for another group of

infants it changed to a string like "wo-fe-wo" (again different syllables, but this time in a new order, "same / different / same"). It was
found that the first group treated "ga-ga-ti" and "wo-wo-fe" as
equivalent, but that the second group of infants treated "ga-ga-ti"
and "wo-fe-wo" as different. The ability to process different sound
strings as sharing basic order relations is important for language
learning, because ultimately grammar involves the representation of
a set of abstract structures. It remains an open question, however,
whether this ability in young infants is specific to linguistic inputs,
or whether it is simply a more general capacity to detect "same" versus "different" patterns—an ability that they may use for any environmental input, be it auditory, visual, or sensorimotor.

The new research on young infants reveals the emergence of sensitivity to grammatical relations. But this tells us nothing about how
children come to realize that *meaning* is conveyed by word order. At
what age do children show sensitivity to changes in meaning given
by different linguistic patterns? To answer this question, Roberta
Golinkoff, Kathy Hirsh-Pasek, and their collaborators used the preferential looking technique (see Figure 4 in Chapter 2). They focused
on infants who were at the single word stage, and tested their comprehension of contrasting utterances to ascertain whether they were
sensitive to differences in meaning conveyed by differences in word
order.

During the trials, seventeen-month-old infants were presented
with intermodal visual-auditory stimuli: they saw images of two
events while simultaneously hearing a sentence emitted from a loudspeaker. The infants were observed to ascertain whether they looked
longer at the display that matched the sentence they heard or the
one that did not. For example, they heard utterances like "Big Bird's
tickling Cookie Monster. Find Big Bird tickling Cookie Monster," as
two images appeared on two video monitors. On one side, the video
image showed Big Bird tickling Cookie Monster and on the other
side, Cookie Monster tickling Big Bird. Prior to the experiment, the
researchers checked that all the infants knew the names of these
well-known TV characters and chose verbs representing actions appropriate for this age group. Given that both the action and the

characters were exactly the same in the two displays, the toddlers' correct interpretation of the three words could only be based on word order. If the infant only noticed the terms "Big Bird," "tickling," and "Cookie Monster" in isolation, rather than processing the order in which they occurred, it was predicted that he would look at each display for an equal length of time. If, however, he was attending to word order, then he should look significantly longer at the image that matched the sentence as a structured whole. The findings revealed a surprisingly early awareness of grammatical form. The seventeen-month-old children looked significantly longer at the display that matched the sentence they heard. We can therefore conclude that, despite their young age, the toddlers were sensitive to the way in which different word orders convey different meanings in English.

The same methodology was used to investigate more complex sentence structures. At age two, most children's sentence production is still fairly rudimentary. Data show, however, that by this age sensitivity to complex grammatical forms is surprisingly well developed. In fact, two-year-olds are able to correctly process the differences between grammatical structures such as transitive versus intransitive verbs. Transitive verbs take a direct object, as in the sentence "Big Bird is flexing Cookie Monster." Intransitive verbs, by contrast, do not (for example, "Big Bird is flexing with Cookie Monster"). In this case, the experimenters chose verbs that toddlers were unlikely to know, to rule out the confounding effect of prior experience. Once again the preferential looking technique was used.

In the experiment, one screen showed Big Bird pushing Cookie Monster up and down to make him flex, while the other showed both the characters flexing up and down next to one another. As in the previous experiment, both the screens both showed the same characters and very similar actions. Yet toddlers as young as twenty-four to twenty-seven months correctly interpreted the sentences and looked longer at the screen that matched the sentence they were hearing. The data revealed that these toddlers were sensitive to the distinction between these two types of verb well before their own productions displayed anything like this level of complexity. It seems that the mere presence of an unbound morpheme (in this case, "with") was sufficient for the toddlers to differentiate between intransitive and transitive sentences.

In this chapter, we will time and again see that infants' sensitivity to grammar vastly outstrips their own production of grammatical markers. Why is this so? Many psycholinguists working on Western cultures believe that the answer lies in intonation patterns of child-directed speech, which may facilitate the packaging of grammatically relevant groupings. So infants' comprehension of language displays sensitivity to grammatical form well before their productions contain any grammar. But while exaggerated prosody may highlight grammatical groupings for the Western child, it cannot be crucial for learning grammar. As Eleanor Ochs and others have shown, there are non-Western cultures in which children successfully learn the grammar of their native tongue without the benefit of the exaggerated intonation of motherese.

The social context of natural dialogue also helps the infant interpret what he is hearing. Input to young children is almost always rooted in the here and now, with lots of pointing and similar paralinguistic gestures. At the very earliest stages of language acquisition, adults rarely talk to young children about absent objects, people, and events, or if they do, it is usually about things very familiar to the infant. This helps to lower the processing load (the amount of mental activity) on the child as he tries to create representations of the nouns and verbs used in speech, and thus allows him to focus more on grammar. This is why in experiments such as those described earlier, the processing load is reduced by supplying images and sentences together, so that infants do not need to conjure up representations of Cookie Monster and Big Bird from memory, or create the syntax to refer to their actions. If the experiment required the child to actually produce sentences in order to show his knowledge of grammar, he would have to retrieve from memory the specific words to use, work out how to order them, add the appropriate morphology, and simultaneously attempt the tricky task of producing the relevant sounds. For the young child, language production can therefore be a very costly process that may lack the supportive context provided by language comprehension tasks. So it is not surprising that children are slower to use grammatical speech than they are to understand it.

The head-turn and preferential looking techniques have helped revolutionize our ideas about early comprehension of grammatical knowledge and continue to assist researchers in unraveling the mysteries of grammar acquisition. We no longer rely solely on production data. Nevertheless, the progressive changes in children's productions, and particularly the errors they make, remain a rich source of information about how children learn to speak grammatically.

## Learning to Produce Grammar

Word combination, one of the earliest forms of grammatical speech, usually begins once children have between 50 and 150 single words in their productive vocabularies. This is also the time when some grammatical morphemes start to appear. When children initially produce grammar, their language often sounds rather like the abbreviated language of telegrams ("Daddy gone," "Mummy shoe," "See big car"). This is why, in the past, this type of early output was referred to as telegraphic speech. At this stage, toddlers omit indefinite and definite articles, as well as prepositions and the like. They also leave out morphemes like plural "s," progressive "ing," and possessive "'s." The term "telegraphic," however, is misleading because such morphemes are not omitted from the language of telegrams, where the aim is to keep the number of words, but not the number of morphemes, to a minimum ("Boys arriving Sunday"). So the notion of a "telegraghic stage" is now obsolete because it fails to fully capture the true features of children's early word combinations. Even though children at first omit important grammatical morphemes, from the moment that they say two words together, they have taken the first important step toward becoming a grammatical speaker.

### THE FIRST MORPHEMES

The longitudinal studies of Roger Brown and his colleagues in the 1960s were a pioneering influence on language production research.

Data collected on their three child subjects—known as Adam, Eve, and Sarah—catalogued the language that these American children produced from the very beginning of their first words until their fourth birthdays, by which time they had become relatively fluent speakers. Brown's extensive studies also identified the order in which grammatical morphemes appeared in each child's output. Although the children differed as to the age at which each morpheme was produced, Brown found that the morphemes appeared in the same order for all three children. Research on other children has since confirmed the general order of morpheme emergence in English.

It is well known that children produce some grammatical markers by chance in copied utterances. Brown therefore developed a specific criterion for accepting a grammatical structure as "acquired." He selected three successive samplings of a child's output. He then measured whether or not the marker in question appeared at least 90 percent of the time in its obligatory contexts. Take, for instance, the plural morpheme "s." Brown assessed whether children applied the plural rule to nouns whenever they were referring to more than one referent. Using this criterion, he was able to identify the first fourteen morphemes to be produced by his three subjects. The list that follows shows their order of emergence:

1. Addition of present progressive "ing" ("Baby running"), to express an action that is continuing in the here and now.
2 / 3. Simultaneous appearance of the prepositions "in" and "on" ("Daddy in garden" or "cat on chair"), to express location.
4. Addition of plural "s" ("more biscuits" or "two cats"), to express number.
5. Usage of irregular past tense ("dog came home" or "Daddy went work"), to refer to something that has already happened.
6. Addition of "'s" ("Mummy's hat" or "Teddy mine's"), to express possession.
7. Use of uncontracted copula verb "to be" ("I am a good girl" or "Mummy is nice").
8. Use of indefinite and definite articles "a" and "the," where nouns had hitherto appeared without articles.

9. Addition of regular past tense "ed" ("walked," "jumped"), to express past time.

10. Addition of third person singular regular ("Daddy walks," "Baby jumps"), where these had hitherto been expressed as bare stems ("Daddy walk").

11. Use of third person singular irregular ("Daddy has hat on"), where these had hitherto been missing ("Daddy hat on").

12. New addition of uncontracted auxiliary verbs ("he can go," "she will like it").

13. Use of contracted copula verb "to be" ("Daddy's nice." "I'm hot").

14. Use of contracted auxiliary verbs ("he'll go home now" or "she'd like an ice cream").

As mentioned, although there are significant individual variations in the age at which toddlers produce these grammatical forms, it has been found that the order of acquisition holds across children.

Common errors made by young children indicate how tricky certain structures are to acquire. Take the examples of the plural on nouns or the past tense on verbs. Many toddlers make a mistake when pluralizing words like "foot" or "sheep" by saying "foots" and "sheeps." Such errors usually occur after they have been reproducing the correct plural forms "feet" and "sheep" that they hear their parents use. Similarly, they often suddenly start using the incorrect past tense "goed," "comed," and "hitted" after having produced the irregular forms of these verbs correctly. This behavioral pattern has been described as U-shaped. Children seem to go through a stage when they overgeneralize rules such as add "s" or add "ed," applying the rules to all forms including the irregulars before reverting to the correct forms. Why is this so? For many years, this behavioral pattern was thought to signify that children initially use each correct form as an independent, fixed lexical item. They then discover rules (such as "add 'ed' to verbs to express the meaning of past time"), which they start to apply indiscriminately to all verbs. In fact, recent reexamination of longitudinal transcripts of child output in the CHILDES database has revealed that children make these overgeneralization errors on average only 2.5 percent of the time. Mistakes such as "comed" and "goed" actually coexist with correct usage of "came" and "went," and most of the time children use the correct form at all ages. It is more likely, then, that rather than follow a U-shaped learning curve, children acquire grammatical forms progressively. It is due to the overall processing load on language production that their use of correct forms is at times inconsistent.

New research into past tense marking has led some researchers like Steven Pinker to argue that language production involves two very different processes. The first entails mental computation of a rule (in this case, add "ed" to a verb stem). That is, when the child utters the word "walked" in a sentence, he does not retrieve the complete term "walked" from memory, but only the verb stem "walk." He then uses the grammatical rule "add ed" and generates "walked." The second process relates to irregular forms and does not involve the mental computation of a grammatical rule at all. Rather, it consists of direct retrieval from the mental dictionary of complete past tense forms. Thus for an irregular verb like "go" there are two mental dictionary entries, "go" and "went." "Went" is not derived by transformation from "go." Depending on what the child wants to say, one or the other is retrieved as a whole term from memory. For regular forms, by contrast, there will be a single entry (like "walk"), plus a general rule (add "ed") for forming the past tense.

If Pinker's dual-process theory is correct, why do overgeneralizations like "goed" occur at all? He argues that such mistakes represent the child's occasional failure to directly retrieve the correct irregular form "went" from the mental dictionary. In such cases, the child resorts to applying by default the past tense rule to a retrieved term. But not all researchers agree that language involves the dual processes of mental computation of grammatical rules and mental dictionary retrieval. Kim Plunkett, Virginia Marchman, and others argue that both the regular and irregular past tense are computed the same way. The question continues to generate heated debate among language acquisition researchers.

Occasional overgeneralizations of grammatical marking persist for several years during development. Sometimes we even catch ourselves doing this as adults when we are talking quickly and not thinking, particularly with similar-sounding verbs. So the resemblance between "fly" and "cry" can sometimes give rise to a mistaken "I flied," by analogy with "I cried," in the otherwise grammatically correct output of a forty-year-old. But we should not underestimate the advances made by the child when he begins producing past tense "ed" and plural "s" with a variety of words, even if this sometimes leads to errors. As an exercise, say aloud the following words and note in your mind the sound of each of the endings: "walked," "climbed," "ended," and "pears," "nuts," "oranges." Although written language involves a stem with the addition of an identical marker "ed" or "s," children learning to produce spoken language face a much more complex task. In each of the these examples, as in all normal speech, the actual sound added is a function of the sound that precedes it. So when you said the words aloud, your articulatory system actually had to compute a different sound for each ending: "walkt," "climbd," "ended," "pearz," "nuts," and "orangez." Identical morphemes with different phonological realizations are called allomorphs. In acquiring grammar, therefore, children not only have to learn to add the relevant markers, but they also have to discover how to pronounce the bound morphemes as they vary across different productive contexts.

Overgeneralization of bound morphemes is not the only error characteristic of early production. It has been found that very young children also tend to omit unbound morphemes, like articles, from their output. Why? There are several possible explanations. It may be that young speakers experience general processing limitations in their capacity to produce speech and have to drop parts of a sentence when it is too long. Another reason may be that unbound grammatical markers involve deeper processing than content words. LouAnn Gerken devised a clever way of testing these alternative hypotheses. She adapted the imitation technique to explore why twenty-six-month-old toddlers leave out words like "a" and "the" in their repetitions. Toddlers were required to repeat two types of utterances, such as:

(1) "Pete gorpa ko wug"
(2) "Jeff reshes the pag"

These two utterances contain the same number of syllables, so length of utterance is held constant. The syllables in (1) do not resemble real English words and have no grammatical functions. By contrast, the third person singular "es" and the article "the" in (2) do have a grammatical function. Gerken showed that even though both phrases are of equal length, toddlers repeated all the syllables in (1) perfectly, whereas they left out "es" and "the" in their repetition of (2). This suggests that when processing (2), toddlers leave out grammatical morphemes not because sentences are too long to reproduce, but because the demands of computing the grammar are too heavy at this young age. The fact that toddlers drop the bound morpheme "es" and the unbound morpheme "the" does not indicate that they have failed to process these morphemes. On the contrary, it actually shows that they have processed them, and this has led to processing overload. In sum, what children say—and fail to say—is not always a good indicator of their grammatical competence.

## THE FIRST SYNTACTIC STRUCTURES

As children increase their use of grammatical morphemes, they are also simultaneously expanding their syntactic productivity by combining and moving words in multiple ways. For English-speaking children, word order is a crucial grammatical device. They learn to vary word order to express different meanings. So "Daddy car" may mean "Daddy's car," whereas "car Daddy" may be the child's way of bringing a passing car to his father's attention. Furthermore, children often select certain types of words as "pivots" around which they build a host of expressions. "More" is a frequently used pivot, that expresses recurrence (or a wish for recurrence)—for example, "more juice," "more jump," "more peekaboo," "more teddy." Disappearance / non-recurrence is often expressed with the pivot "allgone," as in "allgone juice" (I've finished my juice), "allgone jump" (I've stopped jumping), "allgone peekaboo" (we've stopped playing peekaboo), "allgone teddy" (I've hidden teddy). Alison Gopnik and Andy Meltzoff have argued that children tend to include in their outputs only those pivots (recurrence, disappearance, and the like) that they already understand cognitively. So cognitive development constrains the productivity of pivot use. Each time a new concept is acquired (such as recurrence), the corresponding pivot word (like "again") can be used to express a large number of meanings when combined with the many other single words already in the child's vocabulary ("again juice," "again Daddy," "again jump," "again book"). At one point, the use of pivots was thought to characterize a universal stage in all children's grammatical development—the pivot grammar stage. It is now considered to be only one of many possible pathways through which some children increase their expressive powers. Nonetheless, Martin Braine's pivot grammar was a very important step in child language theory, because it represented one of the very first attempts to characterize child grammar in its own right—previously it had been simply defined in terms of the adult end-state grammar.

As they progressively increase their syntactic abilities, children also start adding words that describe properties of objects, as in "pretty cat," "big truck," and "Lucy Mummy," as well as the location of objects: "Daddy bed," "doggie garden," and "juice kitchen." At the earliest stage of single word production, the toddler produces only single words to convey similar meanings. Although Martin Braine's pivot grammar seems relatively unconstrained as far as which words can be combined, Paul Bloom has pointed out that in fact the children's two-word combinations are not totally unconstrained linguistically. For example, toddlers may say "big boy" but never, it seems "big he." Nothing at the level of meaning makes the latter utterance illegal. So toddlers entering the word-combination stage must already be aware of certain grammatical constraints.

Initially, syntax and morphology are often expressed separately. For example, location or possession might be expressed syntactically by word combination alone in utterances such as "Daddy bed" and

"Lucy Mummy." Similar ideas might be expressed by morphological marking on single words—for example, "Lucy's." By the beginning of the third year, however, this partial grammar will be replaced by complete phrases that integrate both syntax and morphology, as in "Daddy is in bed" and "that's Lucy's Mummy."

## Assessing the Complexity of Children's Speech

Once word combination gets well under way, children's language production improves rapidly. But how can we actually quantify the complexity of children's grammar? Simply counting the number of words strung together in each utterance tells us little about grammatical progress. In order to address this problem, Roger Brown devised an ingenious method of analyzing child speech to account for both the length and complexity of every utterance. For each production in his longitudinal data, a Mean Length of Utterance (MLU) was calculated. MLU records not only the number of words in the utterance, but also the number of grammatical markings. For example, the sentence "Daddy eat red apple" has four words and an MLU value of four. In contrast, the sentence "Daddy eats apples" has an MLU of five. It is shorter than the previous sentence but more complex, because it has three words plus two grammatical markers (third person singular on "eat" and plural "s" on "apple"). This method of analyzing child output allows researchers to differentiate between children who are simply stringing word stems together and those who may be producing shorter utterances but are demonstrating more complex grammar.

Between the ages of two to four years, MLU increases rapidly from a length of about two to an average of eight or more, with utterances by then generally taking the form of complete sentences. Words like "and," "if," and "but" start to appear more often. Whereas earlier questions were merely two-word utterances ("Where toy?" "What that?"), now children ask questions in increasingly grammatical ways: "What's that called?" "Why is she doing that?" "Is Daddy still in the kitchen?" "When is Mummy coming home from work?" For parents, this progress can turn out to be rather irritating. This is a time when children seem to ask questions only for the sake of asking, as in this typical exchange between a mother and her two-and-a-half-year-old:

> *Child:* Why that boy go home?
> *Mother:* Because his mother thought he was tired.
> *Child:* Why he tired?
> *Mother:* Because he hasn't slept all day.
> *Child:* Why he not sleep?
> *Mother:* Because they went to a party.
> *Child:* Why they go to party?
> *Mother (exasperated): Because!*

While such dialogues often seem more like a game than real conversation, they are nonetheless ideal opportunities for learning grammar. Note that in these exchanges the mother does not correct the child's grammar, although in some non-Western societies children are actually encouraged to imitate correct adult grammar. Research on American children suggests that children's grammar rarely improves simply through parental correction. In cases where children are corrected, researchers have found that generally the child does not heed the parental example:

> *Child:* Daddy goed to work.
> *Mother:* Yes, that's right, Daddy *went* to work.
> *Child:* Daddy goed to work in car.
> *Mother:* Yes, Daddy *went* in his car.
> *Child:* Daddy goed his car very fast.
> *Mother:* Ah ha, Daddy *went* to work in his car. Say *went* to work, not goed, Daddy *went* to work.
> *Child:* Daddy *wented* to work.

Clearly the child's own grammar, more than the repeated maternal model, guides his speech. Correction only has a very indirect effect at this early stage of grammatical development because the child is focused on using increasingly complex sentences to convey increasingly precise meanings, not on producing correct grammatical forms.

By the time children approach their fourth birthdays, their MLU has increased exponentially, and they pay much greater heed to correct grammar. They have by now become rather fluent speakers and start to use far more complex sentence structures. These include co-ordinated sentences, as well as relative and subordinate clauses:

> "My Mummy goes to work and my Daddy stays home to look after me."
> "It's Jenny who's got my new toy."
> "Watch what I'm doing."
> "Can I have another biscuit when I've finished my juice?"
> "Where did you say he hid my book?"

We can see that in just twenty-four months, between the ages of two and four, children make huge leaps in their use of grammar. And they do this without any explicit teaching. So is grammar learned over the course of development, or are we born with a grammatical mind? Are our human predispositions language-specific, or do they involve more general aspects of cognition and / or social interaction? Such questions form the backbone of the theoretical debates about where grammar comes from.

## Theories of the Acquisition of Grammar

As we have seen, adherence to grammatical form begins some time in the third year of life. Like other aspects of language acquisition, however, there is wide variation among children, with some toddlers starting to use rudimentary grammar as early as fourteen months and others showing no signs of grammar in their speech until well after their second birthday. If grammar were innately specified in the infant brain and simply triggered by hearing the correct forms, why would it take so long to manifest itself? In such a case, one might expect grammar to be an inherent part of the child's output from the start. After all, by the time infants reach their first birthdays they will have had considerable exposure to linguistic input and, as we saw, they already have a significant receptive vocabulary. The average three-month-old has already had approximately 900 waking hours or 54,000 minutes of auditory input. And these calculations do not even take into account the last three months of intrauterine life when, as we learned, auditory learning is already seriously under way. By one year, then, when first words begin to emerge, the infant has had a great deal of language experience. This lengthy period of linguistic exposure could be considered more than ample to support substantial learning of grammar. For those who believe that the basic structure of language is innate, the delay in grammatical output is explained by the late expression of grammar-relevant genes.

Theoretical opinions concerning the process that allows children to crack the grammatical code remain deeply divided. As we saw in the introduction to the book, at one end of the theoretical spectrum are nativist approaches that argue that an abstract form of "Universal Grammar" (UG) is built into the human brain and underlies all human languages. Such theories begin with the premise that evolution has provided the human brain with innate structures for language. Rather than resulting from exposure to a language, these structures are considered to be there from the start and simply triggered by the language that fills the child's environment.

At the other end of the theoretical spectrum are those approaches that argue that the linguistic input itself contains sufficient information about the structure of language for the child to acquire grammar. Such theories propose that general learning mechanisms are called upon when acquiring grammar. Between the two extremes are a number of other approaches that place varying emphases on the effect of factors such as stages of cognitive development or the social environment, which are argued to play crucial roles in helping the child become a grammatical speaker. Descriptions of some of the principal theories of language acquisition follow.

### STRUCTURAL APPROACHES

Noam Chomsky's structural approach to human language has been the major influence on many psycholinguistic theories of a nativist persuasion. Chomsky's own theory has undergone several changes since its original form in the mid-1950s, culminating most recently in the minimalist theory. Full details of his framework go well beyond the confines of our book, so we will keep our account general and refer the reader to the references at the end.

Throughout his theoretical revisions, Chomsky retained a number of general assumptions about the nature of human language that are relevant to the acquisition of grammar. As a starting point, the theory states that language is a system that makes infinite use of finite resources. Simply put, one can create an infinite number of sentences from a finite number of morphemes, words, and phrases. Take the following sentence, for example:

> The ice-cold girls, who had been in the lake for much too long at this chilly time of year, looked blue to the priest riding past on his aging donkey.

It is highly unlikely that you have ever heard these thirty-one words together in this order before. Yet you have no problem understanding and creating an accurate image in your mind, simply from interpreting the words and grammar of the sentence. This is because syntax and morphology enable us to group and manipulate words endlessly, creating new meanings all the time in ways that are immediately understandable to others.

For Chomsky, a second aspect of language that gives it infinite potential is its recursive quality. Once created, sentences are not merely strung together. They can also be embedded in one another. So, for instance, the sentence "The boy kissed the girl" can become "The boy who kissed the girl is happy," or even "The boy who kissed the girl who ran away is happy," and so on. This quality of human language again gives it infinite powers of expressiveness.

These and other unique features of grammar have led Chomsky and his disciples to make claims about the innateness of language. Everyone agrees that there must be some innate component to the human capacity to learn grammar, because we are the only species capable of it. And everyone agrees that children need linguistic experience to learn the actual words that make up their particular native tongue. But nativist theorists maintain that it is the formal constraints that govern how words are structured, combined, and moved within sentences that are universal and innately specified. Thus, language is presumed to be innate at the structural or grammatical level. Chomsky calls this inherent human capacity "Universal Grammar." It embodies, on the one hand, a set of invariant principles that underpin every one of the world's spoken and signed languages and, on the other hand, a fixed set of parameters whose settings differ from language to language. The principles are deemed to be common to all languages, while the parameters are set according to the child's experience of the particularities of his native tongue.

The invariant principles of UG govern the organization of phonology and the lexicon, as well as how structured groupings of words are formed and how they can or cannot be moved within a sentence in order to form questions, relative clauses, passive constructions, and the like. It is particularly important to note that the principles operate on structure-dependent parts of sentences, not on sequences of single words. Structure dependence defines how words form grammatical groupings. Take again the case of question formation illustrated earlier in the chapter. In order to ask a question, we can turn the sentence "The boy is leaving" into "Is the boy leaving?" It might seem that doing so simply involves a rule for finding the first verb and moving it to the beginning of the sentence. But this is not so. Consider the next, very similar sentence: "The boy who is tall is leaving." To turn this into a question we cannot just apply the earlier rule. Doing so would create *"Is the boy who tall is leaving?" which is ungrammatical. (Linguists use asterisks to denote ungrammaticality.) What is important is not the position of a particular word. Rather, it is the grammatical function of the word to be moved within the clauses making up a sentence. So, in our "tall boy" example, the first "is" is part of the embedded relative clause and functions as part of the predicate ("who is tall"). The second "is" is an auxiliary verb in the main clause, and it is this verb that moves to form the question "Is the boy who is tall leaving?"

Other principles of movement pose constraints on the subjects and objects of embedded clauses. Thus we may say "Who do you think loves Jack?" but it is ungrammatical to say *"Who do you think that loves Jack?" This is because the subject of an embedded clause cannot be extracted to form a question while retaining the relative marker "that." Yet this is not the case for objects of embedded clauses where you can retain the relative marker. So "Whom do you think that Jack loves?" is just as grammatical as "Whom do you think Jack loves?" These examples of subject extraction (the movement of the subject slot of sentences like "Jack") show that we cannot simply generalize from other surface forms, such as object extraction (the movement of the object slot of sentences) to work out the rule for subjects of sentences.

Chomsky argues that because children and adults never make errors like the asterisked examples above, they must be born with a knowledge of grammar that stops them from making incorrect generalizations of movement rules. The underlying structure is simply not evident in what the child hears. This notion of invisible structure led Chomskyans to argue for innate structure. Furthermore, utterances addressed to the child are full of false starts, unfinished sentences, and ambiguous contexts, so are misleading even if the child were able to derive abstract structure from surface forms. The language the child hears is open to too many erroneous generalizations and therefore, Chomskyans argue, learning or experience cannot alone explain how the child avoids making such errors. As stressed above, the invisible structure of the adult grammar is not revealed in the input to the child in any transparent way. This is often referred to as "the poverty of the stimulus" argument.

Several theorists have also stressed that parents rarely correct grammatical errors. Parents tend to correct errors of meaning, or they encourage children to add polite forms, like "please," to their speech. But they rarely seem to provide consistent corrective models of grammar upon which to learn. Therefore, it is maintained, children must be born with the linguistic knowledge that makes them avoid false generalizations. They must already "know" how sentences are broken down into grammatical chunks, as well as which groupings allow for structure-dependent movement and which do not. Chomsky argues that the invariant principles that determine the structure-dependent movement principles and that hold for all possible human languages make this sensitivity possible.

Chomsky maintains that each child is born not only with a set of invariant principles, but also with a number of parameters. It is the setting of parameters that make individual languages differ from one another. Parameters have optional settings (usually two), and it is now that the child's particular linguistic experience comes into play. The models provided by the input allow him to set each parameter in one direction or another. So the parameter settings of an English-speaking child will differ in certain respects from those of, say, a child learning Italian and, in other respects, from a child learning Swahili. One example is the "null-subject" or "pro-drop" parameter. In the theory it has two settings: either (1) subjects of sentences do not have to be marked explicitly (the subject position in the sentence can remain empty), or (2) the overt marking of subject position is obligatory. Italian and English illustrate this contrast. In English, the subject of a sentence must always be overtly mentioned (with the exception of imperatives like "Go home"). You cannot simply say "going." It is necessary to mention who or what is "going," as in "I'm going," "it is going," "they are going," and so on. Similarly, it would be incorrect just to say "snowing." One must include a dummy subject known as an expletive: "it is snowing." Experience of English from a very early age teaches the child that generally he cannot drop the subject of sentences in his language. According to Chomsky, the child's brain therefore sets the pro-drop parameter to the "*non* pro-drop" setting.

If the child had grown up in Italy, however, the story would be very different. In Italian, it is perfectly grammatical to express the three-word sentence "I am talking" with the one-word utterance "parlo" (or "parla" for "he is talking"). The subject of a sentence is given by the morphological marker ("o" versus "a") on the ending of this regular verb "parlare." The child learning Italian, therefore, will discover that in his language subjects do not need to be overtly expressed. He will thus set his pro-drop parameter to the opposite setting from that used by the English-speaking child.

There is some disagreement among theorists as to whether or not parameters already have a default setting at birth. Nina Hyams argues that the Italian-speaking child will not need to set his pro-drop parameter because it already has the default pro-drop setting. Only the English-speaker child will, according to Hyams, need to change the default setting to non-pro-drop.

Another parameter is the so-called head-direction parameter. Some languages, like English, have a standard word order subject, verb, object (SVO). The subject is first but the order of elements in the verb phrase (VO) is verb before object, as in "The boy kisses the girl." This characteristic word order in English means that English is referred to as a head-initial language. Other languages, like Japanese, have SOV as their standard word order. Here again the subject comes before the verb, but the order of elements in the verb phrase is the opposite of English. So the Japanese equivalent of our example would be "The boy the girl kiss." Japanese is therefore referred to as a head-final language. Once again, according to Chomsky's theory, the language-learning child will discover, through exposure to his native tongue, whether to set the head-direction parameter to head-initial or head-final.

Parameter setting does not contradict the notion of an inherent, invariant Universal Grammar. This is because, Chomsky claims, the huge variety of world languages only differ from one another in a very limited number of ways, and as a result of parameter settings. But the theory postulates that the setting of parameters actually does far more than simply differentiate one language from another. It is thought to equip learners with invaluable shortcuts to grammar, thereby reducing the amount of actual linguistic exposure needed for subsequent learning. This is because many aspects of a language covary. In other words, once a parameter is set, it automatically leads to a number of other, often seemingly unrelated constraints on a particular grammar. So, for example, the theory maintains that once a child learning English has set his pro-drop parameter to the non-pro-drop setting, he will then automatically know, without further experience, that it is also obligatory to use expletives (the meaningless "it is" in "it is snowing"). And the Italian-speaking child, having set his parameter to the pro-drop setting, will automatically know, again without further experience, that expletives are unnecessary. He will simply say "nevica" (snowing) for "it is snowing." Likewise, once the English-speaking child has set the head-direction parameter to head-initial, he will automatically place prepositions before noun phrases ("my book is on the table," not "my book is the table on").

And, the argument goes, he will be able to do so without necessarily having heard anyone use prepositions. Chomsky calls this type of grammatical knowledge that flows from parameter setting "entailments." For Chomskyan theory, then, parameter setting plays a vital role in rendering the learning of specific languages rapid and efficient.

As adults, we take our grammatical knowledge for granted, and even if we stopped to consider how we might have come to master our complex grammar, we certainly have no recollection of having learned it. According to Chomskyan theory, this is because every infant's brain comes equipped with the full set of principles and parameters, which require only minimal language-specific experience to be activated. The structural approach to grammar acquisition therefore claims that Universal Grammar constitutes the child's initial language faculty. Universal Grammar exists prior to any linguistic experience and gives the child the ability to acquire any of the world's languages. Depending on where he is born and raised, the child can just as easily learn Swahili, Russian, Japanese, or Urdu as he can English or Italian. While experience of a specific language is necessary for learning words and for setting the innately specified parameters, nativist theories regard experience as secondary to the grammatical capacities that they claim were created by evolution.

Innate grammatical knowledge is also described as tacit. Unless you are a student of linguistics and study language formally, you are thought to be totally unaware of the principles that govern movement within the sentences you produce or the settings of different parameters. You do, of course, notice errors and know whether sentences are grammatical or not. But most often you are incapable of explaining why. This is why our tacit grammatical knowledge is sometimes referred to by nativists as an "instinct," part of a biological plan common to all humans.

In a sense, Chomsky considers language acquisition to be almost instantaneous, triggered by the input. Triggering is thus proposed as an alternative to learning. To "learn" grammatical rules requires a large number of clear-cut examples in the input and, as we pointed out earlier, Chomsky believes natural input to be too opaque to reveal underlying structure. Triggering, by contrast, places far less burden on the input. It is seen to allow language development to progress rapidly, constrained only by the mechanism of maturation, which leads to some structures appearing later than others. For Chomskyans, then, grammar proceeds along a predetermined maturational schedule. And throughout development, the child's grammar, however simple, is claimed never to violate the principles of UG.

Chomsky's theory aims to specify *what* is learned as the child acquires grammar. But it does not, as a theory, explain *how* grammatical structures are learned. Many nativist theorists adhere to the Chomskyan structural account of the adult end-state grammar, but have pointed out that the theory does not sufficiently address the actual course of language development. A schedule of acquisition is assumed, but not explicitly accounted for. So although the principles of UG stipulate how movement is constrained within grammar, the theory tells us nothing about how the child actually comes to discover which constraints pertain to his particular language. Nor, for instance, does the theory explain how the child knows which actual words operate as subjects, objects, verbs, or the like in his language. An account is lacking of how children go about mapping the relationship between universal grammar and the particular grammar of their native tongue. And if children do not start life with some form of Chomskyan UG, how do they derive structure and meaning from the actual language that they hear? The need to address such issues has led to the development of theories particularly concerned with the *process* of grammar acquisition.

### BOOTSTRAPPING APPROACHES

Bootstrapping hypotheses have been developed to explain how the child might acquire the grammar of his native tongue by paying attention to different features of the language. The general idea is that the child can use one part of the linguistic system (such as phonology) to advance learning at another level of the system (such as syntax). In other words, these theories propose that infants' knowledge of one aspect of the input can act as shortcut to learning about a new aspect of the system (allowing them to pull themselves up by their own bootstraps, so to speak). Three main hypotheses have been put forward: (1) prosodic / phonological bootstrapping, (2) semantic bootstrapping, and (3) syntactic bootstrapping.

### Prosodic / Phonological Bootstrapping

Prosodic bootstrapping is based on the fact that languages not only group words into larger structural units such as phrases, clauses and sentences, but also package these syntactic units within prosodic envelopes. A prosodic envelope conveys the idea that those words that go together syntactically also form part of the same intonation pattern. This approach also offers an explanation for how children discover, through intonation, syllable and word boundaries, as we discussed in Chapters 3 and 4. But the theory includes more than just prosody. It also involves the role of rhythm, stress, phonetics, and phonotactics (that is, which combinations of sounds are permissible in a language). This is why it is also referred to as the "phonological bootstrapping hypothesis."

To discover syntactic boundaries at the phrase and clause level, infants need to focus principally on prosodic information. The central tenet of the theory is that the way intonation packages together certain chunks of language mirrors, to some extent, the structure of grammar. This does not mean, however, that there is a straightforward, transparent mapping between prosody and syntax. Rather, it is argued that prosody offers a relatively good, probabilistic clue as to where clausal boundaries might lie, even before the child attempts to analyze their meaning. From this perspective, Peter Jusczyk and his collaborators have hypothesized that infants, from a very young age, pay particular attention to such prosodic envelopes in speech, thereby storing in memory chunks of language that are suitable for subsequent syntactic analysis. So theories of prosodic bootstrapping are more about finding grammatical groupings in the speech stream than about discovering meaning.

We already came across the importance of prosody in Chapter 3. When a typical Western mother is speaking to her child, her exaggerated intonation, pauses, and the like give moderately strong clues about syntactic groupings like noun phrase, verb phrase, and prepositional phrase. The hypothesis, then, is that children's representation of linguistic input includes some automatic bracketing around syntactically relevant chunks. In a sentence like "Look, the boy is patting the dog with his hand," we don't say "Look the boy . . . is . . . patting the . . . dog with his . . . hand." Rather, we tend to group our productions into grammatically relevant packages that mark the beginnings and ends of the noun phrase, the verb phrase, and the prepositional phrase. So, prosodically, this sentence tends to be packaged as "The boy . . . is patting the dog . . . with his hand," marking the different phrasal units. Furthermore, within these units are distinct stress patterns that help to separate different elements, such as the article from the noun. Articles and other unbound morphemes are usually unstressed and of relatively short duration, in contrast to the pronunciation of nouns. Similar phonological differences hold for all types of phrasal groupings: another example is verb phrases where auxiliary verbs are less stressed than main verbs ("they are RUNning").

According to the phonological bootstrapping hypothesis, these naturally occurring intonation packages help the infant to bracket the input automatically into relevant syntactic groupings. From this viewpoint, then, there is more direct information about syntax in the input than Chomskyan theorists allow. This would consequently render certain aspects of language learnable on the basis of relatively simple input. It would also mean that, while the child needs to be equipped from the start with the relevant perceptual capacities to be sensitive to such prosodic bracketing, he would require a much less elaborate universal grammar than is assumed by Chomskyans. So the phonological bootstrapping hypothesis aims to discover how, assisted by his innate processing capacities, the infant is able to build up adequate linguistic representations for grammar to be acquired. It is postulated that prosodic representations provide a scaffold for syntactic analyses upon which subsequent semantic analyses can be performed.

Critics of this theory have argued that the reliability of prosodic cues to syntax has been overestimated, even in the case of motherese. They point out that prosodic boundaries often do not coincide with syntactic boundaries. It is argued therefore that prosody alone cannot get language acquisition off the ground. While prosody does provide one very useful cue, it cannot help the child know which of the prosodic groupings maps onto the noun phrase, the verb phrase, or the prepositional phrase. It is also difficult to see how, though prosodic bootstrapping alone, the child could make the conceptual leap to meaning.

### Semantic Bootstrapping

Steven Pinker developed the semantic bootstrapping hypothesis to explain how the child might discover the mapping between meaning and syntax. Pinker's emphasis on semantics does not preclude his belief that children's initial representations are syntactic from the start. In contrast to other theories, the semantic bootstrapping hypothesis aims to account for how the child might initially use *meaning* to bootstrap the particular syntax of his native tongue.

Pinker makes several assumptions about how the child proceeds. Before the child can understand or produce grammatical language, he first needs to have learned the meanings of many nouns. Second, the child must be able to construct a semantic representation of the input sentence by using a combination of the real-world context and the meanings of individual words in the sentence. Third, Pinker argues that sentences addressed to the language-learning child must be accompanied by nonsyntactic cues like the special intonation of motherese. Given our knowledge of language input in certain non-Western societies, there must exist alternative cues to the prosody of motherese. The input must also obey the general form of simple declarative sentences of the type noun phrase plus verb phrase (like "the boy is hitting the girl"). Fourth, according to Pinker, the child must have prior, innately specified knowledge of certain linguistic universals. This knowledge will allow the child to know instinctively, for example, that (1) agents of transitive verbs (usually the actor of an action like "the boy kisses the girl," where "the boy" is the agent) are expressed as subjects of basic sentences, (2) things directly affected by actions are expressed as objects in the verb phrase (the girl in our example), and (3) names for concrete objects and persons are nouns. Pinker further believes that from the very start, children's linguistic representations already take the abstract forms of noun phrase, verb phrase, prepositional phrase, and subject / object of sentence.

Pinker maintains that initially the child focuses on interpreting sentences in relatively transparent contexts. Upon hearing "The boy is patting the dog," for example, the child needs to know what the words "boy" and "dog" mean before he can even start a grammatical analysis of the sentence. Then, upon seeing the accompanying action (boy touching the dog's back), the child can use this real-world situation to make the formal linguistic analysis, mapping "the boy" to the subject noun phrase, and "patting the dog" to the verb phrase containing a direct object. In other words, to get syntax under way, the child initially extracts an appropriate semantic representation for a verb by mapping the extralinguistic context onto the syntactic string and by inferring what the speaker is trying to convey. In this way, the child is able to learn that "pat" means to move your hand on something in a certain way, as he can infer from the extralinguistic context. He can also derive from the linguistic context that "pat" is a transitive verb that must take a direct object. If the child later hears "the boy is running," he can again combine his knowledge of the meaning of "boy" with the transparent situation being referred to, to conclude that "run," a new word, is the verb phrase and means to move quickly. He can further derive that "run" is an intransitive verb that takes no direct object, because in this case the object slot in the verb phrase is not filled. According to Pinker's theory, the interpretation of verbs is made on the basis of a combination of the child's perceptual and cognitive mechanisms, mapped onto innately specified syntactic structures for noun phrases, verb phrases, and the like. Thus, it is by semantic bootstrapping—the mapping of sounds such as "pat" or "run" onto mental representations of semantic concepts—that the child can then learn the syntactic restrictions on transitive and intransitive verbs.

The central claim of the semantic bootstrapping hypothesis is that children use innate *semantic* entities (like a thing, causal agent,

action, thing being acted upon, thing changing state, or path trav-
eled from source to goal)—the meaning of which they can already
understand—to infer that input sentences are made up of instances
of the corresponding innate *syntactic* universals (noun, subject, verb,
object, preposition, and so forth). Of course, there are exceptions
to the general rules. For instance, not all subjects of sentences are
agents (as in "the boy got kissed by the girl" where girl is the agent
but boy the subject of the sentence). Pinker argues, however, that semantic bootstrapping is a good initial default strategy to get syntax
off the ground. In fact, research shows that the majority of utterances addressed to children in the early stages of language acquisition are simple, active sentences of the type "Mummy's driving the
car." Linguistic analyses of child-directed speech show that the notion of an initial prototype, where the subject is also the agent, does
indeed correspond to the structure of the simple sentences that
mothers use when talking to their toddlers. And this is considered to
be a significant aid to learning during the early period of grammar
acquisition. Later, when input to the child is more complex, semantic bootstrapping will no longer suffice, because by then sentences
are not always simple declaratives where subjects are always agents
and the context is always the here and now. Adults talk to older preschoolers using, say, passive sentences where the subject is the patient and also refer to absent objects (as well as to past, future, and
even imaginary events), rendering direct mappings from semantic
entities to syntactic universals far more difficult. But early on, semantic bootstrapping might indeed offer one way of initiating the
acquisition of grammar.

*Syntactic Bootstrapping*
Semantic bootstrapping showed how meaning could help the child
derive grammar. It is a theory of the acquisition of syntax. Syntactic bootstrapping, by contrast, shows how syntax can be used to
discover meaning. So they are not rival theories, but rather begin
their explanations at opposite points. Semantic bootstrapping occurs when children proceed from understanding something in the
world to mapping it onto linguistic structure ("world-to-language"

mappings). When children use syntactic bootstrapping, they rely on the syntactic structure of language to get to meaning ("language-to-world" mappings).

Critics of Pinker's hypothesis have argued that although semantic bootstrapping may work for some verbs, it cannot be the sole basis for learning all verbs. This is because even when verbs refer to the here and now, not all real-world situations are transparent. How, for instance, could children differentiate between verbs like "to see" and "to look," since the real-world situations to which these verbs refer could be identical? The same holds for the verbs "to chase" and "to run away." Barbara Landau and Lila Gleitman argue that toddlers, once they know some nouns, do not rely on prior semantic knowledge but rather use the *syntactic* contexts in which verbs appear to work out their meanings. The verbs "to chase" and "to run away" could refer to identical scenes (a dog chasing a boy, or a boy running away from a dog), depending on the perspective taken—so referring to the real-world context alone will not help the child understand the subtle difference in the meanings of these two verbs. But the two verbs do not behave in the same way syntactically. The verb "to chase" requires a direct object, whereas the verb "to run away" requires an indirect object introduced by "from." Likewise, the verbs "to see" and "to look" have different syntactic frameworks, with the first taking a direct object, the second an indirect one with the preposition "at."

Parental input seems to highlight differences in closely related verbs by reserving certain contexts for one type of verb and a different context for the other type. In a longitudinal study of one American mother's input to her child, Landau and Gleitman found that only the verb "to look" appeared as a bare imperative, as in "Look at that!" whereas only the verb "to see" appeared as a bare question, as in "See? That's a dog." The restriction of linguistic contexts in the parental input could therefore provide the child with potential syntactic clues to differentiate verbs close in meaning. Such examples demonstrate how semantic bootstrapping alone cannot always be used in the acquisition of language, even during the early stages. Nonetheless, while syntactic bootstrapping explains the acquisition of particular kinds of verbs, it is hard to see how grammar as a whole could get off the ground based on syntactic clues alone. Children must already also have some knowledge of vocabulary items, particularly nouns, as Pinker previously argued.

It is important to stress that while their specific emphases differ, the three bootstrapping approaches are not mutually exclusive. The child learning grammar may use each strategy at different points in development or when faced with specific kinds of linguistic problems. The general ability to bootstrap—be it prosodically, semantically, or syntactically—represents a useful shortcut to building up various parts of the grammatical system. One tenet on which the three approaches tend to agree is the existence of some form of innate universals. But there are many developmental theories of grammar acquisition that do not support the notion of innately specified linguistic knowledge. Other aspects of development, including social interaction, the richness of the structure of the input, the relationship between language and cognition, and domain-general processing are offered as alternative explanations of the acquisition of grammar. We now consider each of these in turn.

### SOCIOPRAGMATIC APPROACHES

Sociopragmatic theories offer a very different perspective on the acquisition of grammar. Here the focus is primarily on the social context within which language is experienced and learned. The aim of such an approach is to understand the characteristics of social interaction that might allow some aspects of grammatical structure to become salient to the child. Joint attention, turn taking, and the sequential information that characterizes discourse are all seen to play an important role in language acquisition. It has been argued that very early on infants become sensitive to the special features of human interaction, and through them become increasingly attuned to the intricacies of the linguistic content. This ensures that general features of language remain both fascinating and salient to the child before he is able to understand the words themselves. But most importantly, according to sociopragmatic theories, the child is able to actually use what he has already learned about the structure of human interaction as a basic template upon which to map grammatical rules. The very nature of social interaction, then, is considered to provide the child with a window onto grammar.

One of the pioneers of this approach, Jerome Bruner, examined in detail the content and structure of social interactions in which children participate in English-speaking, American middle-class families. His aim was to discover whether children were able to infer grammatical structure concerning word order, or case relations (relations such as agent, patient, or recipient of actions) by making analogies with the way people interact. These ideas have been further developed by Jean Mandler in terms of primitive relations that infants may represent and that are readily mappable onto language—such as agent, patient, actions, with what object, moving across what path, from where and toward what goal, and whether the event is completed or repeated. If the child paid attention to such relations involved in who did what to whom and how, he could then build up a representation of agent, action, and patient and map these onto the syntax being used in simple declarative sentences. These representations could thereby provide clues, it is argued, to the structure of word order in a language.

Unlike Pinker's semantic bootstrapping hypothesis, there is no notion here of innately specified, abstract linguistic categories like noun phrase and verb phrase, nor mention of any form of innately specified universal grammar. Rather, the sociopragmatic approach tends to claim that mappings from meaning to syntax are carried out directly on what the child actually hears rather than on the underlying deeper grammatical structure of an utterance. In the sentence "the boy kicks the ball," the child needs to identify "the boy" as the actor, not that "the boy" is the subject of a sentence.

Bruner's ideas have inspired a large body of research that has aimed to reveal how child-parent interactions might shape the acquisition of grammar. The work focuses on examining the different types of language addressed to children as well as the special adult-child patterns of discourse instigated by both parties. In sociopragmatic theories, input is seen not merely as a trigger for grammar, as in nativist theories, but also as a serious contributor to the child's growing language capacity. It is important to recall that these claims were made on the basis of data gathered primarily from English-speaking, middle-class families and therefore may not be generalizable to all children. In such environments, child-directed speech has been found to be characterized by habitual routines, such as question / answer exchanges. These are argued to provide the child with a number of clues to grammatical structure. For example:

> *Mother:* Can we put your shoes on now? Shall Mummy do it?
> *Child:* Me do-it!
> *Mother:* OK, you think you can do it? Go on, try without Mummy's help. Go on, you can try.
> *Child:* Can do-it!
> *Mother:* Can you put your shoes on? Yes, you can!
> *Child:* Shoe on. Can do-it.

The mother's repetitions, her use of auxiliary verbs like "can," and the series of prompts and questions that she uses to sustain the dialogue all help the child isolate different aspects of the incoming language. Such parent-child exchanges are typical of the observational data gathered by sociopragmatic researchers from which they derived a number of assumptions about the learning of grammar. The special features of child-directed speech are argued to provide crucial clues to word order, the use of auxiliaries, and the formation of questions. It has also often been noted that with young infants parents and caregivers do not really use dialogue to convey information. Rather their focus is on engaging their young child in conversation and on sustaining his attention to linguistic exchanges. The information content of such exchanges is often redundant and secondary to the act of interaction itself. This is why question and answer routines about already known facts form the largest part of early conversational exchanges, with the adult continually prompting or initiating further responses from the child. In such exchanges, adults demonstrate how sentences can be restructured from statements to questions, and vice versa. Caretakers commonly reformulate and expand on children's utterances in this way. Thus, in cases where the child's utterance is incomplete, the caregiver might instinctively integrate it into a larger sentence or simply add the missing part, unwittingly providing alternative grammatical models.

As children develop, parents actively tune their speech to the child's growing abilities. They gauge the child's current level of expertise and, as Bruner put it, progressively "up the ante" by slightly increasing the complexity of the exchanges to challenge the child a little further. Catherine Snow has shown that child-directed speech is very different grammatically from adult-directed speech. This is not to say that adults do not use correct grammar or that they are intentionally "teaching" grammar to the child. Rather, the dialogues happen to facilitate the child's learning by repeatedly presenting a rather narrow and simple set of semantic relations and syntactic structures. Adults do this automatically. They seem to be aware that they are communicating with a less competent speaker than themselves and construct their syntax accordingly.

Data on the relationship between maternal input and child output have mainly focused on child vocabulary growth, rather than grammar. Researchers have shown that the child's output is affected by the frequency of the occurrence of certain words in the language directed at them. Social interaction, then, may have a general facilitating effect on vocabulary, on the child's conversational abilities, and on teaching social routines like "hello," "bye-bye," "please," "thank you," and the like. But does it really have a specific effect on the learning of grammatical form? In a series of studies, Erika Hoff-Ginsberg investigated whether certain aspects of the input can be used to predict children's syntactic progress. One of her findings showed that the amount of question and answer routines used by mothers is related to the timing of the emergence of auxiliary verbs in their children's output. This suggests that the nature of the input that the child hears could have a direct effect on the timing of grammar acquisition, and not solely on the growth of vocabulary. But the true extent of this effect on syntax remains unclear.

Sociopragmatic research has also focused on the relationship between maternal speech and children's early use of morphological markers. Michael Jeffrey Farrar identified four properties of maternal reformulations and used these to assess how useful child-directed speech actually is for learning to produce appropriate morphology. The first property concerned whether the maternal reformulation followed directly after the child's utterance. The second related to whether the reformulation maintained the semantic topic of the child's utterance. The third looked at whether the mother's recast version incorporated some of the child's own words. And the fourth concerned whether the mother actually reformulated the child's utterance by adding to it, or simply corrected it. Farrar used these four measures to analyze transcripts of spontaneous mother-child interactions.

The study had two main findings. First, it was only when the parent's utterance was a reformulation rather than a simple correction that it had an impact on the child's subsequent use of morphemes. Second, this only held for the child's use of plural "s" and of present progressive "ing," and not for other morphemes such as definite and indefinite articles, past tense "ed," and so forth. In two areas of morphology, then, it appears that parental reformulation can help children notice the special role that some parts of words have in modifying meaning. It is the frequency of reformulations, rather than corrections, that can have an effect on the speed with which children learn the plural and progressive morphological markers. But as we saw, there were many cases where parental input had no effect at all on children's morphological progress. Indeed, we know that in some non-Western cultures, where reformulations are rare but where parents expect children to imitate a correct model, there is no long-term adverse effect on the overall learning of grammar.

Despite the relatively weak results of the above study, it is important to note that the aspect of language where parental input does seem to help is a relatively important one. Learning to add plural and progressive markers represents a significant step in acquiring grammar, because these mark crucial distinctions between nouns and verbs. Once acquired and consistently used, this grammatically relevant distinction between nouns and verbs could pave the way for subsequent morphosyntactic progress. Nonetheless, it is noteworthy that Farrar's results demonstrate only a very limited effect of maternal input on the time course of the acquisition of grammar. Alone, the sociopragmatic approach cannot explain how children growing up in varied linguistic and social environments become competent in many aspects of grammar.

Sociopragmatic approaches generally fail to explain how complex and subtle grammatical rules could be generated simply from representing language interactions. Social interaction does not in and of itself provide the child with enough information to build up such a complexly structured system as grammar. In a series of studies, Erika Hoff-Ginsberg and Marilyn Shatz demonstrated that the simplified infant-directed speech of motherese is just not refined enough structurally to account for the order in which most grammatical rules are acquired by children. Despite nearly two decades of research on the effects of maternal input, the data have simply confirmed the original finding: a very limited influence of mother's language on the acquisition of only a few morphological markers. Mother-child interaction seems to have potentially more of an effect on vocabulary learning than on the acquisition of grammar.

Sociopragmatic approaches to language acquisition originally set out to demonstrate that the structure of social interaction could provide a model for the structure of grammar. But this claim has not been borne out by the data. On the positive side, this body of research has convincingly shown that conversational exchanges between adults and children can play a role in language development by (1) directing the child's attention to language, (2) promoting a positive attitude toward linguistic exchanges, (3) stimulating conversational turn-taking, (4) teaching social routines, (5) improving the intelligibility of the child's pronunciation, (6) facilitating segmentation through such techniques as exaggerated prosody and repetitions, and (7) providing some feedback in the form of correct models and reformulations. All of these features of parent-child interaction are claimed to reduce the processing load for children, thereby drawing them into the process of learning grammar. But such approaches reduce the role the child himself takes in actively

discovering the intricacies and complexities of grammatical structure in his linguistic environment.

## COGNITIVE APPROACHES

The most influential cognitive approach to the acquisition of grammar is based on Piaget's general theory of child development. For his
disciples Hermine Sinclair, Ioanna Berthoud-Papandropoulou, and
others, the acquisition of basic grammatical structures is directly dependent upon the child's level of cognitive development. According
to Piagetian theory, all learning—be it of language, number, space,
and so on—is underpinned by a common set of cognitive mechanisms. Unlike the nativists and the sociopragmatists, those who adhere to the Piagetian school of thought believe that there is nothing
special about learning language. No innate linguistic knowledge nor
specific social models are invoked to explain how grammar is acquired. From the cognitive viewpoint, language acquisition is analyzed in the same way as are the development of memory, motor
control, object recognition, drawing, number, and so forth.

For Piagetian theorists, the child is considered to pass through
several general cognitive stages during development. These include:
(1) a sensorimotor stage (from newborn to about eighteen months),
when the child's understanding of the world is based solely on the
effect of his actions on the world, (2) a symbolic stage (from eighteen months to about four to five years), when the child forms internal representations of the world, (3) a concrete operational stage
(from about five to eleven years), when the child can reason about
tangible objects and relations, and finally, (4) a formal operational
stage (from about twelve to sixteen years), when the child can reason
about hypothetical situations and abstract concepts.

While the child is in the sensorimotor stage, Piagetians argue that
he cannot represent concepts in terms of arbitrary symbols and is
therefore not ready to learn the arbitrary mapping between words
and meaning. The onset of language is seen to represent the beginnings of a symbolic stage around eighteen months, at which point
the child is believed to be able to think about objects, actions, and
events that are no longer present. Language-processing capacities

are therefore not considered to be language-specific in any way. Rather, they are thought to be simply part of general processing. By this Piagetians mean that the child's brain uses the same processing mechanisms not only for learning to categorize objects and people, or to analyze spatial relations, but also to learn language. For Piagetians, grammar acquisition is not based on capacities that are developed specifically for learning language.

Thus, according to Sinclair, the same cognitive capacity allows the child to fit a set of Russian dolls together and permits her to embed clauses and understand sentences like "The boy whom the girl hit started crying." Similarly, the cognitive mechanism used to understand that when an object simply changes its shape other features like its weight, volume, and quantity remain unchanged (for example, when a round ball of play dough is elongated into a thin sausage), is considered to be the same as the mechanism used to understand that the meaning of the active sentence "the boy pushes the girl" remains unchanged when it is transformed into its corresponding passive sentence, "the girl is pushed by the boy."

While they differ in the emphasis they place on either cognitive or social factors, there is some common ground between sociopragmatic and cognitive approaches. Neither accepts that the child is born with language-specific processing mechanisms. Both invoke the interaction of very general learning mechanisms and specific aspects of the environment to explain language acquisition. For sociopragmatic theories, it is the structure of the dynamics of human interaction that are of prime importance. Piagetian cognitive theory, on the other hand, tends to downplay the role of social interaction in favor of the role of the physical environment. According to the cognitive approach, language is simply one of many inputs that the child experiences in the physical environment. At every step of language acquisition, the child is thought to be constrained by what he can assimilate into his already existing cognitive structures, and by how those structures can accommodate new inputs, be they morphosyntactic or relevant to the principles of physics, number, space, and time.

There is no doubt that cognitive development plays some role in language acquisition. But it is highly unlikely that general cognitive mechanisms alone will be able to explain the process of becoming a grammatical being. Piagetian theory fails to address how children go about actually segmenting the speech stream into grammatically relevant parts, and ignores how they might map words onto verb and noun phrases merely using general processing. It also cannot explain all the data that point to early infant sensitivity to lexical and grammatical constraints prior to the onset of the Piagetian symbolic stage (at eighteen months).

In a child's journey to language acquisition, it becomes increasingly clear that he must use multiple sources of information to learn his native tongue. The process of acquiring grammar is dynamic. In our view, language acquisition will not be fully explained by focusing solely on either domain-general or domain-specific processing mechanisms. Both must play a contributory role. There are now a number of processing models that integrate general cognitive and language-specific theories in an attempt to understand how the child treats the linguistic input as a problem in its own right.

## PROCESSING APPROACHES

### The Operating Principles Approach

Daniel Slobin was one of the first developmental psycholinguists to propose a series of operating principles that children might use to acquire grammar. Initially Slobin presented these in terms of general cognitive principles applied to language, but Slobin's more recent theory includes language-specific principles. He lists a very large number of operating principles, so we will only focus on some of the main ones here, to give an idea of how they are claimed to support the acquisition of morphological markers and word order. Slobin bases his theory on a huge body of cross-linguistic data from children learning different languages throughout the world. Rather than using adult grammar as a model from which to infer child grammar, as Chomsky and others do, Slobin looks at children's own productions to infer the types of operating principles involved in building up what he calls a basic child grammar. Note that he bases the principles of this child grammar on production data. In a sense, then, Slobin's basic child grammar is a performance grammar, which means that the theory is based on children's own productions and the structures that they pay attention to in the speech that they hear. By contrast, Chomsky proposes for the child a competence grammar, which means that the theory is based on children's sensitivity to the abstract characteristics underlying adult language.

Slobin's theory addresses two aspects of early grammar: word order and the way in which children acquire grammatical morphemes. With respect to word order, he begins with the assumption that children build representations of prototypical scenes that are salient and occur frequently in their lives. These are the first representations onto which they try to map the sentences that they hear. Aspects of real-life scenes get reflected in the child's early production grammar in the following ways: "Daddy kick ball," "Daddy got racket," "Daddy going," "Daddy in house, go garden," "allgone food," "more kick." When referring to prototypical scenes, the speaker—be it child or adult—takes a particular perspective. Take the following changes of perspective for a single scene:

> I'm pushing the car across the garden with a stick.
>   (neutral)
> It is I who am pushing the car across the garden.
>   (focus on agent)
> It's with a stick that I'm pushing the car.
>   (focus on instrument)
> It's across the garden that I'm pushing the car.
>   (focus on path)
> It's the car that I'm pushing across the garden.
>   (focus on patient)

In each case the scene is identical, but the perspective taken by the speaker differs. These rather unnatural sentences are more typical of written English. In spoken English, we normally use stress to mark perspective:

> *I'm* pushing the car.
> I'm pushing the car with a *stick*.

I'm pushing the car across the *garden.*
I'm pushing the *car.*

For some languages like French, however, one cannot add stress to certain words. If we take the first example above, in French, "je" (I) cannot be stressed, so the use of another formulation like "c'est moi qui. . ." (It's I who. . .) is necessary to mark perspective. Slobin emphasizes that such cross-linguistic differences will affect language acquisition on two levels. First, they will determine which operating principles are more important in a given linguistic environment. Second, they will affect the word order that children might initially use to refer to prototypical scene ("car garden" versus "garden car"). Young children use their early grammar to mark the perspective they have taken. Therefore the previous series of adult perspectives might be expressed by a twenty-four-month-old child as:

"me push"
"stick car"
"car garden"
"push car"

So, for Slobin, it is not concepts like noun phrase and verb phrase but the perspective that children take on scenes that will determine their early uses of word order.

With respect to other aspects of grammar that his theory addresses, two major types of linguistic operating principles are claimed to be involved in early grammatical production. The first type includes principles for converting heard speech into stored data that the child can then use to construct his basic child grammar—what Slobin terms "perceptual and storage filters." The second type of principles are those that are used to organize the stored data into linguistic systems—what Slobin terms the "pattern makers." Details of the perceptual and storage filters were initially developed in Slobin's early work in the 1970s, and have since been refined by both Slobin and Ann Peters. These principles include, for example, one that instructs the child to pay particular attention to the ends of words (last syllable), which often carry morphological information; stress; and the beginnings of utterances (first syllable). This principle applies both to single words and to quite long formulaic units. In sum, this principle stipulates that the learner should pay attention to and store any perceptually salient stretches of speech.

Another perceptual and storage principle stipulates that the child should keep track of the frequency of occurrence of every unit and pattern that he has stored. This helps the child discover which of the components that he has noticed are the most reliable cues to grammar. Another principle, in contrast, focuses on these reliable cues to help the child discover whether stored segments tend to be preceded or followed by units that occur together in speech strings. This is thought to help the child discover, for instance, that articles like "a" and "the" always precede nouns, and that verbs tend to follow nouns. Of course, there are numerous exceptions to such rules in complex sentence structures, but Slobin's principles are intended to work for early language, which is made up of very basic word-order sentences. In general, then, perceptual and storage filters are seen to help the child single out important, grammatically relevant structures in the speech stream.

The second type of operating principles—the so-called pattern makers—includes principles for discovering and storing grammatical morphemes and their meanings. One example is the principle that stipulates that the child should extract any two units that share a similar-sounding portion, segment off that portion, and then store the common portion and the residue as separate units. So, for example, when hearing the phrases "the dog walked" and "the dog barked," the child should identify the common portion "ed" from "walked" and "barked." He should then store "ed" as one unit and the residue units "walk" and "bark" as separate units, instead of simply storing two whole-word units "walked" and "barked." According to the theory, it is now that the extralinguistic context comes into play, helping the child to discover a common meaning (past time) for the shared linguistic unit that he had extracted.

Having proposed a set of operating principles used to construct the basic child grammar, Slobin focuses on how these are used by the child to discover what is or is not grammaticized in his native tongue. Languages differ as to which principles will turn out to be the most useful. For example, the English-speaking child must learn to mark number in his language (e.g., plural "s," or "it" versus "they") and semantic gender ("he," "she"). By contrast, a French-speaking child needs to learn to mark number, semantic gender, and grammatical gender. So the French-speaking child must also learn that "the table" is "la table" (feminine) and not "le table" (masculine). Every noun in French has arbitrary masculine or feminine gender, and this affects not only the noun, but also modifiers such as adjectives, which must have gender (and number) agreement with the noun ("les tables brunes," "le chien brun"—the brown tables, the brown dog). But, while English marks the difference between animate and inanimate pronouns (he versus it), French does not. For a Chinese-speaking child, things are different again. He does not need to learn to mark either number or grammatical gender in his language. Furthermore, children learning some East Asian, Southeast Asian, and American Indian languages have to learn also to mark shape and size grammatically. In such languages, whenever a noun is used, obligatory markers are included to denote the referent's shape and size. In yet other languages, like Turkish, the learner must always add a marker to distinguish between whether what he is saying is something he personally observed or something he simply knows by hearsay. So languages differ considerably in their obligatory markers. Unlike nativist theories, which claim that all children face a very similar language acquisition task, Slobin focuses on the fact that children from different linguistic communities confront rather distinct language-learning challenges as they progressively discover the ways in which their native tongue grammaticizes different aspects of the physical and social worlds.

Slobin's theory of basic child grammar covers a wide range of other principles, too numerous to mention here, which are claimed to further assist the child in building up increasingly complex morphosyntax to ultimately achieve the adult grammar. The language-specific principles are said to operate in conjunction with a number of general problem-solving principles. These include principles that help the child strengthen representations, link production and comprehension, and reorganize memory entries.

Slobin's processing principles differ from Chomsky's structural principles in that they neither prespecify nor are based on adult end-state grammar. For Slobin, adult grammar is progressively built up during development and not given from the start in the form of a universal grammar. So the basic child grammar is deemed to be qualitatively different from adult grammar. The principles that operate at the basic level are not the same as those that operate in adult processing of grammar. Slobin claims that the young child uses different strategies than the adult to break down the speech stream, and that his mappings are more rudimentary. By contrast, Chomsky proposes that the child obeys Universal Grammar throughout development. Chomsky's language learner is therefore more passive than Slobin's. Chomsky's child does not construct his grammar; it is given to him. Slobin's child, by contrast, uses innate processing mechanisms to actively explore the linguistic environment to discover language-relevant units.

Slobin's principles provide a detailed description of what children might actually be doing to acquire a productive grammar from the speech that they hear. He appears to have worked backward from children's output to how they might have processed the input. The principles have been devised to explain different types of grammatical productions and, as a result, they are rather unconstrained. Any number of new principles could potentially be added to the list, if something unusual turned up in children's productions. There are no formal, internal constraints to the theory, and there is nothing that confines the child to a limited set of principles. In theory, then, the child's basic grammar could embody an ever-increasing number of different principles that might make language learning slow and laborious. It also remains difficult to see how Slobin's basic principles would cope with the constraints of later, more complex syntactic structures. Finally, it is unclear how the different principles interact dynamically in the course of development. The issues of the order in which principles are applied to each utterance, as well as the competition between principles that must arise as the child grows increasingly proficient at processing grammar, are not addressed. This leaves us wondering how the transition between basic child grammar and adult grammar actually occurs.

### The Competition Model

A more dynamic processing model, also heavily based on cross-linguistic research, is the competition model, which was first developed in the 1980s by Elizabeth Bates and Brian MacWhinney. One of the important advances offered by the competition model is to bring together two crucial aspects of language: the significant differences found between individual learners within each language, and the rich statistical nature of co-occurrences in the linguistic input. These theorists consider language to be probabilistic rather than deterministic in nature. In other words, rather than having a fixed Universal Grammar that is determined in advance and applied rigidly at all times, Bates and MacWhinney argue that even adults constantly recompute grammatical structure to accommodate every new utterance that they hear.

Perhaps more than any other area of development, language acquisition is characterized by huge individual variation. Children can begin producing words anytime between nine months and two years, and start adding grammatical form anytime between fourteen months and three years. It is therefore crucial to examine what it is about language that causes such developmental differences. Maturation alone cannot account for this substantial individual variation. Moreover, although language learning varies from child to child within a specific language community, the general patterns of acquisition show strong commonality across all languages. The competition model therefore attempts to uncover the dynamics of the various aspects of language acquisition that result in this combination of individual differences and common ground.

The distinguishing characteristics of specific languages play a crucial role in the Competition Model. By comparing a series of perfectly grammatical sentences in Italian with their literal English translations, it becomes apparent just how varied the particular expressions of grammar are across different languages. The sentences below show six different types of word order, all of which are quite acceptable in Italian, but only one of which is grammatically correct in English. Word order is determined by the positions of the subject (S), the verb (V), and the object (O). In Italian, a great deal of variation in word order is permitted in order to reflect the speaker's perspective on his or her statement. As we can see, word order cannot play the same role in English; instead, stress is often used.

(1) *(SVO):* Io mangerei un primo
This translates literally to,"I would like to eat a first course." SVO is the typical English word order, hence the literal translation is grammatical in (1). But the following examples show just how different Italian and English word orders can be and how stress in English replace word order changes in Italian.

(2) *(OSV):* La pastasciutta Franco la prende sempre qui.
This translates literally to "Pasta, Franco it orders always here." Translating with correct grammar and stress would instead give, "Franco always orders *pasta* here."

(3) *(VSO):* Allora, mangio anche io la pastasciutta.
This translates literally to "Well then, am eating also I pasta." Translation into proper English would give, "Well then, *I'm* also eating pasta."

(4) *(VOS):* Ha consigliato la lasagna qui Franco, no?
This translates literally to "Has recommended the lasagna here, Franco, right?" and can be rendered in English with appropriate stress as, "It's *lasagna* that Franco recommended here, right?"

(5) *(OVS):* No, la lasagna l'ha consigliata Elisabetta.
This translates literally to"No, the lasagna it has recommended Elizabeth" and in proper English becomes, "No, *Elizabeth*, recommended the lasagna."

(6) *(SOV):* Allora, io gli spaghetti prendo.
This translates literally to "In that case, I the spaghetti am having," which means in English, "In that case, I'm having *spaghetti.*"

Note how restricted English word order is in comparison to Italian in these examples provided by Bates and MacWhinney. In every case, we have to revert to the standard SVO word order to make the English translation grammatical and add stress to make the right translation. So why is so much variation permissible in Italian, but not in English? Because of some fundamental differences between the grammars of these two languages and the way in which they encode the speaker's perspective. In English, word order is fairly rigid and morphological marking is impoverished. If one changes the order of words in English, one risks changing meaning ("the boys hit the girl" does not mean the same as "the girl hit the boys"). We cannot vary word order freely because there are no obvious clues on the ends of words as to who is the agent, who is the patient, and which protagonist the verb relates to. So in English words cannot be easily moved around to convey different perspectives. Instead we generally use stress to do so ("the *boys* hit the girl" or "the boys hit the *girl*"). To determine meaning, the English listener has to give more weight to word order, and to determine perspective he has to focus on stress. By contrast, in Italian, word order is not the principal cue to meaning. Rather, it conveys the speaker's perspective. It is the rich morphological marking of Italian that conveys meaning. Thus, to determine the meaning of a sentence, the Italian listener's attention must give more weight to word endings than to word order, and to ascertain perspective, he must pay more attention to word order.

According to the competition model, cues such as stress, intonation, rhythm, morphological marking, and word order are always in competition, and these different types of cue interact dynamically every time children or adults hear a sentence. While examples of all these cues can be found across different languages, as we have just seen, the weight of each type of cue in determining the meaning of an utterance differs between languages. A certain type of cue crucial to one language may be incidental to another. So the young child learning English must adopt a different set of strategies and rely on different cue weightings than does the child learning Italian or other languages. How do children detect what cues exist in their language and which are the most reliable for mapping between grammatical form and meaning?

This is specifically the question that the competition model sought to answer. Looking at a number of different languages, Bates and MacWhinney identified which cues are most prominent in the input, which are the most reliable, valid, and consistent, and which carry the most meaning. As mentioned, in English word order is, in general, a very strong cue to meaning. In an English sentence, if the first position is occupied by a noun, this is a prominent and reliable cue that the noun is the subject of the sentence ("boy" in "the boy is jumping"). At the same time, the subject in the first position is generally also the agent (as in the sentence "the boy kissed the girl"). There are, however, exceptions to this second cue (for instance, "the girl is kissed by the boy," where "girl" is the subject but not the agent of the sentence). In processing such passive sentences, competition between different cues arises. In order to compute the meaning, the child must override the first position and word order cues, and focus on the changed grammatical structure introduced by the tense of the verb and the preposition "by."

For the competition model, semantics and pragmatics also play an important role in language processing. For instance, if the child hears "the car was washed by the girl," his pragmatic knowledge (that cars simply do not do washing, they get washed), will compete against the cues from word order, which by default suggest that the first noun is the agent. Interestingly, it has been found that around the age of six, as English-speaking children become increasingly aware of the importance of word order, the dominance of this syntactic cue may temporarily override sensible pragmatic interpretations. This may lead the young child, still unable to correctly understand passive sentences, to try to solve, for instance, "the car was washed by the girl" by suggesting that the word order car, wash, girl must mean that the windshield wipers have squirted water onto the girl and "washed" her. This is evidence of the growing drive to become a grammatical being. Initially young children rely heavily on pragmatics and semantics, but as their knowledge of grammar increases, cues from syntax can temporarily become overly strong. This tendency demonstrates how different types of cue dominate at different developmental stages and in a variety of linguistic contexts. Of course, for the Italian-learning child, for whom word order will always be a weak cue, there would be no question of trying to override the most pragmatically plausible interpretation.

As we can see, the strongest cue in one language might be one of the weakest cues in another. Analyses of child production have shown that in English SVO word order is the earliest cue used by children to determine sentence roles (agent, action, patient) and the strongest cue at every point in development. By contrast, subject-verb agreement is a weak cue at every stage of language acquisition for the English-learning child. The opposite is true for children learning Italian or Spanish.

Excessive adherence to word order by the English child at one stage of development suggests that the competition between cues in young children may be more restricted than in adults. The adult brain allows the competition between different cues to determine meaning, whereas for the child, when a new cue becomes prominent it can temporarily carry more weight than it should, thereby impeding competition. So in order to reach the dynamics of adult competitive processing, children first have to learn which cues are available and reliable in their language (the cue validity), then allow the competition between them to operate freely in order to reach a viable interpretation. Bates and MacWhinney propose that to process sentences correctly, children progressively broaden both the number of cues they use and the ways in which cues compete. According to the competition model, then, the course of language acquisition will necessarily differ across languages with respect to when and how children acquire elements of grammar. The order in which different grammatical forms are processed—word order, morphology, stress, semantics, or pragmatics—will reflect their cue validity in the language.

Bates and MacWhinney have provided a great deal of cross-linguistic evidence that confirms their hypotheses about cue validity. But what is equally interesting is that they also found cases that did not conform to their predictions. For instance, there is the example of sentences with embedded clauses, which involve long-distance agreement between subject and verb. Take the following sentence: "The boys who fought over the most popular girl were late for school." Here the plural verb ("were") is structurally related to the plural noun "boys." But "boys" and "were" are far from one another, whereas the singular word "girl" is right next to the plural verb. A simple sequential analysis of the words as they appear would lead to the ungrammatical "the girl were late." Since the interpretation of embedded clauses is more complex and places a heavy burden on memory, the plural cue on the verb might not initially be used by the child, even though he is already able to use cues from plural markers in simpler sentences. To account for this, the model incorporates the idea of cue cost. Cue cost refers to the amount and type of processing needed when cue validity is held constant. So for the young child, the most valid combination of cues may not always be used if cue cost is very high. In fact, it is suggested that one important aspect of development consists in learning to balance cue cost relative to cue validity. Then, as memory grows, cue cost becomes less of a determinant in weighing competing cues, and grammatical processing becomes less constrained.

Bates's and MacWhinney's model emphasizes the way in which cross-linguistic comparisons can help the researcher identify how individual children approach the task of learning their language. The tenets of their model differ from Slobin's in important ways. Most relevant to our current discussion is that the competition model focuses on how children and adults process language in real time. Second, unlike Slobin's model, which addresses only language acquisition in children, Bates and MacWhinney argue that their model also applies to the adult end state. They propose that the same language processes continue to operate throughout life every time a person hears language. In their view, there is no such thing as a static grammatical rule. Every time adults hear language, they recompute the statistical probabilities of the different cues in each sentence, in order to derive meaning. This is called on-line or real-time processing.

The competition model proposes that children and adults all possess a set of fundamental mechanisms that are relevant to processing the rapidly fading, sequential sounds (or visuo-manual signs) specific to language. Importantly, these mechanisms are not believed to be the same as those used for processing space, number, and the like. Unlike nativist theories, but like Slobin's approach, the competition model describes mechanisms that do not impart grammatical structure or meaning. Rather, they help children discover such structure in the speech that they hear. Furthermore, the efficiency with which these mechanisms operate is said to be dependent on the stage of development that the child has reached, as well as on both the strategies that each individual brings to the language-learning task and the particularities of the language to be learned.

Some aspects of the competition model may remind the reader of Steven Pinker's updated model, where he makes use of the notion of multiple partially-informative cues for language learning. The two approaches differ in significant ways, however. For Bates and MacWhinney, there is far more grammatical information in the surface form of the linguistic input. This information is believed, in and of itself, to allow the child to discover the structures of grammar. Pinker, by contrast, considers the discovery of linguistic structures to be based on innate representations of abstract categories like subject or object that are not directly obvious in heard speech. For the competition model, by contrast, categories like subject or object emerge from the identification of agents or patients or from the expression of perspective by the speaker. In other words, the child is not born with the abstract categories of subject and object. Instead, the competition model sees language as dynamically computed at all times, with linguistic information represented internally as a network of probabilistic (rather than deterministic) connections between forms and the meanings that they typically express. Pinker takes a more static and deterministic view. Linguistic categories such as subject and object are considered to be autonomous, distinct formal categories that exist in universal grammar from the very outset of language learning. For Pinker, then, the child learns how to map what he hears onto the preexisting abstract categories, whereas for

Bates and MacWhinney abstract categories emerge out of what is learned.

The competition model also contrasts sharply with Chomsky's deterministic view of language acquisition. Chomsky considers adult end-state grammar to be the result of evolution and not of progressive language learning. For him, language acquisition is not something in which the child is actively engaged, but is simply something that happens to the child when he is placed in an appropriate setting. Where individual differences play an important role in the competition model, in Chomsky's theory they are relegated to a minor role, and the special characteristics of particular languages are merely triggers for parameter setting. In contrast, for the competition model, both interindividual and cross-linguistic differences are crucial for explaining the process of language acquisition and the principles of adult real-time processing. Unlike the more static theories of how children acquire grammar, the competition model represents an important step forward in our discovery of how children come to process grammar across developmental time and across different languages.

## CONSTRUCTION-BASED APPROACHES

While the competition model focuses on comprehension, a promising new approach to early language production is based on how the child actually uses concrete examples to progressively build up grammar over time. Developmental psycholinguists such as Elena Lieven, Julian Pine, and Michael Tomasello argue that the child does not discover grammar; he slowly constructs it. They call this a construction-based process. This theory suggests that human evolution has provided us with both language-relevant and more general sociocognitive processes that together enable children to acquire grammar. From this viewpoint, grammar is in no way innately given. Rather, the toddler uses his ability to rapidly process real-time, sequential input (spoken or signed), as well as his general capacity to detect recurring patterns in that input, in order to very gradually build a more abstract grammar from the specific, concrete examples that he hears. It is the focus on concrete examples of specific grammatical structures rather than on abstract, generalizable rules that distinguishes this approach from Slobin's model.

The construction-based theory rests on two central tenets. First, it is argued that young children's linguistic skills (and perhaps even adults') are much less abstract than previously believed. Children's productions reflect not the existence of abstract categories and rules, but their knowledge of specific lexical items and specific grammatical structures. Second, unlike Pinker, construction-based theorists propose that children do not initially learn how to combine word categories (such as nouns, verbs, and so forth). Rather, their learning is often based on whole syntactic patterns, or constructions, as kinds of linguistic gestalts or wholes, with their own unique forms and functions. In other words, if a toddler utters "dog biting bone," this does not indicate that he necessarily possesses categories like subject, verb, or object and has combined them to form a "sentence." Rather, the construction-based theorists claim that it is more likely that the utterance has been learned as a whole and then used as a basic pattern or template from which to create other, similar utterances with the same structure, like "cat chasing mouse" and "Daddy washing car."

In-depth analyses of data from parental diaries tend to support this theoretical position about the concreteness of early child grammar. One of the greatest advantages of the continuous parental diary is that it includes information about not only what the child actually has said but more importantly about those utterances that the child *never* produced. When children fail to use a grammatical structure with all the words they know, we can deduce that they do not possess an abstract rule but rather are imitating a concrete example. So the lack of generalization to new exemplars is as informative to the researcher as those actually produced.

When generalization does occur, it is far more limited than previously thought. One study by Elena Lieven and her colleagues demonstrated that between the ages of two and three years, children's language can be analyzed in terms of a relatively small number of "slot-and-frame," or "fill in the blank," patterns from which children generate large numbers of utterances. These patterns are often based around one or two specific words or phrases that have open "slots" into which the child can place a variety of other words already present in his repertoire. For example, children might produce the following pattern as their earliest grammatical utterances:

MORE + X
WHERE + X

in which words like "drink," "apple," "woof-woof," "car," and "Daddy," can take the X slot. Another common pattern is:

WANNA + X

into which words like "cookie," "book," "drink," "go-byebye," and "get-down" can be slotted.

At first, variables like X are filled with single words. But as children develop, whole phrases may fill the X slot. The number and length of slot-and-frame patterns forming the child's repertoire grows to incorporate more complex utterances like "I can't + X" or "where's + Y + gone?" Slot-and-frame patterns may also be combined such that the child might produce "where + more + X + gone?" Children can be extremely productive with these patterns. But it is important to reiterate that the patterns are argued to be lexically specific, that is, they are based on particular words or phrases and not on abstract categories like noun phrases or verb phrases.

Michael Tomasello and his collaborators used the construction-based approach to ascertain how a specific aspect of grammar, verb structure, develops in the child's productions. They have shown both in naturalistic observations and through controlled experiments that children initially build up particular patterns of utterances around particular verbs. The child's knowledge about how to use one particular verb does *not* automatically generalize to other verbs. So if the child learns how to use the verb "to give" in the utterance "the girl gives a book to the boy," this does not indicate that he knows how to use all verbs with three slots or what are called "arguments." If he wants to express a different perspective, such as "the boy gets a book from the girl," he will have to learn how to use the verb "to get" separately. In other words, initially each verb's grammatical structure is learned individually in just the way that children have heard it being used by a parent or caregiver.

Many researchers have acknowledged the significance of slot-and-frame patterns for the very earliest stages of multiword speech. Indeed, a similar idea lay behind the notion of a pivot child grammar originally proposed by Martin Braine in the 1960s to account for two-word utterances. Until the development of the construction-based theory, however, researchers failed to recognize the possibility that the development of children's grammar might for several years continue to be built on *specific* grammatical applications rather than on abstract grammatical knowledge, even when they are using full sentences.

As we have seen, the construction-based approach challenges claims about the existence of an abstract grammar early in development, by suggesting that what children are really learning is where to place particular words within recognized examples. In order to do so, they capitalize on their capacity to process the input as a sequence of recurring patterns, rather than retrieve ready-made, abstract linguistic structures. Of course, it could be argued that if the child were able to use the argument structure of the verb "to give" correctly, even though he cannot yet use the verb "to get," this still reflects the existence of some abstract and innate knowledge. But this type of reasoning imposes the theory onto the data, rather than letting the data constrain the theory, as good science would dictate. The construction-based approach starts from the child's actual productions and makes no assumptions about the nature of the child's linguistic representations other than those to which the data directly point. Consequently, a more psychologically realistic picture of children's actual language production emerges—one that allows the researcher to identify the points at which the child progresses from slot-and-frame productions to more abstract generalizations. This movement toward more abstract and adult-like constructions is deemed to be a very gradual process, carried out in a piecemeal fashion for each new structure encountered. The theory is very different than the notion of an immediately abstract Universal Grammar, which is believed to support the child's productions.

Current research within the construction-based framework is concentrating on the relationship between patterns in the speech that children hear and patterns pertaining to children's own speech. Such comparisons then help to identify the developmental moments at which the children's patterns become less tied to specific items and begin to resemble more adult-like, productive sets of structures. To further test the validity of the theory, researchers are also starting to examine languages whose grammatical structures differ from English. The approach also suggests that cultural differences (the existence or lack of motherese) will play less of a role in language acquisition than often presumed. The child is thought to extract whole structures from both infant-directed and adult-directed speech. The construction-based theory may therefore be more applicable cross-culturally and better explain the individual differences that are so prevalent in early language development.

The data yielded so far have serious implications for any paradigm that uses adult-like formal grammars to describe children's language. Construction-based approaches imply that children's speech should not be credited with the kind of syntactic competence of which adult grammar might be composed—namely, abstract categories and combinatorial rules. Instead, it is argued that specific words and specific utterance patterns form the building blocks for language development in children. Construction-based research supports a theory of language acquisition that is psychologically based because such research suggests that children's linguistic skills are closer to their other social and cognitive skills than some linguists and psychologists have hitherto believed. But it offers a more formalized and less descriptive approach to the analysis of actual child output than that found in some cognitive and social theories. Finally, if successful, the construction-based theory may even challenge current models of adult end-state grammars. Indeed, as suggested above, it may turn out that adult grammar is actually far less abstract than Chomsky claims, and that our spoken (or signed) language is stored as particular words and phrases, with schooling required to bring out the more abstract categories of written language. The continuity between child and adult spoken language organization suggests a more natural progression in learning.

## Modeling Language Development

A rather different approach to exploring language acquisition tests theories through computer modeling. The most commonly used models—connectionist models—employ networks whose processing is designed to approximate that of the network of connections between cells in human brains. In other words, connectionist modeling of language uses computer programs designed to mimic the information processing that takes place in the brain as language is learned over time. Figure 6 shows a very simple network, composed of an input layer that receives language data, a hidden layer wherein more compressed representations of the data are formed, and an output layer that yields the linguistic output. Each time an input passes through these three layers, tiny adaptations are made to the connections so that the next time the same input is processed, the output is slightly closer to the targeted one.

Let us use the English past tense as an example, because we discuss it in several other parts of this book with respect to real child data. Learning the past tense is not straightforward because there are regular forms and irregular forms. Somehow the child's brain needs to learn to produce both, and many have assumed that innate knowledge must underpin this capacity. Connectionist modelers such as Jeffrey Elman, Virginia Marchman, Kim Plunkett, and Michael Thomas suggest an alternative explanation that does not require innate linguistic knowledge. In order to test hypotheses about the innateness and specificity of language learning, connectionists offer a picture of how sophisticated but nonlinguistic mechanisms might be used to learn about aspects of grammar such as the past tense. What is shown is that with a powerful learning device and a richly structured and varied input, neural networks are indeed capable of learning rules without prior (innate) linguistic knowledge.

In connectionist experiments a network might, for example, be presented with numerical formulae representing the regular present

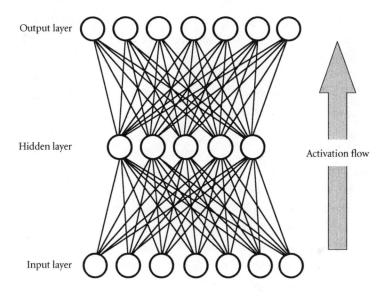

Output layer

Hidden layer

Activation flow

Input layer

*Figure 6*    Three-layer network

tense "walk" and the irregular present tense "go" at the input layer, and then, by being fed numerous different examples of present or past tense over numerous trials, be slowly trained to produce the past tense "walked" and "went" at the output layer. Every time the network produces an output, it is given a tiny amount of feedback as to how far off it is from the target output. The network, like the child, will obviously not be successful at first. Initially it will just produce random responses. But progressively, and through tiny adjustments to the hidden layer, the network will learn to produce the past tense on the output layer. These connections are strengthened each time the output is correct. Yet by paying attention to what the input offers overall, the network, like the child, will learn that the ending "ed" occurs frequently in the past tense and so will try using it more often—that is, it will strengthen connections to that output. This will cause a temporary overgeneralization of the regular form to irregulars, producing "goed" instead of "went." Connections will then strengthen with respect to the irregular but more common forms, in order to develop a neural route for irregular past tense formation. Competition between the connections for different outputs will be such that any not used frequently will be weakened. Note that the network was not given prespecified "knowledge" or rules about abstract grammatical categories (such as regular and irregular past tense). The information in the hidden layer was initially random. The knowledge that allowed the network to become progressively "grammatical" *emerged* as a result of processing the concrete exemplars and repeatedly comparing the input to the correct output. It is during such learning that the "grammatical knowledge" comes to be represented in the hidden layer.

These network models obviously do not precisely mirror real child learning. Children do not learn the past tense in isolation from the rest of their linguistic or cognitive systems or apart from their physical and social environments. A computer network does not behave like the brain of a real child growing up in the real world. Nonetheless, connectionist modeling offers new tools for answering questions about the extent to which innate knowledge is or is not essential for learning grammar. Artificial networks give us a picture of how connections might be progressively built up from repeated exposure to the input without prior knowledge and with general, albeit sophisticated, learning mechanisms that could also be applied to nonlinguistic information. Connectionist modeling is a new but promising area of language acquisition research. Connectionism might well act as a testing ground for theories like the construction-based one discussed earlier, with the construction-based paradigm providing more realistic child language data to modelers. This interaction between connectionism and construction-based approaches to child grammar could yield some exciting advances in the field of developmental psycholinguistics.

## Conclusion

The many different theories discussed in this chapter have contributed to our understanding of how children may acquire grammar. Structural, nativist theories have highlighted the subtle complexities of the end-state adult grammar that they claim the child has to ultimately acquire. Bootstrapping theories, in contrast, have centered on the actual process of learning adult grammar. Sociopragmatic and cognitive approaches have turned the focus to the social and physical environment in which language learning actually takes place. Processing approaches point to the crucial role of cues offered by the input language itself. They have highlighted the importance of using cross-linguistic data to understand individual differences and the dynamics of language processing in real time. The construction-based approaches have tried to identify the child's own grammar, which is thought to be built progressively from specific lexical items and grammatical structures discovered in the speech of parents or caregivers. And finally, connectionist network models have shown how grammatical rules can emerge without innate knowledge or language-specific mechanisms. Although some of these theories appear to be mutually exclusive, we believe that a comprehensive explanation of how all of grammar is acquired will ultimately have to be constrained by aspects of each approach.

# 6 | BEYOND THE SENTENCE

As we have seen, a great deal of acquisition research focuses on language at the levels of the word, phrase, clause, and sentence. But everyday language is not simply limited to vocabulary and full sentences. We engage in discourse, which involves both dialogic exchanges and lengthy monologues like storytelling. This level of language entails yet another set of rules and conventions that the child has to learn to understand and use. Unlike the full sentences studied in Chapter 5, a characteristic feature of real dialogue is that much is actually left unsaid. When we speak to one another, we automatically take for granted both shared knowledge and the ability of our interlocutor to make inferences. Take the following example:

> Jimmy was playing in the garden barefoot. His toe landed on a sharp nail, and he had to be rushed to the doctor.

The conclusion to the story tells us that Jimmy wounded himself, but this is not explicitly stated in the text. It is not necessary to do so, because we can infer this part of the story from our general knowledge. As a speaker we know that we can leave out certain pieces of information without causing ambiguity. Inference and shared knowledge are very important aspects of discourse. Imagine if we had to state every little detail in a totally literal way. Conversations and stories would become very heavy.

A second important feature of discourse is that many responses are truncated and indirect. This is especially the case in dialogic exchanges. Take the following example:

*Speaker A:* Where are you going after you've finished?
*Speaker B:* Home.

This is the sort of natural answer that we would expect. But what if discourse did not provide us with such shortcuts? The answer might have to resemble something like:

*Speaker B:* I am going home after I have finished this.

Most responses to questions would seem very odd and pedantic if left as a full sentence. Both of the responses from Speaker B are linguistically correct, but the first answer meets the conventions of discourse, while the second is far less appropriate pragmatically. In real dialogue, therefore, the speaker must not only respond to the content of the conversation or story being told, but also continually gauge his interlocutor's knowledge in order to strike the right balance between saying too much or too little. This comes naturally to the fluent speaker, but it is yet another aspect of language that children must learn and, as we will see in the first part of this chapter, it is not as automatic as it might seem.

The pragmatics of dialogue represent only one facet of discourse. While conversations often involve an exchange of short sentences, they also often include storytelling, or narratives, which are structured with a beginning, a middle, and a conclusion. Sharing what you did yesterday, offering your opinion on a television program you have just watched, or giving instructions about how to get from A to B all entail stringing a number of sentences together into a complex and coherent whole. The linguistic rules and conventions that operate across sentences at the *inter*-sentential level are often quite different from those that govern the *intra*-sentential level. This, too, is something that children have to learn.

## Learning about Dialogue

Children are introduced to the pragmatics of dialogue long before they begin to produce language and acquire grammar. Even in the first weeks of life, interaction between parents and infants assumes, with vocalizations or simple gestures, the turn-taking and reciprocity typical of later linguistic exchanges. Within this nurturing communicative context, infants learn to initiate and lead interaction. Later, as cooing turns to babbling and then to first words, infants begin to accumulate knowledge about how to answer different types of *speech acts*. Speech acts describe the differences among, say, questions that require verbal answers, statements that require no action, commands that require action responses, and so forth. Thus children need to learn that language requires a variety of different kinds of responses, which might also involve compliance, refusal, acceptance, or rejection.

While this ability is a vital step in discourse development, there is much more to dialogue than learning how select a response to a question or statement. The child has to learn to interpret both the form and function of the speaker's utterance, and to maintain the conversation by initiating further responses and creating links between utterances. She therefore has to realize, for instance, that an utterance starting with the word "where" is both a question (form), and a request for information (function). Of course, the principle function of a question is to initiate a response, unlike a statement such as "that's a truck," which does not necessarily invite the child to a verbal response. Toddlers learn early on these different relationships between form and function.

Research on child-child verbal interaction has shown that during the first three years, children's dialogic abilities are restricted. Their exchanges are not real dialogue but consist mainly of sequences of initiation-response turns concerning a vaguely defined overall topic. From roughly the age of four, however, children begin to develop more sophisticated discourse skills, allowing them to create links both within and between exchanges in order to maintain longer stretches of dialogue. They also begin to select responses that fulfill a feedback function by both responding and initiating within a single utterance. As we will see, it takes several years to complete the complicated process of becoming a proficient conversationalist.

As we have seen throughout the book, most parents in Western cultures tailor their behavior toward infants and toddlers to provide a supportive environment for language development—and not just

through the use of motherese, but in the very way that they interact
with the child. From the first moments of life, most of the infant's
movements, gurgles, and facial expressions are responded to by the
parent as meaningful and become incorporated into dialogue-like
interaction. The way in which adults attune their actions and utterances to infant behavior provides an early model of conversational
structure. The difference between the following two examples illustrates this nicely:

(1) *Mother (carrying baby):* Are you tired? Is it time for a little sleep,
    now?
    *(Lays baby down in the cot. Baby gurgles with contentment.)*
    *Mother:* Yes. That's just what you wanted, a nice little sleep.

(2) *Mother (carrying baby):* Are you tired? Is it time for a little sleep,
    now?
    *(Lays baby down in the cot. Baby wriggles and cries.)*
    *Mother:* No? So is it not time for sleep yet? Let's sing a song, then.

Here we see how the mother initiates and builds up a question-
response structure around the child's actions. She does so in such a
way that any response by the infant can be interpreted as an "answer" to her question, and can then be integrated into a reciprocal,
turn-taking interaction. It is the mother who translates the child's
actions into verbal responses. At first, adults initiate such exchanges
and let the infant's responsiveness set the pace for the interaction.
But within a matter of weeks, babies learn to purposefully attract
their parents' attention and therefore to be initiators. This represents
the very first step in taking an active role in discourse.

As babbling gets under way, proto-conversations between parents
and infants take on other characteristics of real dialogue. By the end
of the first year, the baby's babbling rises and falls in intonation to
mimic questions and statements. Babies also incorporate into their
interactions proto-imperatives (asking for something to be done)
and subsequently proto-declaratives (pointing out something in the
environment), by vocalizing and gesturing simultaneously in order
to direct the adult's attention. By this time, toddlers can differentiate
between yes-no questions; questions using who, what, where, when,

and why; and statements, and they learn to respond differentially to each. In fact, long before they can actually interpret precisely what is being said, they show awareness that utterances with rising intonation require a response. But before the age of two, their responses are very limited and consist mainly of either actions, repetitions of part of the adult's utterance, or routine answers that may or may not be semantically correct, but maintain an appropriate form. So a fifteen-month-old may answer his parent as follows:

> *Father:* Do you want to go in the car?
> *Toddler:* Car.

Here the toddler repeats the final word in order to sustain the dialogue. Alternatively, he may produce a specific type of answer that demonstrates his awareness of dialogic form:

> *Mother:* Shall we go to the park?
> *Toddler:* Swings.

In this second example, the child shows his sensitivity to the context of the question and adds his own contribution to the dialogue.

Analysis of early parent-child dialogue suggests that at this stage it is not the meaning (literal or intended) of dialogue to which the child responds. Rather, it seems that during the first two years of life, children build up categories of utterance-response pairs. These are based on real-world contexts, the intonation of the speaker, and the initial words of an utterance. For instance, at this stage they tend to answer all questions beginning with "wh" as meaning "where" or "what." They also display an action bias whereby they will look for mention of an action in the utterance that they can act upon. It is only from about age three that children really begin to demonstrate a wider knowledge of the semantics and pragmatics of discourse and can respond to questions such as "why" and "when" with semantically appropriate answers. This is also the time when the use of connectives (like "and") and auxiliary ellipsis (responding to a request with "yes, I will" instead of "yes, I will go and get that cup for you") becomes more established.

The pairing of speech act types with standard responses is obviously not sufficient to allow the child to partake in longer stretches of conversation. For any utterance a person makes, there are a great number of possible answers to choose from, even within the response categories a child might construct. Nevertheless, by the age of four, children are able to answer most questions appropriately, and by five they have mastered the art of initiating and sustaining relatively well-structured conversations.

As we suggested earlier, a child's simply being sensitive to the form of an utterance does not provide her with enough information to select an appropriate answer and maintain dialogue. She also has to learn about the speaker's intention vis-à-vis both the meaning of the utterance and its function in promoting or ending further conversation. A question such as "Did you play that game again at school today?" is intended as a request for information, but also propels further conversation with links to previous dialogic exchanges ("that game again" refers to a previously discussed subject). Such an utterance can be described as multifunctional. Children have to learn how to both interpret and produce such dialogue-relevant utterances.

Adult-led conversations provide the linguistic context within which young speakers can attain a multifunctional level of dialogue with considerably greater ease than when conversing with a peer. Studies of parent-child interaction in Western cultures show that adults guide and probe children in order to sustain the dialogue and convey their intentions. But analysis of the development of child dialogue within child-adult exchanges can be misleading and result in the attribution of too much competence to the child. This is because adults play an unequal and predominant role in conversations with very young speakers. An alternative approach has been to look at children's dialogic exchanges with their peers. This approach has allowed researchers to conduct longitudinal studies following the conversational progress of children over several years, to see how new skills develop and are incorporated into discourse.

Conversations between young children are not as flexible as those between adults and children. This is because feedback (those utterances that simultaneously respond and initiate and are responsible for creating and sustaining coherent conversations) is largely absent from early child-child dialogue. Conversations between children younger than five consist mainly of sequences of initiation-response pairs, which constitute short, closed exchanges. They begin and end with one topic and are rarely incorporated into subsequent exchanges.

The following represents a typical conversational exchange between two three-year-olds:

> *Alex:* I'm gonna put it there.
> *Nicki:* Over there.
> *Alex:* On the green box.
> *Nicki:* Yeah, put it on top.
> *Alex:* You wanna do it?
> *Nicki:* Okay.

We can see that although each child is answering the other's utterance directly and appropriately, there are no openings for further conversational links. The exchange is terminated when the action being discussed is performed. Further dialogue may indeed carry on with the same topic, but is unlikely to refer directly to the previous linguistic exchange.

By the age of four, children increasingly respond to the *structure* of discourse, rather than simply to its content. They now acknowledge each other's answers verbally and attempt to link their responses to earlier utterances in order to keep a conversation going. Also quite common is the use of tags, such as "isn't it" or "aren't they" at the end of utterances to initiate and sustain dialogue.

> *Jimmy:* Alice isn't my best friend anymore.
> *Dylan:* Why?
> *Jimmy:* She was mean. She told her Mummy I took her bike. But I didn't. I just borrowed it. You saw me, didn't you?
> *Dylan:* Uh huh, she's a liar. I'm gonna tell on her.

Although these four-year-olds are sustaining a complex exchange and elaborating on their answers, it is not until the age of five or six that children's conversational skills really take off. The greatest development is the ability to provide feedback in dialogue—to combine more than one response into a conversational turn, so as to respond to an utterance while simultaneously initiating further talk. The use of auxiliary ellipsis also provides a useful means of keeping the dialogue going. As we mentioned earlier, an ellipse is a response that takes part of the answer as implicitly given. For instance:

> *Question:* Do you think it's going to rain tonight?
> *Answer:* It might.

On its own, the answer is meaningless, but as an ellipse following the question, it provides an answer: "Yes, I think it might rain tonight." In order to respond in this way, the child must reach a sophisticated level of interpretation, have a good understanding of the speaker's intention and current state of knowledge, and learn what to leave in and what to omit. It is not surprising, therefore, that the ability to take part in long structured sequences of dialogue takes the best part of a decade to develop.

## Learning about Narrative

One of the principal forms of discourse is the narrative. When we are in the middle of a social interaction, we are usually unaware that, as we speak, we are constructing a story with both an overall structure at the level of topic and an internal structure at the intersentential level. This involves guiding the listener through a beginning, a middle, and an end while linking the string of sentences together through linguistic devices such as tense marking, connectives, and pronouns. Such devices allow us to refer back to things said earlier, to leave things unsaid, to link events, and to progress through the narrative smoothly without having to elucidate and reiterate every detail. These are the kinds of issues that children face when learning how to follow and produce narrative.

Narrative differs from dialogue in several specific ways. Conversational exchanges, particularly with children, often contain vital cues from the here and now that can be very different from the clues available in intersentential forms of discourse. In dialogue, for instance, the pronoun "it" can be accompanied by a point or eye movement toward the intended referent. The child is thus able to easily ascertain the subject of the dialogue. But in narrative or extended discourse, pronouns have to be anchored in the linguistic text itself. They refer back (in what is called an anaphoric reference) to something already mentioned in the story. Note, for example, the pronouns "she" and "her" in the following narrative: "Jenny was very intelligent. She went to one of the best schools in the country, which her mother had attended also." In order to be able to retrieve or deduce what a pronoun refers to, it is necessary for the listener to have already built up a representation of the preceding intralinguistic context. This is how we are able to visualize in our minds a picture of what is being described or recounted when we are listening to a story. In dialogue, especially with children, exchanges are more often grounded in the extralinguistic context of the here and now.

In contrast to dialogue, narrative production cannot rely on the extralinguistic context. The speaker needs to sequence and organize a number of sentences in such a way that they hold together linguistically for the listener. So for the child, narrative is harder than dialogue both to understand and to produce. But, as Jerome Bruner has stressed, it is through narrative that children develop a sense of self. By being able to share their experiences and thoughts, they create their own autobiographies and get a better understanding of the world around them.

Narrative involves both coherence and cohesion. Coherence refers to the way in which the content of the narrative, or the topic, is held together and elaborated. Narrative cohesion, in contrast, refers not to content and overall structure, but to the linguistic devices employed to link sentences together and to relate background or old information with new foregrounded information as the discourse unfolds.

How do children learn to process the complex discourse devices of coherence and cohesion in order to both understand and produce well-formed narratives? Acquiring the principles of discourse represents one of the final steps in the complex road to language acquisition.

## NARRATIVE COHERENCE

The primary goal of telling a story is to communicate an immediately understandable account of events, thoughts, and feelings, with appropriate temporal and causal connections. Stories may originate from the storyteller's own experiences or pertain to fiction. In order to succeed in narrative, the speaker must establish an overall structure within which all the elements of the story can be fitted. Detailed analyses of story grammars (sometimes referred to as macrostructures or scripts) have shown that narratives are consistently made up of several identifiable parts, which form a hierarchy. This general structure has been shown to be universal across all cultures and languages.

At the top of the narrative hierarchy is a setting and an episode. The setting refers to the time and space in which the story takes place, as well as the persons involved. The episode refers to the sequence of discourse events involved in the narrative. These usually comprise an initiating event that triggers a series of other, goal-oriented events, as well as an action plan, an outcome, and finally, a judgment or summing up of that outcome. The content of each part of the story can be infinitely varied, and the speaker is free to choose how long or short each part will be.

While narrative clearly represents a very flexible communicative form, it is nonetheless constrained by its structure. If the speaker violates the order of the episodes, for instance, this can render the story harder for the listener to understand. The aim of discourse is to keep the listener interested and maintain social interaction. Therefore, it must be coherently structured from the start. One has to link characters, contexts, and events in a way that immediately makes sense. Imagine explaining a recipe to someone but changing the order of the preparation steps and introducing the different ingredients at the wrong time—the outcome would not be very appetizing. In a similar way, a narrative that does not hang together properly will not be very palatable to the listener. This is why narrative coherence is so important.

Two teams of researchers, headed by Jean Mandler and Nancy Stein, have examined the structure of adult narrative as a starting point for studying the development of discourse coherence in children. They define a coherent story in terms of the sequence of goal-based actions. So a good story includes the following:

1. The introduction of an animate protagonist capable of intentional action;
2. An explicit statement of the desires or goals of the protagonist;
3. The overt actions, linked temporally and causally, carried out in the service of the protagonist's goals;
4. Outcomes related to the attainment or nonattainment of these goals;
5. Some evaluation or summing up the outcome.

Research has shown that children as young as three are capable of telling coherently structured, albeit rudimentary, stories, as long as these are accounts of real-life events that they have experienced both physically and emotionally. Events that make young children laugh or cry, or make them angry, sad, jealous, and such, are easier for them to recount as well-structured narratives than those in which they have no personal emotional involvement. This is because the child forms strong representations of emotional experiences—representations that provide ready-made content for the ensuing narrative account. With such experiences, therefore, the child is not faced with the task of computing the story parts and structure from scratch. Stories that are more complex and whose events were perhaps experienced indirectly or are purely fictional, require more extensive, real-time computation. In these cases coherence suffers in the very young speaker. Thus, although personally experienced stories are quite well structured in young speakers, the ability to produce well-structured fictional stories does not occur until significantly later in development.

As we can see, the content of a story and how it relates to the child's social experiences play an important role in early narrative production. The same is true for story comprehension. If the story being told is sufficiently simple and conforms to a canonical story structure that preserves temporal and causal order with a clear beginning, middle, and end, then four-year-olds have little difficulty following it. If the story content is more complex and the coherence is not canonically ordered, however, then it takes some years developmentally for children to display proficient understanding. Much of the research on narrative comprehension focuses on issues of memory, but here we will focus on narrative production and children's judgments of what constitutes a successful narrative.

A series of experiments has compared what children themselves judge to be a "good story" and how this affects the stories they tell. It was found that children younger than five accept as good both goal-based narratives and non-goal-based narratives. This acceptance is mirrored in their storytelling, which often takes the form of strings of temporally related events that (to the adult listener) seem to lack a goal. In goal-based narratives, by contrast, the story parts are causally related and progress toward a specific conclusion. Here is an example of a non-goal-based narrative:

John got up from the chair. He put his coat on and left the room. Alice said hello to him when he walked past her.

Upon hearing such a narrative, we are left thinking, "So what?" But very young children find temporal sequences like this acceptable as a "good story" because they have identifiable characters who perform clear-cut actions in a normal temporal sequence. By contrast, school-age children, like adults, are far less likely to accept such non-goal-based narratives as "good stories." They clearly expect both temporal *and* causal connections to exist between events that form a story.

The different narrative expectations of younger and older children have implications for research. Because children at different ages do not always share the same conception of what a "story" is, measuring simply the length and number of story episodes that they tell will not fully differentiate their levels of competence. Rather, it is crucial to take account of the presence or absence of both temporal and causal connections within their stories.

So how do children link story parts coherently? A study by Nancy Stein and her team assessed storytelling abilities in children ages five, eight, and ten to see how coherence differed across these age groups. The experimental task required the children to tell three stories based on three different starting stems. Each stem consisted of two statements, as in the following:

> *Fox story:* Once there was a big gray fox who lived in a cave near a forest.
> *Alice story:* Once there was a little girl named Alice who lived in a house near the ocean.
> *Alan story:* Once there was a little boy named Alan who had many different kinds of toys.

Children were asked to repeat the stem provided, and then to tell a "good story" about the character introduced in the stem. They were told that their stories could be as long or as short as they liked. After producing each story, they listened to a tape recording of it and were asked to rate whether or not it was indeed a "good story." If they deemed it was not good, they were encouraged to improve it. The aim was to ensure that the production data to be analyzed was considered by children themselves to be acceptable. It turned out that the vast majority of children in all age groups left their stories unchanged.

Each story produced by the subjects was categorized according to the degree of coherence achieved. The five classifications used by Stein and her collaborators are given below, along with relevant examples of children's productions:

> *No structure:*
> Once there was a boy named Alan who had a lot of toys. He had lots and lots of toys.

> *Descriptive sequence:*
> Once there was a big gray fox who lived in a cave. He was mean and scary. He had big giant eyes and a bushy tail . . .

> *Simple temporal action sequence:*
> Once there was a little girl named Alice who lived in a house near the ocean . . . In the morning she'd get up and go out, and take a swim. She comes in, eats lunch. She goes back out. She plays on the sand.

*Reactive sequence:*
Once there was a girl named Alice who lived down by the seashore. Alice was in the water, floating on her back, when along came a shark and gulp, gulp, that was the end of Alice.

*Goal-based sequence of events:*
Once there was a big gray fox who lived in a cave near the forest. One day the fox got sick and wanted someone to come and visit him. He looked outside but nobody came. So he got up . . . and put up a sign saying, "Come in and visit me." And then everybody came in, except that none of them came out 'cause he ate 'em all up. He was a pretty smart fox and they were pretty dumb.

Results showed that the oldest children generally produced causal goal-based narratives with fairly diverse phraseology. By contrast, the youngest age group tended to produce more simple descriptive or temporal action-based narratives. Having said that, it is important to note that 83 percent of the children younger than six told at least one goal-based story. This clearly demonstrates that the ability to produce a coherent narrative structure already exists in the five-year-old. What seems to have presented a problem for younger children was relating goals to actions in a sequence of fictitious events. They appeared to have difficulties with those stems that could not be related to their own real-life experiences. Such fictitious accounts pose a problem for the young child because they demand the simultaneous computing of story content and story structure. This explanation is supported by the fact that these young children do not show the same difficulty in forming a goal-based and coherent structure if the story they are telling is relevant to their own experiences. In general, children of this age also show little difficulty recounting a much-heard bedtime story or sharing a personal experience in detail.

One of the strategies that young children use to overcome the problem of integrating goals and actors within a fictitious narrative is to limit their stories to a single protagonist. This reduces the processing demands generated by story content and structure, and allows the child to concentrate on integrating the events around a single focal point. Older children are not restricted in this way. They experience little difficulty in producing stories with several interrelated branches of characters and events. The progress in narrative production is surprisingly fast if one considers the complex processing demands of producing a coherent story. From the age of three or four, when the ability to form narrative first appears, narrative coherence increases steadily. By seven or eight, the child not only is able to retell a popular fairy tale in a coherent abbreviated version containing all the principle characters and the most important events, but also can create and tell imaginative stories.

In conclusion, provided they are already familiar with a story's emotional and causal content, very young children display—through their comprehension and their own storytelling—some knowledge of what constitutes the coherent structure of a narrative. At first, this narrative competence is not as developed for novel and / or fictitious stories. With development, children increase the complexity of their narratives by introducing more than one character, and by being able to generate goal-based accounts with multiple embedded episodes. These now include stories that are totally fictional and novel. One of the reasons why younger children find it tricky to introduce more than one character in their stories may be due to the difficulties of finding the right linguistic devices (for example, pronouns) to keep their story from becoming ambiguous. We now turn to this aspect of narrative development.

### NARRATIVE COHESION

Narrative cohesion refers to the specific linguistic devices that hold sentences together and link them to one another. These include the use of pronouns (such as "he," "she," "they," "it," "this," and "that"), temporal and causal connectives (like "and," "then," "next," "while," "when," and "because"), and other linguistic tools such as ellipsis, which we discussed in the section on dialogue. Initially, children use these markers deictically. Deixis refers to something that can be pointed out in the here and now. For example, "that dog" is used deictically when the animal is present and can be referred to by pointing or looking; when "that dog" is used anaphorically, it must have been mentioned in the prior linguistic context. For deixis, there need not have been any prior or further verbal reference in order for the sentence containing the pronoun to make sense. And this is how children initially use pronouns. But gradually, as children begin to experiment with narrative, they start to use these same linguistic markers to refer to people, things, or events within the discourse itself.

Achieving narrative cohesion is a huge step forward in language development because it enables children to share with anyone and in any context their personal thoughts, experience of past events, and invented stories without having to rely on the information provided by the here and now. As children start to produce narratives, they learn that the markers they have hitherto been using to form grammatical language at the single-sentence level now take on specific discourse functions. These functions include, for instance, making clear (by using different linguistic terms) who is the main protagonist of a story and who are the subsidiary characters. The use of pronouns versus full noun phrases provides subtle linguistic clues about differences in the status of the characters in a story. Cohesive devices also involve marking information as either given or new. For example, simply by positioning information differentially within sentences it is possible for the speaker to indicate linguistically the extent to which information can or cannot be presupposed.

Presupposition can be based on one of two things: mutually shared knowledge that exists prior to the discourse ("the elevator man had an accident last night" presupposes it is a man we both already know), or information set up by the prior discourse ("a man came to mend our elevator last night and he had an accident"). It is a universal feature of all languages that presupposed information tends to be placed toward the beginning of a sentence, while information that is new or cannot be presupposed is placed in the final part of the sentence. The position of a piece of information is thus a major clue to its narrative status.

Appropriate grounding of information (foregrounding and backgrounding) also helps a story maintain cohesion. Grounding is the means by which speakers indicate what is of primary focus in their discourse and what is subsidiary. Take the statement "While I was speaking on the phone, Jane had her baby." In this sentence "Jane had her baby" is clearly of primary focus, and is foregrounded by changing the tense from past progressive ("was speaking") to past perfect ("had"). Situating the phrase "Jane had her baby" at the end of the sentence also implies that this information is of primary focus. The first part of the sentence, "while I was speaking on the phone," represents subsidiary information—background context for the main event. These and many other linguistic devices are combined in a cohesive narrative to ground information and highlight its status.

It is important for the child to learn that the rules for making a grammatical sentence are not necessarily the same as the cohesive principles that govern grammatical discourse. In narrative, as well as in dialogue, we sometimes violate the grammar that pertains to the single sentence. For instance, in a single-sentence utterance, a pronoun usually designates the most recently mentioned referent. So, in the isolated sentence "Sarah thought she should go home now" the pronoun "she" clearly refers to Sarah and it could not be replaced by a second use of "Sarah" without implying the presence of two different people called Sarah. In discourse, however, a pronoun need not always refer to the most recent referent. Here is an example where the pronoun in the fifth sentence is far removed from its antecedent (an old man), and yet the meaning is perfectly clear because of the coherence of the overall story structure and its internal cohesion:

> This is the story of an old man who loved gardens. Because of his age, he had to employ two gardeners who were actually boys from the local school. One of the boys helped cut the lawn. The other boy did digging and planting. He paid them well so they did the job with enthusiasm.

As we can see, the cohesive use of pronouns in discourse is not governed simply by their use in the local sentence, but also by the hierarchical structure of the narrative as a whole. Within the simple story about the old man are many subtle clues as to who is the main character and what pieces of information are primary and secondary. In this case, the combined use of coherence and cohesion establishes a well-structured and unambiguous account. But it is important to note that it is theoretically possible to create a narrative that is cohesive without being coherent, or coherent without being cohesive. Take the following example:

> There's a little boy. He is thirty years old. He hates water, so he jumped into the river. And when he was twenty, he decided to drive his car with a girl. Then she jumped into the water.

In this story, all the referents are introduced properly and then subsequently referred to anaphorically. The narrative can therefore be described as "cohesive," but it makes little sense because its contents lack coherence. The events are badly sequenced and poorly linked causally. The story contains no initiating event, no goal-related sequence, and no outcome. This is a theoretical example of cohesion without coherence.

The story below, by contrast, is an example of well-formed coherence with poor cohesion:

> This is the story about the boy. Sadly the boy fell in the water. The boy gets wet. The boy found his car and his friend, and goes home. Before they go home, Jerry fell in the water. The boys are rather silly.

In this second story, the narrative incorrectly presupposes that the listener would know who "the boy" in the opening sentence is. Different verb tenses are inappropriately used throughout. It is also unclear to whom the proper name, Jerry, refers. Nonetheless, the content of the story is coherently structured, with a beginning, development, outcome, and judgment on the outcome. Of course, neither of these narratives meets the criteria for a good story. As we can see, coherence and cohesion are both vital to story structure, and the child has to learn to strike a balance between the two.

## THE DEVELOPMENT OF NARRATIVE PRODUCTION

Cohesion and coherence interact at all times during discourse processing, although they have tended to be studied separately in children. In this section, we focus particularly on how children learn to use cohesive devices in their own storytelling.

One of the most extensive studies of the production of narrative cohesion in children is a cross-linguistic investigation using a set of pictures called the Frog Story. The study was headed by psycholinguists Ruth Berman and Daniel Slobin, together with collaborators from all over the world. The original study covered English, German, Hebrew, Spanish, and Turkish. Their approach has since been applied to most other European languages and has been used in a wide range of non-Western or uncommon linguistic environments including Morocco (Arabic); Australia (Arrernte, Guugu Yumithirr, Warlpiri); Botswana (Kgadlagadi); United States (Kickapoo, Lakhota); Papua New Guinea (Kilivila, Yupno); Solomon Islands (Longgu); Malaysia (Malay); China (Mandarin); Japan (Japanese); Belize (Mopan); Gabon (Myene); Uganda (several Nilotic languages); India (Tamil); and Mexico (Totonac, Tzotzil, Tzeltal, Yucatec). Narrative production has also been studied in several sign languages (American Sign Language, Sign Language of the Netherlands), as well as with various populations of language-impaired and cognitively impaired speakers. The experiments were carried out on preschool- and school-aged children (three- to nine-year-olds), as well as adults, in these many languages. The subjects were selected to reflect different stages of language development within varying linguistic contexts. As an investigative tool, the Frog Story has proven very useful in eliciting basic information about how children structure stories.

The Frog Story is a book selected from popular children's literature that contains twenty-four pictures with no text. It illustrates a story about a boy, his lost frog, and his various attempts to find it. The same picture book was used with every subject in every language. During the experiments, children (or adults) were simply asked to tell a story from the sequence of pictures that they saw in the book. The analysis focused on how children mark time, space, the perspective taken (agent versus patient), and connectivity. Researchers noted the tense of verbs, the use of locative markers, whether children used active or passive sentences, and how they linked one sentence to another. They then analyzed several aspects of the narratives produced: (1) how children encode events in language through choice of perspective (is X giving Y something, or Y taking something from X? Is X chasing Y, or Y being followed by X?); (2) how children group narrative events hierarchically; and (3) the range of expressive options children use as a function of their level of language development.

It was found that cognitive skills play a large role in determining the range of perspective-taking options available to children, but there are also language-specific influences. Interestingly, results showed that children learning languages like English and German focused primarily on *manner* of movement, and were therefore more likely to describe events in the pictures by selecting action verbs like "walk," "run," "jump," "crawl," or "drive," which describe the type of action performed by the character. These are called "manner verbs." Children learning languages like Hebrew, Spanish, and Turkish produced different descriptions for the same pictures. They focused on *direction* of movement rather than type, using expressions like "go into," "go out of," "go through the room." These are called "path verbs." The focus on path is not because these languages lack verbs describing manner of movement. Rather, it is because in these languages the child would have to say the equivalent of the more complex "he exited the house running" instead of "he ran out of the house." Where these languages differ, then, is in whether the main verb describing a motion event is a manner verb or a path verb.

As we have seen in other chapters, different features are more salient in some languages than in others, and children become sensitive to this early on. So the Frog Story research showed how the characteristics of a native language also influence the perspectives taken in narrative production. In addition, the data have shown that children start with single event descriptions. As they get a little older, they learn to string events together with cohesive markers. Finally, the oldest subjects progress to use the more elaborate syntactic devices that express temporal and causal relations between events, as well as explicitly mark episode boundaries and plot structure. Details of the findings are fascinating, but the full account goes beyond the scope of our single chapter on narrative. We therefore refer the interested reader to Berman's and Slobin's book.

The Frog Story study offers an incredibly rich database. But because the book chosen for the studies was ready-made for the commercial market rather than carefully crafted by researchers, it is not suitable for research requiring experimental manipulation. In order to capture the development of children's use of cohesive devices in narrative production, other researchers have devised specially controlled experimental materials. In one study, children between the ages of four and nine were asked to tell a story from some simple picture books that had been designed to constrain the different narrative options available. Ninety native French speakers and 150 native English speakers were shown a complete series of six pictures from which to tell a story. In addition, a further 180 French and English children, between the same ages, were shown just one picture taken from the middle of the book. The single picture represented an important event in the middle of the story, containing two characters. The action it involved could either be interpreted as "giving" or as "taking," depending on the perspective of the narrator. The aim of the research was to ascertain how the linguistic description of an identical picture might differ when it was given as part of a whole narrative versus as an isolated event.

Unlike the analysis of the Frog Story, this study focused on answering several questions about how children fill the subject slot of each sentence in their narrative, depending on their choice of cohesive device. For instance, do they use full noun phrases with indefinite or with definite articles? At what points in the story do they introduce the use of pronouns? And when do they use zero anaphora? A zero anaphor is an empty slot or placeholder that appears between a connective like "and" and a verb, when the referent of the verb is given by the preceding linguistic text. In other words, it is a placeholder for a pronoun that does not need to be mentioned overtly. For example, in the sentence "Harry read the book and went to sleep," a zero anaphor stands between "and" and "went," instead of the pronoun "he" or the repetition of the proper name "Harry," which can be taken for granted. Simply put, the subject of the verb phrase "went to sleep" is not expressed but is linguistically present in the deep structure of the sentence.

The principal areas of interest in this narrative study were children's (unconscious) decisions about when to use different cohesive markers. Analysis of the data also focused on those spontaneous self-corrections by the children that were used specifically to maintain cohesion. These occurred at points in the discourse when any one of the following markers—full noun phrase, pronoun, or zero anaphor—would have been grammatically correct. But the children nonetheless tended to self-repair in order to clarify the status of the referent as a principal or subsidiary character in the story. For instance, they might say "the girl said goodbye to the lady, and then the girl . . . and then she went home."

Based on hypotheses about the development of cohesive devices, the pictures composing the stories in the experiments were structured so that the status and sex of the characters could be manipulated by the researcher. For one story, then, the main character was obvious and the subsidiary character was of the same sex. This presented the potential for ambiguity if a pronoun was used. In another story, there was no clear main character, and it was left to the children to establish character status. And in a third type of story, there were two main story characters of different sex. Such manipulations of story structure allowed the researcher to compare the development of cohesive skills by looking at subtle differences in storytelling both within and across different age groups.

The findings of this study are too extensive for us to cover in totality, so we will focus on only one story type. We will see how children of different ages tell stories about two characters of the same sex—stories, then, in which use of a pronoun in the subject slot of each sentence could make the story ambiguous. In the experiments, each child was shown a series of six pictures bound together like a book with no text, and asked: "Tell me a story about what is happening in the pictures." The following examples represent two versions of this type of story. In one case, the six images depicted the following scenes (in order):

> *Picture 1:* A little girl, dressed in green, is walking along by herself.
>
> *Picture 2:* The girl sees a woman selling ice creams.
>
> *Picture 3:* The woman hands an ice cream to the girl (or the girl takes an ice cream from the woman).
>
> *Picture 4:* The girl walks away, licking her ice cream.
>
> *Picture 5:* The girl trips and drops the ice cream (or the ice cream falls to the ground).
>
> *Picture 6:* The girl is crying.

In a second set of pictures, the story possesses an identical internal, underlying structure but different surface realization.

> *Picture 1:* A little boy, dressed in red, is walking along by himself.
>
> *Picture 2:* The boy sees a man selling balloons.
>
> *Picture 3:* The man hands a balloon to the boy (or the boy takes a balloon from the man).
>
> *Picture 4:* The boy walks away holding his balloon by a string.
>
> *Picture 5:* The boy lets go of the balloon (or the balloon flies off into the clouds).
>
> *Picture 6:* The boy is crying.

As we can see, both stories have a clear main story character, a momentary introduction of a subsidiary story character of the same sex (which makes the use of the pronouns "she" or "he" potentially ambiguous), and a return to the main character. Picture 3, in each case, could be described in two different ways, depending on one's perspective. This gives children the choice to put either the main character in the subject slot (by using a verb like "take"), or to opt for the subsidiary character (by using a verb like "give"). This was the picture in each story that was subsequently described as an isolated event by the control groups. It was predicted that by middle childhood, but not before, different accounts of Picture 3 would be given, depending on whether it was embedded in a more extensive narrative. Picture 5 in each case also offered two different potential interpretations within a story. One could either describe the picture by making the main character the agent (by using verbs like "drop" or "let go"), or by focusing on the object (describing the ice cream or balloon as "falling" or "blowing away"). Again, overall structure of the narrative, rather than the local perspective, determines the perspective from which the child might describe Picture 5.

It was hypothesized that if the four- and five-year-olds use noun phrases and pronouns only deictically (to actually point to the referents in the pictures), rather than anaphorically (to refer back to the linguistically established referents), then they should see no problem in using the same pronoun for two different story characters of the same sex. Furthermore, a cross-linguistic comparison would be expected to yield further insight into the narrative difficulties faced by French-speaking versus English-speaking children. In French there is even more potential ambiguity of reference because the word "glace" (ice cream) is feminine in gender. All French nouns take gender marking, even if inanimate. So the same word "elle" can refer to people, meaning "she," and to objects, meaning "it." Therefore the use of the pronoun "elle" could refer not only to either the girl or the woman, but also to the ice cream. Likewise, "ballon" is masculine, so the pronoun "il" (he or it) could refer to the boy, the man, or the balloon.

Given the simple structure of the short stories, these experiments revealed a very clear developmental progression in the use of cohesive devices for discourse. First, the vast majority of children in all the age groups produced narratives that accurately described the content of what was depicted in each picture. The way in which they did so, however, changed substantially between the ages of four and nine. The youngest children—four- and five-year-olds—used markers predominantly in their deictic functions, despite the potential ambiguities that this might cause.

Here are a couple of typical examples of stories told by four- and five-year-olds:

> The girl's got a green dress like mine. She's coming out of her house and there there's a lady selling ice creams. She [pointing to girl] wants

a vanilla ice cream. So she gives her one and she walks off licking it. And there she's dropped it so she's crying her eyes out. I dropped my ice cream in the cinema once but I didn't cry. She's silly.

There, he's walking along. He's got a hat on 'cause it's sunny. He wants a balloon . . . a green one. He has to pay so he gives him the money and he (indicating referent with a head gesture toward the man) gives him a nice green balloon. It's got a string so he can hold it. Oh, it's windy and he's gonna let go and now he's lost it so he's crying. That's the end.

In both of the above examples, the child introduces the referent directly with either a definite noun phrase ("the girl") or a pronoun ("he"). If the researcher couldn't see the pictures, she wouldn't know who was doing what to whom. But this ambiguity is clarified through the use of extralinguistic devices such as pointing and head movements, as well as through the addition of deictic locatives like "there." For the youngest age groups, therefore, children's definite and pronominal devices refer to the pictures, not to an internal representation of the linguistic text. Although the string of pronouns used throughout these young speakers' narratives is ambiguous if interpreted only within the linguistic context, the pronouns are nevertheless deictically interpretable within the extralinguistic context to which the child refers.

Six- and seven-year-olds produced a very different kind of narrative. Interestingly, although they showed definite progress toward intralinguistic cohesion, their story content was often more impoverished than that of the younger children. What seems to happen at this later developmental stage is that children realize that the story requires intralinguistic structure. But their use of cohesive devices is not yet flexible enough to coordinate simultaneously coherence and intralinguistic cohesion. Cohesive devices are used rigidly, but cohesion is strongly expressed. In order to overcome ambiguity of pronominal reference, children of this age tend to preempt the subject slot of every sentence for the main story character only. Here are two typical examples of this cohesive strategy:

There's a little girl who's going out for a walk. She sees an ice cream van and buys one. She walks off in the sun. But then she drops her ice cream by mistake and starts to cry.

There's a little boy in red and he sees a balloon man and he takes a balloon and he goes off holding it. But he lets it go and loses it, so he starts to cry.

In both of these narrative examples, the main character is referred to in the subject slot of every sentence. The subsidiary characters (ice cream lady / balloon man) are barely mentioned, and never in the subject slot. This slot is reserved exclusively for the principal character in each story. The child seems to do this specifically to maintain cohesion and avoid pronoun ambiguity. But in doing so, the coherence of the story may suffer and lead to impoverished content.

As we saw in the earlier examples, in the narratives of children in the four- and five-year age groups Picture 3 is described from the point of view of the subsidiary character ("he gives him a nice green balloon"). In other words, the youngest narrators describe each picture separately, rather than integrating them into a single perspective. Six- and seven-year-olds, by contrast, describe all the pictures from one perspective, putting the main story character in the subject slot of every sentence in their narrative. This strategy has been called the thematic subject constraint, or TSC. Children choose the theme of their story and the main character of that theme, then opt for the cohesive strategy of preempting the subject slot for the thematic subject. There is clearly less detail in the stories produced by these somewhat older children. Cohesion is vastly improved compared to the younger group, however. This is a particularly interesting stage in narrative development, because it demonstrates how children tackle the difficult task of balancing coherence and cohesion, and how this takes some time to acquire.

For the oldest age group—children ages eight and nine—the TSC continues to constrain narrative output. But this is done far more flexibly. Like the six- and seven-year-olds, the storytellers who are eight and nine choose a theme and a principal character. But rather than rigidly preempting the subject slot for this character, they preempt pronouns in the subject slot for their main character. If a subsidiary character is placed in the subject slot, then it is referred to with a full noun phrase. This helps to maintain the status differentiation. By this age, then, children have learned to use *differential* referential expressions (pronouns, definite, and indefinite articles) to indicate the changing role and status of the characters as the story unfolds. We see this development in the following two examples:

> This is the story about a little girl who's taking a walk in the sunshine. She notices a lady selling ice cream and, as it's hot, she decides to buy one. The lady hands her a cornet [ice cream cone] and she walks off to enjoy it. But suddenly she trips on a stone and drops the ice cream, so she starts to cry because it starts to melt in the sun.

> A little boy is walking home. He sees a balloon man. The balloon man gives him a green balloon, so he happily goes off home with it. But the balloon suddenly flies out of his hand and so he starts to cry.

Note how once the main story character (a girl / a boy) has been introduced with an indefinite noun phrase in the opening sentence, it is then referred to consistently with a pronoun. In contrast, a definite noun phrase is used to refer to the subsidiary story character (the ice cream lady / the balloon man), in order to clearly mark their difference in status in the narrative. Note, too, that the pronoun for the main character is not always used to refer to the most recently mentioned referent ("She notices a lady selling ice cream and . . . she decides to buy one"). Children of this age thus use pronouns preferentially (although not exclusively) to refer to their representation of the overall story structure built around the main character.

At this final stage of narrative development, then, the use of different cohesive devices allows the storyteller to not only refer to each character, but also to distinguish between the roles each character plays within the total story structure. The consistent appearance throughout a stretch of discourse of a pronoun like "he" in the subject position itself provides the listener with additional information beyond semantics. Through this strategy, the speaker can convey that the word "he" not only refers to a singular human male, but also indicates the main story character. Likewise, the marked use of a full noun phrase in the sequence of episodes provides additional information about the discourse role of the subsidiary character (continued use of "the balloon man" designates him as a subsidiary story character). The very fact that pronouns and full noun phrases are used in multiple ways by older children is the hallmark of a well-structured, cohesive narrative.

Data from the single picture condition also provided interesting insights into the development of cohesion in children's narrative discourse. In this follow-up experiment, a group of children who had not seen the full stories was asked to describe an isolated, single picture. These descriptions provided valuable comparative data upon which hypotheses about narrative development could be further tested. When Picture 3 was presented in isolation, children of all age groups showed a strong tendency to place the "balloon man / ice cream woman" in the subject slot, using verbs like "give," "hand over," or "offer" ("the man's giving the boy a balloon," "the woman is handing an ice cream to the girl"). Of course, these pictures were designed to suggest this interpretation. Yet this very natural interpretation of the scene in Picture 3 is particularly interesting in light of the narrative data produced by the six-year-olds. Remember how, in their stories, the children placed the main character (the boy / the girl) in the subject slot for this particular picture? By contrast, when describing this very same picture in isolation, children of the same and other ages always placed the other character in the subject slot. This demonstrates how children's desire to convey discourse structure in narrative will if necessary override the most natural description of a single picture.

From the studies discussed in this chapter it is clear that we must think beyond children's mere mastery of linguistic forms like full noun phrases and pronouns. There is no point in counting, for instance, how many pronouns children of a given age group produce in their narratives. What is important is each pronoun's *function* within the narrative. Since every referential expression has multiple functions, it is a child's ability to orchestrate the interplay of all these functions, in particular the dialogic and narrative functions, that constitutes discourse mastery. Discourse marking does not involve using *new* grammatical structures. Rather, it requires learning to use existing structures in new ways. It is noteworthy that markers can function differently at the discourse level than at the sentential level. This is why we argue that learning to take part in discourse involves storing in memory not just words, but the multifunctional status of the linguistic markers. Each time a referential term is needed, the child now has to choose between the variety of linguistic devices that fulfill different discourse functions. At the single sentence and purely grammatical level, choice of a referential expression is dictated by the semantic characteristics of the referent. Is it animate or inanimate, male or female, singular or plural? In contrast, at the discourse level, as we have seen, the child needs to convey a great deal more information through his selection of the cohesive devices.

The storybooks used in the study discussed here were purposely very simple in structure, and are not therefore representative of all child narrative. Evidence from more complex narratives may reveal that the TSC strategy is not as rigid as these data suggest. Nonetheless, a number of studies in a variety of different languages, like French and Turkish, have shown that the subject slot of sentences within narratives is used by children to convey important information about discourse cohesion.

While coherence and cohesion fulfill quite different roles in the development of narrative production and comprehension, it is important to stress that they do not develop separately. They are intimately entwined and yet have often been studied in isolation from one another. Although research has made huge advances in our understanding of the acquisition of discourse skills in children, there remains a need for further studies that examine how coherence and cohesion relate to one another dynamically at every stage of children's progressive discourse development.

## Conclusion

Producing well-formed discourse, both dialogue and narrative, involves taking into account a great number of factors simultaneously.

These include (1) the time, place, and causality of the events described, (2) the grounding of information, (3) the amount and nature of prior knowledge shared by speaker and listener, and (4) the specific cohesive devices that both provide additional information about the hierarchical structure of the story episodes and help describe the relationships between characters and events. As adults, we perform all these linguistic feats simultaneously and automatically when taking part in discourse. For the child, however, integrating all of these aspects of language requires a lot of practice. This is why, even though children can make grammatical distinctions at the sentential level at a relatively early age, the full mastery of discourse is a milestone of late development.

# 7

## ATYPICAL LANGUAGE
## DEVELOPMENT

From the evidence presented in the previous chapters, it is apparent that language development is a resilient process that is successfully completed by the vast majority of children. A small percentage of children, however, do experience difficulties with language learning. A number of very different factors can cause the acquisition process to differ from the norm. Some of these factors are general to development, while others are specific to language acquisition. For instance, disabilities such as deafness or blindness play a significant role in determining how the child becomes a fluent language user. In such cases, both the child and the caregivers must use special strategies to overcome the specific difficulties faced by the learner. But the outcome in both cases is that the deaf or blind child will ultimately become a proficient communicator. For the deaf child, the drive to communicate is fulfilled by acquiring one of the many sign languages of the world. If his parents are hearing and do not know a sign language, the child will create a relatively rich gestural communication system until he can be immersed in a deaf signing community. And he invents this system without the benefit of any real linguistic input. For the blind child, in contrast, the language learning task involves acquiring a spoken language without the help of visual cues. This may seem straightforward, but try closing your eyes and listening to someone talking to you for ten minutes. You will find that you may have to guess quite a lot because you cannot see where your interlocutor is looking or pointing. You might even be tempted to peek to determine the emotional state of the speaker—is he attempting to deceive you, or telling the truth? Now imagine facing this task as a two-year-old trying to actually learn language, not just follow it. It soon becomes obvious that some sensory problems, which at first may seem relatively unrelated to speech, can nonetheless change the normal course of language acquisition.

Certain types of genetic disorders or developmental traumas can also lead to atypical language. In Down syndrome, language is one of several cognitive faculties affected. Similarly, children who suffer severe social deprivation early on—such as institutionalized children or feral cases—may develop a gamut of cognitive impairments of which language is just one component. There are also individuals who, as a result of genetic mutations or injuries to the brain, may seem to develop normally in all other cognitive and physical domains, but show Specific Language Impairment (SLI). By contrast, some genetic disorders cause serious deficits in almost all areas of cognitive development except language. This includes children with Williams syndrome, who seemingly excel in language. It appears, then, that language development can be differentially impaired and differentially spared, an important issue that we will examine in detail.

As we shall also see, the study of atypical language provides another perspective on the processes of normal language acquisition. Unraveling how language learning can go wrong can help us tease apart the various factors involved in the normal case. Such research is also vital for the implementation of early intervention programs for children at risk of language impairment. Data show that adverse environmental factors, such as being hospitalized for a lengthy period at a young age, have less of an effect on language acquisition in normal learners than in children with genetic or acquired disorders. It has also been found that, in general, the linguistic input directed at atypical language learners is impoverished and may itself cause secondary problems that further exacerbate language acquisition. Clearly there is a need for positive intervention as early as possible, to provide atypical children with the supportive linguistic environment that they need. Research into very early remediation—and by "early" we mean from the first few weeks of life, through the entire prelinguistic period and beyond—is an area of study that we hope will begin to take center stage in developmental psycholinguistics during the twenty-first century.

## Atypical Language Learning Due to Sensory Deprivation

### LANGUAGE LEARNING IN DEAF CHILDREN

One of the most fascinating cases of atypical language acquisition is that of congenitally deaf children. To most of us, sign languages remain a mystery, and it is a common misconception to view this medium of communication as an embellished form of gesturing. Nothing could be further from the truth. There is, for instance, a huge difference between "signed English" and British Sign Language or American Sign Language. The latter two are real languages. Signed systems, such as manually spelled English, have been created to directly translate, item-by-item, particular spoken languages into gestural communication systems. But these are not languages. Such impoverished gestural systems are not used in deaf communities, nor do they possess vital features of real sign languages. They have been developed mainly for use by hearing parents or hearing teachers of deaf children. Interestingly, even when a deaf child is using a gestural system quite fluently, once he is introduced to deaf people within a native signing environment, the genuine sign language he is exposed to will immediately take precedence and will quickly replace the old gestural system.

There are numerous different sign languages in the world. They all possess complex grammar and rich vocabularies that are as individual to each language as those of any spoken language. They bear no relation to the local spoken tongue, nor do they resemble each other. Furthermore, contrary to what one might imagine, the many different sign languages of the world are not the result of local variations on a basic gestural template. The signs and grammatical markers that make up the languages of the deaf are particular to each sign language. Their grammars can be as complex in structure and the word signs as arbitrary in nature as are the grammars and words that make up spoken languages. Indeed, American Sign Language (ASL) is as different from British Sign Language (BSL) as spoken English is from Russian, French, or Swahili.

Like spoken language, signing makes use of subtle grammatical distinctions in order to convey meaning in discourse. Signs can be stressed, the tone of the signer can be communicated, and strings of signs can take the form of questions, statements, declaratives, relative clauses, plurals, and so forth. Some of these grammatical differences are expressed by the use of facial signs (like raising eyebrows) or body movements, rather than only signing with the hands. Sign languages thus offer as valid and rich a means of communication as any spoken language. And for the deaf child, the process of acquisition is as natural, fascinating, and ultimately rewarding as for the hearing child learning her native tongue. Deaf children are therefore capable of reaching precisely the same levels of language acquisition as hearing children. That is not to say that the way children process language is exactly the same in both cases, however. Research using the Event Related Potentials method of brain imaging shows that the part of the cortex normally used for auditory processing is taken over by the visual processing of language in the deaf individual, so as to compensate for the missing sensory input.

When we look at the linguistic development of deaf children, it is helpful to initially make the distinction between deaf children of deaf native-signing parents, and deaf children of hearing parents. The learning experiences of these two groups differ significantly. In the long run, almost all of these children eventually learn one of the many recognized sign languages of the world. But children of deaf parents who use a native sign language in the home are at a distinct advantage, because they learn language in much the same way as hearing children acquire their native tongue. These deaf children progress through the same stages of language acquisition as their hearing counterparts.

Most of the studies of language acquisition by the deaf child have been carried out in Western communities such as England, the United States, the Netherlands, Italy, and Sweden. What has been found across these communities is that like the hearing infant, deaf children are initially exposed to a form of sign motherese (where signs are exaggerated and occur over a wider signing space than is used for adult-directed signs). Like hearing babies, they also proceed through a stage of babbling, but in the manual mode, trying out a very wide variety of different hand shapes. These are progressively narrowed down to the hand shapes relevant to their native sign language. They then go on to produce individual word signs, followed by a sign vocabulary spurt. Next comes the production of two-sign combinations, and finally, strings of signs displaying increasingly complex grammatical structure and content. The overall pattern of language development is similar to that of the hearing child.

Early on, toddlers acquiring sign language express the same restricted set of semantic relations as those learning a spoken language (for example, locatives, as in "Mummy garden"; possessives, as in "Tommy truck," referring to himself; or adjectives describing or modifying object properties, as in "big dog.") Like hearing children, they also seem to avoid making certain kinds of grammatical errors. Then, eventually, the deaf child learns to include all the morphological and grammatical structures of his sign language (plural, present progressive tense, relative clause, question formation, foregrounding and backgrounding, and so forth) to produce fluent and eloquent signing. It is now that the child incorporates facial signs to structure complex sentences, as well as changes in body position to convey different discourse markers when telling narratives.

As was the case with spoken language, children's errors in sign language are often important clues to the acquisition process. Although most signs are arbitrary, those for "you" and "I" are common across sign languages and simply involve pointing to the interlocutor or to oneself. Yet during development, deaf learners even treat these signs as arbitrary markers. Laura Pettito showed that deaf children often go through an initial stage where the signs for "you" and "I" are correctly used. A little later in language development, however, deaf children begin to make errors when using these signs: they point to the interlocutor when they wish to express "I" and to themselves when they wish to express "you." Why is this so? It is thought that such mistakes occur as a result of signs becoming increasingly more arbitrary for the child. He now analyzes the signs formally as conventional symbols, rather than seeing them as a simple extension of natural gesture. So if the adult signer points toward the child when referring to the child, the child copies the sign "point to interlocutor" when referring to himself. This is a particularly striking example of the distinction between the iconic nature of natural gesture and the formal nature of the linguistic sign.

As we can see, deaf children acquire their native sign language as naturally as any hearing child learns to speak. Likewise, hearing children of one deaf parent and one hearing parent grow up bilingual, in much the same way and with the same ease as children learning two native spoken languages. For these bilingual children, there does not seem to be a problem with the shift in modalities from speech to sign. In fact, signs tend to emerge slightly earlier than words, though in the long run this difference has no real developmental significance for either language. One possible reason for early signing is that deaf parents might be more likely to assign meaning to sign babbling than hearing parents are to oral babbling. Prelinguistic gesturing is often given linguistic status, whereas parents of hearing children tend not to interpret babbling as having precise meaning unless the babbles sound very similar to real words. But other than that, for the hearing or the native signing child, the linguistic environment and the process of language acquisition are almost identical. Indeed, the only factor that renders language learning atypical for the deaf is that the language in question is manually, rather than vocally, produced.

The same is not true for deaf children born to hearing parents who use only spoken language. Such is the situation for more than 90 percent of hearing-impaired children. There used to be a strong tendency for parents of such children to choose to communicate with a combination of oral speech and manual sign. Cued speech or signed English are common solutions for such parents. But as we mentioned earlier, these types of communicative systems cannot be given the status of "language" because they lack the complex grammar and arbitrariness of full-fledged linguistic systems. It is becoming increasingly common, particularly in the Netherlands, Sweden, and some parts of the United States, for hearing parents of deaf children to begin learning a proper sign language as soon as they realize that their child is deaf. This learning is driven by the desire to communicate naturally and adequately with their child from the outset. Learning a sign language as an adult is as difficult as learning any second language at a late age. Nonetheless, the advantages for the deaf child of having a parent communicate with him normally in a full-fledged language cannot be overestimated. Such children ultimately surpass their parents and become fluent sign users, demonstrating how resilient children are when acquiring a natural language, even if the input is somewhat impoverished. This points to the importance of establishing a normal linguistic environment for deaf children and of using a proper sign language from the start.

Research with hearing parents who do not learn to sign shows that initially such parents do very little gesturing to communicate with their young infant. This might be because gesturing by a hearing mother to a deaf infant is more self-conscious and pre-planned than motherese (spoken or signed), which hearing or deaf mothers produce quite instinctively. So these infants experience a lack of early signing input and will begin to acquire their parents' spoken language as best they can through rudimentary lip reading. Most deaf children who are thus raised orally are always at a disadvantage because few people can become fluent lip readers without the addition of sound. Of course such infants quickly grow sensitive to all the gestural, facial, and interactional opportunities afforded by the *act* of speaking. But the inability to process the auditory input remains a huge constraint on language learning when there is no sign language model. For such children, therefore, language acquisition can be hindered by lack of sufficient input.

Despite this impoverished input, deaf children of hearing parents turn out to be surprisingly resourceful. Susan Goldin-Meadow and Heidi Feldman have shown that even in the complete absence of any signing, deaf children of hearing parents will eventually develop their very own system of signing in order to overcome their communicative disability. Despite the total lack of a model, these invented "languages" have been shown to involve a very clear differentiation between gesturing and signing. The signs of such invented "languages" are not simple iconic gestures. Rather, these children's languages are made up of signs that become progressively arbitrary and abstract with development. For example, the child might initially invent a hand shape for "duck" based on the waddling movement of ducks. At this early stage, the sign is clearly more like an iconic gesture than an arbitrary symbol. But rapidly the sign becomes abbreviated and increasingly more abstract, so that ultimately the original gesture bears little resemblance to the now stable abstract sign that has taken on the role of a sign word. With a growing vocabulary of invented signs, these deaf children of hearing parents then begin to display the rudiments of grammar, by combining their signs and using variations in sign order to convey differences in meaning. This gives them considerable communicative powers. Yet although all of this illustrates the remarkable resilience of the human drive for language, the linguistic development of these children is nonetheless limited. They will always eventually require proper interaction with native signers outside their hearing family in order to acquire a full-fledged language. When they do enter a signing environment, it is found that such children quickly catch up with their peers and finally get the chance to communicate all their thoughts, feelings, and experiences through the newly acquired sign language. In these circumstances, roles become reversed, with parents learning language from their children.

Although fewer in number, deaf children born to deaf but nonnative signing parents provide a particularly interesting case of atypical language acquisition. Under these circumstances, the deaf parents learned to sign only as adults. So the language model that their deaf children receive is more like that of a second language than a native language. What is interesting is that these deaf children end up with better skills and knowledge of the sign language than do their signing parents. A similar outcome is found in, say, refugee families where the children learn the language of the new country, particularly the grammar, far more easily than do their parents.

As late language learners, adults acquire signs as totalities without analyzing their morphological component parts, so deaf children of nonnative signing parents start the language learning process by copying the frozen signs that their parents use. But, as Elissa Newport and Ted Suppala have shown, the children go on to make a formal analysis of the morphology. Morphology can be expressed in sign by varying certain formal features of hand shape, place of articulation, and movement.

Let us illustrate this concept with spoken words. At first the child may not appreciate the relationship between "zip" and "unzip," and will learn these as completely independent, "frozen" items. With time, however, the child will recognize the relationship between the two words and will store "un" as a morphological marker that alters meaning. He may later even generalize the marker to create the word "unbreak" when he means "mend." Similarly, when he hears "walk" and "walked," he will extract and store "ed" as a morphological marker that changes tense. The same applies to deaf children. They gradually learn to decompose the frozen signs in the parental input into their constituent parts, and to discover similarities across different signs. So if several signs have a common stem or a common morphological marker (like past tense), deaf children learn to mark the separate components by temporarily placing stress on each part. They thereby build up a system of linguistic representations that are richer in structure and meaning than their parents'. This is true for all deaf children who become fluent in a recognized sign language. But for the deaf children of nonnative signing deaf parents, this achievement is even more remarkable, because it shows that they are able to represent morphosyntax in more sophisticated ways than their parents who are providing the model. Similar outcomes have been reported in children from ex-colonies. It is through children rather than adults that such protolanguages as Pidgin English, for instance, are progressively turned into more complex creole languages. The main difference between pidgins and creoles is that pidgins contain only strings of words, whereas creoles become richer by the addition of a simple morphosyntactic structure.

Another interesting example of atypical language learning is that of hearing children of deaf parents. In such cases, where children only interact with their parents and have no regular opportunities to interact with hearing people, they initially simply learn sign language fluently and easily. Spoken language is at first poorly acquired, despite the children's ready access to television. This is because television is not a good substitute for real speech. It provides no feedback to children's actions or attempts to talk (that is, it cannot answer questions, note whether the child understands or not, or repeat and recast utterances). The language in television programs is also, on the whole, adult-directed. For the young child, this is very impoverished linguistic input and does not provide the vital qualities of child-directed language. Television input may have some influence on language learning for children in a normal environment. But for the hearing child of deaf parents for whom television may for a while be the main source of spoken input, it is totally inadequate. It remains to be seen whether programs like *Telletubbies*, where the language is specifically designed for very young children, could help the hearing toddlers of deaf parents acquire spoken language. But it is unlikely that such input will prove to have a significant influence because it still would not provide the vital social contexts in which real linguistic interaction occurs. Hearing children of deaf parents with such limited input will of course soon enter the normal hearing environment of the outside world and become bilingual.

## LANGUAGE LEARNING IN BLIND CHILDREN

Another interesting case of sensory deprivation and atypical language learning is that of blind children. One might assume that spoken language belongs exclusively to the domains of oral output and auditory input. It would follow that the blind child should be able to learn to speak just as easily as the normal child. But we challenged such an assumption in our introduction to this chapter. Consider, for instance, the subtle difference between the verbs "look" and "see." How would you teach a blind infant to make this distinction? Think of all the factors that you take for granted when you speak to a person who is seeing what you are seeing, who can follow your gestures and your facial expressions, whose attention you can direct without the help of extra words, and who can even preempt your next utterance just by noticing what you are looking at. Blind children may get auditory input that is similar to what their sighted peers hear, but they face an extra challenge in making semantic mappings between the utterances they hear and the objects or events to which these utterances refer.

It has been found, for example, that blind language learners have particular trouble acquiring personal pronouns. This may be because we naturally use head movements, eye gaze, or pointing to accompany our use of personal pronouns, and the blind child lacks this additional information. What happens in this case is that early on blind youngsters (and their parents) tend to use proper names and avoid personal pronouns. Another common finding is that blind children use significantly fewer auxiliary verbs like "can," "do," or "will" than their sighted counterparts. This is found to be the case even when the blind toddlers' language is matched for mean length of utterance (MLU) with their sighted peers. Both sets of children produce the expected length of utterances for their age, but the type of words used in their speech differs in important ways. It turns out that this is because the mothers of blind children tend to ask far fewer questions, like "can you give me that?" or "do you want some milk?", and to use far more directives, like "take this" or "come here." The blind child turns out to be less exposed to auxiliary verbs in daily dialogue, and therefore takes longer to learn them. Without realizing it, parents provide subtly different input to the blind child.

It is not only the input that differs in the blind child's language development. Research shows that the acquisition process itself is also somewhat altered compared to that of sighted children. Studies with sighted infants demonstrate that children are more likely to attend to, and try to imitate, speakers they can see *and* hear, as opposed to speakers they can only hear. Paying attention to lip movements plays an important role in the development of the sighted infant's lexicon. Many of the inaudible elements of language, such as the articulatory activity given by the changing shape of the speaker's mouth and clues found in facial expressions, are unavailable to the blind child. This is not to say that these subtleties of speech and syntax are completely lost to them, however. The blind language learner fills in the gaps by developing greater sensitivity to subtle differences in the auditory signals themselves, as well as by sometimes feeling the lip movements of his interlocutors and thereby "seeing" through his hands. He also learns to detect a smile, a grimace, or a change in the direction of the speaker's attention by picking up minute variations in the sounds that speakers emit. It has been suggested that since the part of the infant's brain usually devoted to sight remains undeveloped in the blind child, the visual cortex is taken over for the processing of auditory and tactile input. The sense of hearing (and touch) becomes more extensively developed in blind children, with increased brain volume devoted to auditory input than is the case for the sighted individual.

Like his deaf counterpart, the blind child's drive to become a fluent language user will eventually surmount the obstacles resulting from his sensory deprivation. Children are very creative in their acquisition of language, whatever modality it occurs in.

## Specific Language Impairment

We have stressed throughout the book that language acquisition is an area of child development that is characterized by wide individual variation. Normal ranges for such things as first word onset, vocabulary growth, and early grammar can be very broad. As long as they display adequate language comprehension skills, both the toddler who produces two hundred words by twenty months and his same-age peer who can only utter thirty-five words fall within the normal developmental range. As we have also seen, it is quite common for boys to start speaking later than girls, and yet, by the age of four when most children are speaking fluently, late talkers are on the whole indistinguishable from early talkers. There is, however, a small percentage of individuals—about 5 percent of the total population—that goes on to develop Specific Language Impairment (SLI).

A disorder that exclusively affects language acquisition, SLI occurs in otherwise normally developing individuals. A child suffering from SLI has, by definition, no neurological damage, no oral-motor structural dysfunction, and no sensory impairments; nor has there been any social deprivation. Such a child also possesses a nonverbal intelligence, or Performance IQ, in the normal range (at least 85). Such individuals reach all the typical cognitive and motor milestones on time, but show significant language delay and impairment. They experience difficulties with specific aspects of language comprehension and / or production. Here is an extract from a normally intelligent fourteen-year-old with SLI, repeating a story about the researcher's brother that he has just been told:

> Yesterday jump in river . . . uhm . . . get new shoe . . . shoe wet. Mummy cross. Her looking for brother. Her go everywhere . . . uhm . . . not find him. Hide behind tree . . . uhm . . . very naughty.

If we did not know, we might think that such language came from a very young child or from a foreigner who did not yet know the grammar of English. And yet, in all other aspects of his intellect, this adolescent appears to be as able as any other fourteen-year-old. His very delayed language demonstrates that he does not really know how his mother tongue works.

Although children with SLI differ in the level of severity of their language impairment, the lexical and pragmatic skills involved in communication tend to be somewhat less impaired than the grammatical skills. Problems with morphosyntax are often the most notable. In the dialogue and narratives of SLI children, articles as well as plural and past tense markers are often omitted from their obligatory contexts. The more salient forms that occur at the end of sentences (such as "him" and "her") are more likely to be produced. These often replace less salient forms (such as "he" or "she"), which occur at the beginnings of sentences. In many cases, too, quite elementary morphology seems to be more severely affected than aspects of syntax like word order. Indeed, our fourteen-year-old's difficulty rests neither with the basic ordering of words, nor with the stringing of ideas and utterances together. Rather, the problems concern more subtle aspects of grammar. So in his narrative, the story unfolds coherently, but the subject "he" is replaced by the more salient form "him," auxiliaries and articles are lacking, and tense markers are missing on verbs.

Dorothy Bishop has argued that SLI can be divided into at least six subgroups. The different forms of SLI concern problems with specific aspects of language. At one extreme are those who suffer from verbal auditory agnosia, or word deafness. Such individuals are incapable of understanding spoken language, although they clearly comprehend the meaning of gestures. They do not show any form of hearing impairment and yet they are totally unreceptive to speech. Language production is either completely absent or extremely limited; such people seem unable to use their articulatory system to form linguistically relevant sounds. This type of language disorder is very rare, and little is yet known about it.

Another somewhat less severe subgroup of SLI is known as verbal dyspraxia, and it also is recognized by very poor articulation and limited language production. In this case, however, comprehension reaches a fairly good level. In contrast, children who suffer from phonological programming deficit understand and produce long and complex sentences, but their speech is often incomprehensible. This is due to poor differentiation between individual phonemes. The fourth subgroup is lexical-syntactic SLI, which does not affect speech per se but rather impairs discourse skills—that is, the child's ability to formulate a series of connected sentences in order to maintain a conversation or tell a story. Children suffering from lexical-syntactic SLI have an immature syntax typical of much younger children, although the content of their output is age appropriate. A large vocabulary may coexist with only rudimentary grammar. In addition, these children's comprehension of language that refers to the here and now is considerably better than their understanding of references to hypothetical events and abstract concepts.

The fifth subgroup is called semantic-pragmatic SLI and involves particular difficulties with meaning and the appropriate social uses of language. This deficit also causes problems for comprehension and sentence construction. So while speech appears fluent and is well articulated, the content is often bizarre and sounds echolalic (much as if the child were repeating ready-made phrases rather than constructing novel sentences). Because of their pragmatic difficulties, children with this syndrome also display overly literal comprehension. So if asked, "Do you know what time it is?" the child is likely to reply "yes" without actually telling you the time. Such children cannot make the necessary pragmatic inferences when interpreting indirect speech acts. Another common finding is that these children single out a couple of words in the sentence they hear and respond to these rather than to the sentence as a whole. One is left with the impression that the child participates in conversation without really understanding either what the overall topic is or what is being said about it.

The sixth subgroup, grammatical SLI (G-SLI), also referred to as phonological-syntactic deficit syndrome, has been extensively researched in recent years. This is the group to which our earlier fourteen-year-old belongs. G-SLI affects the acquisition of grammar and therefore seriously impairs the overall development of language. Myrna Gopnik, Mabel Rice, and Heather van der Lely, among others, have suggested that this form of SLI might be held up as proof of the innateness of grammar. They argue that the existence of a grammar-specific impairment implies that we are all born with a genetically predetermined, specialized mechanism for grammar that can be impaired in isolation of other linguistic and cognitive faculties. But as we shall see, the problems of the G-SLI child are not as clear-cut as these theories claim, and we should be more cautious in generalizing from atypical development to the normal case.

Those who suffer from G-SLI generally do not have difficulty learning individual words, but they go on to develop seriously impoverished language production. The errors that these children produce, especially once word combination gets well under way, indicate that certain grammatical structures have not been adequately acquired. It is common for such children to fail to learn the distinctions between certain verbs such as the transitive "drop" (I dropped the cup) versus the intransitive "fall" (the cup fell), which are very similar in meaning but require clues from grammar in order to be learned and used correctly. Omission of obligatory bound and unbound morphemes is also frequent in G-SLI. Various other grammatical structures, such as the addition of the plural marker "s" or the past tense marker "ed," fail to be properly acquired.

Children with G-SLI seem to store words as direct lexical entries without noticing their component parts. So upon hearing the utterance "one apple, two apples," they would make two separate and distinct lexical entries for the words "apple" and "apples," unlike the normal child who would store the noun "apple" and process the plural "apples" as "apple + plural marker (s)." This is not to say that G-SLI children do not understand the cognitive concept of plural, however. Research clearly demonstrates that they do. Rather, it is argued that these individuals have difficulty in expressing such concepts linguistically through the obligatory use of morphosyntactic structures. When they do occasionally produce correct plural forms, it is believed that this is as a result of rote learning rather than grammatical processing. So, for instance, if a G-SLI child correctly produces "one dog," "two dogs," it is likely that he has retrieved from memory first the lexical entry for "single canine" and then a separate lexical entry for "more than one canine." The same holds for past tense forms. G-SLI children are thought to store forms like "walk" and "walked" as two independent and unrelated entries in their lexicon. Interestingly, they show a greater proficiency with irregular verbs (such as "go" and "went") because these are more naturally encoded as separate lexical entries in memory.

Salience of forms in the output plays an important role in the manifestation of SLI. For instance, English-speaking SLI children are more likely to learn the correct plural marker for "horse" than for "book" because the acoustic realization of the plural morphological marker in "horses" ("ez") is more perceptually salient and of greater duration than the sound "s" in "books." Cross-linguistic studies have provided further evidence of the importance of salience. In English, bound morphological markers and articles are vital for grammar, but they do not stand out in the speech stream. This is not the case, however, in certain other languages like Italian. We can better illustrate this with the following example. In English, the present tense forms "jump" and "jumps" both have one syllable and sound almost identical. Only the addition of third person singular "s" differentiates one form from the other, and this distinction is not particularly salient in the speech stream. This tense marker is frequently omitted in the output of English-speaking children with SLI. In Italian, by contrast, first-person singular "salto" (I jump) differs from both third-person singular "salta" (he jumps) and first-person plural "saltiamo" (we jump), in phonologically salient ways. Italian children with SLI do not omit these morphological markers nearly as often as do their English-speaking counterparts. Similarly, unbound morphemes (like the definite and indefinite articles "una," "uno," "la," "il," "lo," "gli," and "le") are very varied and salient in Italian because of their full syllabic status and the fact that they mark differences in both gender and number. This is not the case in English, where "a" and "the" are the only forms and "the" is the same in the singular and the plural. So the task of acquiring certain bound and unbound morphological markers may be more difficult for English-speaking SLI children than for their Italian counterparts. This does not mean that there are no cases of G-SLI among Italian children. There are, but their difficulties are with other aspects of grammar.

What the cross-linguistic comparisons show is that the surface manifestation of SLI can differ from language to language, but SLI exists throughout the world. It is clear, then, that we cannot generalize across all SLI cases for either research or therapy, because the way the syndrome manifests itself will vary in different linguistic environments. Researchers and clinicians must therefore take into account the language-specific aspects of the input that might present special obstacles to those with SLI. This illustrates how crucial it is to examine the complex interaction between the impairment the child displays and the particularities of the language that he is learning.

Dorothy Bishop has proposed a general hypothesis to explain the possible cause of SLI. She has suggested that children with this disorder persist in analyzing language in terms of syllables. Typically developing children, by contrast, move beyond the basic syllable to analyzing language at the levels of onset, rhyme, and phoneme. So, Bishop maintains, upon hearing a word like "cast," the SLI child always stores it as a syllabic representation (the whole word "cast"). In contrast, normal children go on to reanalyze the initial representation "cast," store it subsequently as onset-rhyme "c-ast," and finally break it down into its component phonemes as "c-a-s-t." If a child does not take all these later representational steps, he will fail to abstract linguistic commonalities between different exemplars. He will not notice, for instance, that "cat" and "cast" begin with the same phoneme, or that "last" and "cast" end with the same rhyme and consonant cluster.

It is well documented that in normal development, the way in which linguistic input is represented changes and becomes progressively more analytic over time. But, Bishop argues, children with SLI seem to continue using inefficient, basic modes of representation and therefore cannot process phonemic similarities. These are vital for achieving automatic processing. Indeed, while SLI manifests itself in different ways, the majority of sufferers do appear to share a difficulty in building appropriate phonological representations. As a result, more often than not these children are at risk of also developing reading problems. If Bishop's hypothesis turns out to be correct, future research will need to develop methods for helping children with SLI go beyond syllabic processing.

Another prominent theory in the literature on SLI concerns children's early capacity to process rapid transitions between sounds. As we saw in Chapter 3, only weeks after birth infants are already able to distinguish minute changes in linguistic stimuli embedded within long and complex syllabic strings. The acoustic transformation that produces meaningless strings of sounds like "bitamoti" and "bitomati" takes place over a fraction of a second, and yet the very young brain has no difficulty in detecting such a distinction. This ability is vital to subsequent language acquisition because it allows the individual to hear very subtle variations in sound combinations that produce different meanings.

Paula Tallal and her collaborators have suggested that if an infant has problems with rapid auditory processing in general, then this is likely to have a more serious effect on his representations of linguistic input than on other aspects of cognitive development. This would explain why the child's impairment would manifest itself as seemingly language specific. Tallal's team has developed a computerized program of games that produce lengthened versions of the normal sound transitions that occur in speech. These expanded versions sound less like speech per se, but during trials they are gradually shortened to eventually mirror those found in normal output. These programs are used to test and train children with SLI. It is claimed that such training helps these children not only detect and better process linguistic sound transitions but also, as a result, enables them to process morphological markers without having to be trained specifically on such forms.

We are still some way from discovering the precise causes of SLI. Most researchers, however, accept that SLI has a genetic basis and runs in families. Identical (monozygotic) twins are therefore more likely to share the impairment than are nonidentical (dizygotic) twins. SLI is also three times more likely to occur in males than in females. As a result of such data, a number of psycholinguists have argued that this demonstrates the existence of a genetic underpinning for grammar. Grammar acquisition, they claim, can be independently impaired while leaving the rest of development intact. Indeed, it could be that one day a single gene mutation will be discovered as the cause of the hereditary occurrence of SLI. But it would be incorrect to infer from such findings that the gene involved is the "grammar gene." As we have stressed throughout the book, a huge number of interacting genes (involved in numerous different functions) are likely to play a role in the normal acquisition of language. It might well turn out that a tiny impairment at the level of a single gene can have a huge effect on the expression of a large number of other genes whose protein products ultimately contribute to language acquisition. But it is very unlikely that there are genes that code directly for language in the cortex. This is simply not how genes work, which is why we reiterate the need for caution when implying that the path of normal acquisition can be directly inferred from the atypical case.

We do not challenge the fact that disorders like SLI have a genetic origin, nor that evolution has contributed to creating certain innately specified processing mechanisms in our brains. The question is whether SLI, as a disorder seeming to affect language only, can be used as evidence for an innate processing mechanism dedicated *ex-*

*clusively* to grammar. Must a language-specific impairment neces-sarily result from the malfunctioning of a specific processor devoted only to language? Is it not possible, instead, that evolution has pro-vided us with different types of learning mechanisms that can be used for many aspects of higher-level cognition (including human language), and that there is a much more indirect way for genetic defects to result in a domain-specific outcome like SLI? In other words, could SLI not result indirectly from a malfunction of some aspect of the general developmental process itself? The very case of SLI could in fact be used to support the latter position. If early on the infant's general processing of fast sound transitions were to be even slightly delayed, then certain crucial aspects of morpho-syntactic development might not be acquired at the right time and might subsequently become more impaired than others. This would then initiate a cascade of delays for further language learning. For instance, not being able to notice the sounds on the ends of words may mean that pluralization and tense are not acquired. Grammati-cal dysfunction in this case, then, would actually be the indirect, de-velopmental outcome of a subtle and initially purely acoustic deficit.

The fact that training SLI children solely at the acoustic level can have positive repercussions at the grammatical level lends some sup-port to the idea of a low-level general impairment causing the prob-lem. Data also show, however, that a significant proportion of ado-lescents and adults with SLI do not display any acoustic processing deficits. Nativists have used this finding to rule out acoustic deficits as a possible basis for G-SLI. But this is not necessarily the case. It is feasible that by late childhood or adulthood the acoustic processing defect that caused SLI in the first place is no longer perceptible in standard tests. Children with SLI, of otherwise normal intelligence, might increasingly compensate for the initial acoustic deficit. But this does not necessarily mean that the deficit has disappeared. More sensitive tests than those presently available may reveal that even a very mild form of this acoustic impairment continues to operate in more subtle aspects of language processing during adulthood.

Atypical processing of fast auditory transitions may or may not turn out to be the actual cause of SLI. But such a hypothesis pinpoints the importance of taking a truly developmental approach when explaining seemingly domain-specific disorders. It encourages researchers to consider the interaction between a whole range of cognitive processes, rather than concentrate on purely grammatical functions. Studies should henceforth focus more on early infancy, studying "at risk" populations before the onset of language production and thus before SLI actually manifests itself. In this way, it should be possible to ascertain whether the timing of subtle developmental processes is out of synchrony, and to look at how this increasingly affects the child's processing of complex linguistic input. Due to the way genes interact with each other, we should also seek co-occurring, subtle impairments in behavior that may have nothing to do with language. Indeed, it has been shown that people with language deficits such as SLI or dyslexia (a reading impairment that occurs in normally intelligent individuals) often do display other problems with, say, motor control (for example, they may have minor difficulties with balance while walking). So any genetic defects linked to SLI may not necessarily be exclusively language-specific. They may start out as more general defects that go on to have a stronger effect on language outcome as a consequence of development. To reiterate, it looks unlikely that there are such things as impaired "language genes." Rather, genetic impairments are more likely to act by disrupting the general trajectory of development and, as a result of the interaction between the genes involved, this disruption may in the long run affect some domains much more than others.

The errors and difficulties with grammar experienced by children with SLI are often argued to provide evidence that the computational mechanisms that allow for normal grammatical development are specifically impaired. These mechanisms are considered to be quite distinct from the associative mechanisms that enable us to learn individual words or ready-made phrases (for the distinction between computational mechanisms and associative memory retrieval, see Pinker's theory, Chapter 5). Children with SLI are considered to have an intact associative memory but impaired computational mechanisms. Some researchers have made the opposite claim with respect to Williams syndrome. In the case of this genetic disorder, computational mechanisms are argued to be intact, and it is associative memory that is seen to be impaired.

## Williams Syndrome

Williams syndrome (WS) is a rare disorder with a known genetic cause. It results from a microdeletion of several genes on chromosome 7 and occurs in roughly one in 20,000 live births. The syndrome is of particular interest to students of language acquisition because of the uneven pattern of abilities and impairments associated with it. Although infants and young children with WS are seriously delayed in their language development, adolescents and adults with the syndrome show surprising proficiencies in the linguistic domain, despite having nonverbal IQs in the 40s-70s range. These individuals also display notable impairments with number tasks, spatial tasks such as doing puzzles, planning, and simple problem solving.

Compared with other learning-impaired clinical groups, individuals with WS possess very impressive language skills. They especially enjoy talking, and use long, erudite-sounding words in relatively complex sentences. The following example illustrates WS language from a particularly verbal adolescent. The language stands in stark contrast to the earlier excerpt from the fourteen-year-old with SLI whose Performance IQ was 118. As in the SLI example, the speaker with WS is also fourteen years old, but in this case he has a Performance IQ of only 59. He has been asked to retell the very same story about the researcher's brother:

> Yesterday your naughty brother jumped into a river. It was shallow. He did it on purpose. Now that's a stupid thing to do, isn't it! He got his new shoes all wet and slimy. This made his mum exasperated. He knew he was in trouble, so he hid behind a tree so she wouldn't find him. Oh boy, he'll probably get a whale of a telling off. My mother gets furious if I dare go against her wishes. Was he grounded?

Note how much more complex and grammatically correct this WS story is compared to the SLI one cited earlier. What is also interesting is that the adolescent with WS replaced certain terms used by the researcher (such as "angry," referring to the mother) with more eloquent words ("exasperated"). His tale was also embellished by personal comments on the events and characters that were not part of the original story. In fact, the child with WS sounds rather pedantic for a fourteen-year-old, which is typical of these verbally able adolescents.

Not all children with WS are as fluent or eloquent as this. But researchers encountering for the first time an adolescent or adult with this syndrome are almost always very impressed by the fluency of their language. When one recalls that these same individuals are unable to tie their shoelaces, draw simple shapes, or solve rudimentary arithmetic problems, their language skills are even more surprising. Furthermore, although their speech is excellent, they tend to have difficulty with reading and writing.

Despite the impressive end-state language of individuals with Williams syndrome, for the majority of them the onset of both lexical and morphosyntactic development is delayed. There is, as a result, wide variability in the timing of their language acquisition milestones. In some children with WS, the delay is relatively insignificant. But in many it is substantial, with some three- and four-year-olds having at most a twenty-word vocabulary and no productive grammar, and some five- and six-year-olds barely using two-word combinations. Furthermore, if one examines the profile of early abilities and impairments in infants with WS, the delays that they experience with respect to language turn out to be comparable to those that affect their visuospatial development. It is only with development that language surpasses their spatial cognition.

Some studies have reported that in the early stages of language acquisition, children with WS tend to have substantially larger productive vocabularies than receptive vocabularies, whereas other studies reveal equal levels in production and comprehension. Such a pattern is never found in the normal case nor for most other developmental disorders, where comprehension is always in advance of production. This suggests that children with WS are likely to produce words without fully understanding them and that a characteristic of Williams syndrome is shallow semantic representations. A study by Sarah Paterson looked at 24–36-month-old toddlers with WS, and compared them to toddlers with Down syndrome. Surprisingly, she found that the toddlers with WS were as delayed in language development as those with DS. But whereas the toddlers with WS had equal levels of production and comprehension, those with DS looked more like younger normal controls (matched for mental age) in whom a clear advantage of comprehension over production was found. Thus, toddlers with WS seem to follow a different developmental trajectory than both normal children and those with Down syndrome.

In adolescence and adulthood, the language abilities of those with WS outstrip their levels of intelligence. This stands in sharp contrast to the situation for children with SLI, whose relatively normal intelligence coexists with very poor language proficiency. Can we therefore take the existence of such opposing extremes, or so-called double dissociations, as proof that general intelligence and the acquisition of grammar develop independently of one another? Williams syndrome is indeed frequently cited in support of the claim that there exists in the brain an innately specified module for computing grammar. It is argued that WS is an example of a genetic disorder in which this particular module is left intact, while G-SLI is a disorder in which only this module is affected. In other words, the existence of these two syndromes is seen by some as offering evidence of the Chomskyan argument for an innate computational module for grammar.

There are, however, some serious flaws to this argument. First, it implies that the atypical brain is basically a normal brain with parts intact and parts impaired. This is far from the case. From the moment of conception and throughout embryogenesis and postnatal brain development, the brains of infants with WS develop differently from those of other individuals. The deletions on chromosome 7 are missing from every cell of the developing WS embryo. So right from the outset, the WS brain is growing atypically. Because the human brain develops as a whole organ, it is likely that these genetic deletions will result in overall qualitative differences between the brains of WS individuals and those of normally developing children.

Thus, even though WS morphosyntax may reach seemingly normal levels, there is a real possibility that the processes underlying the acquisition of grammar in WS differ from the normal case. This holds for any syndrome displaying so-called normal behaviors.

If we accept that the brains of children with Williams syndrome follow a different developmental trajectory from the start, then it is hard to see how one region of the neocortex (the part of the brain where higher cognitive functions are processed) could develop on a separate, normal trajectory, leaving the rest of the neocortex impaired. Helen Neville, Deborah Mills, and their collaborators have used Event Related Potentials to measure electrical activity in the brains of people with WS. It turns out that they show particular patterns of electrical brain activity not found at any age in the course of normal childhood development or adulthood. When we look at the real-time processing of language by people with WS, their brains display peaks of activity at different moments and in different locations compared to normal controls. So the pathways in the WS brain have become differently specialized. This once again suggests that individuals with WS have followed an atypical developmental trajectory throughout.

Several of the early studies of WS language have involved only tiny samples of adults that may be unrepresentative of the clinical group as a whole. This can present a problem when there is such wide individual variation. The pioneering work of Ursula Bellugi and her collaborators on initially rather small populations led others to make overly broad theoretical claims and generalizations about the syndrome as a whole. More recently, much larger groups of WS individuals across a wide age range (from nine months to fifty-three years) have been studied. Analyses of the new data have shown that examples of individuals with intact morphosyntax are exceedingly rare. In fact, individuals with WS from a whole range of linguistic backgrounds, such as Italian, English, Spanish, or Hebrew, all display impairments in certain complex structures like grammatical gender agreement across sentence elements and embedded relative clauses. It has become increasingly clear, therefore, that the superficially impressive language skills of individuals with WS may be due to good auditory memory rather than an intact grammar module.

The specific grammatical difficulties experienced by individuals with WS were identified in two sets of studies using different experimental techniques. In one case, a standardized task was used to measure individuals' understanding of grammatical structures. In these tests, participants were required to select from four pictures (by pointing) the one that matched the experimenter's sentence. Even the most able, fluent participants made errors in this task when the experimenter's sentences involved relative clauses. This implies that the processing of some aspects of complex grammar are actually beyond the competence of the individual with WS—a finding that is not always evident in their spontaneous speech.

The other set of studies involved simple imitation tasks and used the same grammatical structures as those causing difficulty in the standardized picture-pointing task. Participants were required to simply repeat a sentence produced by the experimenter. Memory for sentence length was carefully controlled for. In this case, the results showed that most participants with WS were able to correctly repeat quite lengthy sentences of simple structure ("Yesterday I found a red flower growing at the end of my auntie's garden"). These adolescents and adults with WS, however, found short sentences with complex structures more difficult to reproduce ("The boy the girl hit kicked the dog"). When a similar task was performed by normal controls, children as young as six performed well when repeating such embedded sentences. So we see that even in a relatively simple imitation task, people with WS who seem to have normal levels of everyday language nevertheless show real difficulties with complex morphosyntax.

In Chapter 4 we discussed research that examined how typically developing children learn new words. We saw that they abide by four lexical constraints. Similar studies of a group of WS children and adults showed that while they perform fast mapping and abide by the mutual exclusivity constraint, they do not comply with whole object or taxonomic constraints. Unlike normal children, they are as likely to interpret new words as referring to parts of objects as to whole objects. Similarly, they are just as prone to assign the meaning of a new word to the shape or color of an object than to the category to which it belongs. So while they display some of the normal processing constraints, individuals with WS acquire language in a way somewhat different to that used by typically developing children, even in the basic task of learning new words.

A great deal of attention has been focused on Williams syndrome in adolescence and adulthood, when language is particularly fluent. As mentioned earlier, however, studies of infants with WS reveal serious delays in language tasks, comparable to the delays shown by infants with Down syndrome. This is an interesting finding, because the end-state language in adults with WS is a relative strength, whereas language in DS adults is particularly poor. The similarity of impairment in infancy is therefore not mirrored in later life, which suggests that language acquisition in these two disorders does not follow the same developmental trajectory. So in trying to discover how language develops in atypical children, it is important to explore the entire acquisition process, from the infant starting state to end-state adult language. In doing so, we should aim to discover the specific difficulties these children face at the different stages of development. Despite our first impressions of intact and impressive language in Williams syndrome, extensive research now suggests that the fluent everyday language of adolescents and adults camouflages a number of underlying lexical and grammatical problems experienced during the acquisition process. In our view, there is nothing surprising about the fact that WS language is not after all "intact." People with WS follow a different developmental pathway because WS causes a qualitatively different form of brain organization from the start, unlike anything seen in other populations including Down syndrome.

## Down Syndrome

Down syndrome (DS) is a neurodevelopmental disorder caused by the presence of an extra chromosome 21. It is also referred to as trisomy 21. Approximately one baby in every 600–700 births is born with Down syndrome, and about 95 percent of DS children have the extra chromosome in every cell. A small number of cases display what is called a "mosaic" pattern of abnormality with only some cells carrying the third copy of chromosome 21, and this sometimes coincides with a lesser degree of impairment. Unlike WS, there is no missing genetic material in DS, but the extra chromosome causes a serious imbalance in gene expression leading to a highly complex set of physical and intellectual impairments.

Like children with Williams syndrome, those with Down syndrome show noticeable delays in all cognitive functions, but those with DS are better at spatial tasks than at language tasks and the converse holds for those with WS. Down syndrome is associated with severe difficulties with grammar as well as poor articulation. There are one or two rare cases reported in the literature in which DS adult language seems normal, but in general the vocabulary and grammatical development of these children remains at a level of about half their chronological age and then plateaus around puberty, failing to progress any further. Linguistic problems include serious difficulties with various aspects of syntax, phonology, semantics, and pragmatics. For instance, children with DS find consonant clusters particularly difficult to produce, and the pace of their language output is generally rather slow. When DS output is compared with the language produced by normal, younger controls matched on vocabulary levels, the individuals with DS produce fewer morphological markers and fewer references to absent objects or past experiences. In fact, a characteristic of DS language production is its predominant focus on the here and now. Overall, both the content and the structure of DS language differ significantly from the output of typically developing children.

It is tempting when trying to account for language impairment to concentrate exclusively on the atypical child's own speech rather than to look at the wider picture. Yet studies have shown that it is always important also to examine the parental input that the child receives in everyday life. It has been found that, like most parents of atypical language learners, mothers of children with DS tend to use more directives when addressing their children. That is to say, when children generally do not respond in the expected way to the language they hear, adults tend to use language aimed at directing or instructing. Questions and comments are far less frequent in the input that the atypical child hears. In the case of DS, mothers specifically tend to discourage the child from making even temporary overgeneralizations (such as using the word "cat" to refer to cats, dogs, tigers, and horses). Mothers of typically developing children generally accept misnaming as a harmless, temporary stage in the acquisition of a new word, one that the child will outgrow as his vocabulary increases. But parents of DS children tend to interpret such misnamings as potentially permanent lexical errors caused by the child's mental retardation. Consequently, they will interrupt the child's speech every time an overgeneralization is made, and thereby may inadvertently hamper the natural process of language development.

The language of individuals with DS is initially rather similar to the language of young children with WS, in that both are delayed. As soon as language production gets well under way, however, the two syndromes begin to manifest themselves in very different ways. The rate of language acquisition of individuals with WS shows notable improvement with development, whereas language development in DS continues to remain well below expected mental age levels. This remains true for virtually every developmental stage, including adulthood, and applies to the development of phonology, vocabulary, grammar, and pragmatics. In their speech, children with DS tend to omit both bound and unbound morphemes, use only very simple grammatical structures, and display a limited vocabulary. Their narratives are extremely primitive, and they show no sign of metalinguistic awareness.

Nonetheless, one of the reasons why Down syndrome is such an interesting case is that, unlike both normal and other forms of atypical development, a significant dissociation exists between vocabulary and grammar in DS. It is common for children with DS to use as many as 400–600 single words before they begin producing the two-word combinations that herald the beginnings of grammar, whereas a normal child does so at around 150 words. In DS, then, grammatical development falls considerably behind vocabulary growth. This is possibly because grammatical markers have little phonological salience and stress, and children with DS are known to suffer from impaired auditory processing. Although auditory short-term memory and visual short-term memory are both impaired in DS, the former is affected more severely. The opposite holds for WS, where auditory short-term memory is a relative strength. DS children seem to be the only clinical group for which there is a clear dissociation between grammar and vocabulary size during acquisition. This may be one of the hallmarks of Down syndrome language.

## Focal Brain Injury

One clinical group particularly at risk of atypical language development is infants and children with focal brain injury, a trauma to one side of the brain. The long-lasting effects of such hemispheric lesions depend to a great extent on the stage of development at which they occur. Lesions to an adult's left hemisphere can have disastrous effects on his already established, fluent language. In contrast, a left hemispheric lesion in a young child (or even a left hemispherectomy, the total removal of one half of the brain) gives rise to reorganization of language functions to the right hemisphere. The language recovery of such children completely outstrips the recovery of adults. This is because, by adulthood, the structuring of the human brain has become both specialized and localized and thus cannot easily accommodate a reorganization of the brain areas that processed language.

The plasticity of young children's brains means that the right hemisphere can provide an alternative neural substrate for language development if the relevant left hemispheric areas are damaged. In normal right-handed adults, morphosyntax and production of words are predominantly processed by the left hemisphere, while comprehension of words, intonation, and pragmatics are processed predominantly by the right hemisphere. Event Related Potentials (ERP) brain imaging studies have shown that in early childhood there is far more bilateral processing (in other words, both hemispheres are involved in processing words and grammar). It is only with development that specialization and localization of function progressively begin to resemble those of the adult brain.

In the case of children with focal brain injury, damage to one hemisphere results in language processing being taken over and accommodated within the remaining intact hemisphere. Although in these circumstances language acquisition is usually able to progress satisfactorily, there nevertheless remain some very subtle deficits resulting from such atypical distribution of language processing. If a hemispherectomy occurs early enough in development, however, then the differences in language between the atypical case and the normal case are minimal. So under the right circumstances, the right hemisphere alone can sustain the language acquisition process satisfactorily, leading to normal end-state levels.

Research on focal brain-damaged children shows that it is not only timing but also the region where the damage occurs that determine long-term effects on language. When the frontal cortex of either the right or the left hemispheres is lesioned, the child suffers greater delays in language learning than when other areas are damaged. As Elizabeth Bates and her collaborators have shown, however, this is true for only a restricted window of time. Lesions of the frontal cortex affect language more severely if they occur between the ages of nineteen and thirty-one months. As we showed in Chapter 4, this is precisely when most normal children display the vocabulary spurt that coincides with the onset of grammar. Damage to the frontal cortex during this time period can hinder the onset of the spurt and thus be far more detrimental to the progress of grammar than injury at any other period of development.

The long-term effects of damage to the left temporal region of the brain are also time dependent. Between the ages of one and seven years, lesions to this left region have far greater repercussions on language than does damage to right temporal areas during the same developmental period. But left temporal lesions occurring within this period are also detrimental to visual processing, suggesting that the effect on language is indirect and that, in this case, the damage may have more domain-general effects.

The case of focal brain injury provides a nice illustration of how resilient language development can be. The human brain turns out to be able to accommodate important functions in different areas when forced to do so. Where processing tasks occur in the brain is neither totally predetermined nor rigidly fixed. But the brain is not totally plastic. Rather, the neocortex—the part of the brain dedicated to higher cognitive functions including language processing—structures itself during development in accordance with its intrinsic constraints and the child's developmental history.

## Conclusion

By providing a valuable contrast to the norm, the different cases of atypical language learning offer insights into questions related to language innateness and specificity. But caution is always required when generalizing from atypical brains to the normal case. The new brain imaging techniques have shown that language processing can be very different in atypical brains. What the atypical data do demonstrate is that there are numerous alternative pathways to the ultimate goal of achieving adult-like language.

Differences in the input to atypical language learners might also turn out to be important. Research has demonstrated that in general, atypical children are more passive in conversational interaction than normal children, and that adults are less likely to interact with passive children than with active ones. Furthermore, while motherese is indeed often used for atypical language learners as with normal children, it is often an impoverished form of child-directed speech. One common finding is that in atypical cases caregivers respond far less to the actual semantic content of the child's utterances and provide fewer recasts. They also use shorter and less varied utterances and if they ask questions, the questions usually only require a yes / no response. The differences frequently co-occur with language delay. It remains to be seen whether there is a causal link between language impairment and atypical parental input.

Differences between normal and atypical input are in no way surprising, since child-directed speech is predominantly tuned to the child's level of receptive language. Because this level tends to be low (in terms of chronological age) for atypical language learners, it follows that adults will tailor their speech accordingly. The child's inability to respond adequately to whatever linguistic input he does receive may also lead to a partial breakdown in dialogic exchanges. It follows, then, that in some cases the reciprocal interaction between parent and child might fail to adequately support the language acquisition process by remaining at a rather restricted level.

While the theoretical issues raised by atypical development are fascinating, intervention also remains a primary drive behind reaching a better understanding of language disorders. The more we know about typical and atypical language acquisition, the more we will be able to design intervention programs tailored to the specific impairments of each syndrome. This would make it possible for every child at risk to be given a supportive linguistic environment as early as possible in infancy, thus enabling them to reach their full linguistic potential.

# 8

# RETHINKING THE
# NATURE-NURTURE DEBATE

We have reached the end of our journey. It is now time to look back at some of the important issues that were raised as we progressed from the fetus's quickening heartbeat upon hearing its mother's voice to the creative language of the adolescent. If we consider all that is involved in becoming a proficient conversationalist, we can but marvel at the extraordinary feat of language acquisition. Perhaps most surprising of all is the natural ease with which the young child learns to speak grammatically, making use of complex structures early on and achieving relative fluency by the tender age of four. This natural, seamless process is what has inspired so many writers to argue that we must be born with knowledge of language, and that it is this innate capacity that sets us apart from all other species. For many, then, language is what makes us quintessentially human.

In this concluding chapter, we examine this premise from a number of different angles, because it raises important questions concerning the nature of human language and what it means to have language. First, is human language qualitatively different from the communicative systems of other species? If so, how? Alternatively, do the communication systems of different species, be they animal or human, all lie on a continuum? Answers to such questions have important implications for the nature-nurture debate. For instance, if human language is indeed fundamentally special, then how has evolution prespecified language in the neonate brain? Or if human language is a very sophisticated version of a more general animal capacity for communication, then can we conclude that the infant acquires language through experience? If we challenge the existence of a built-in universal grammar, is there still an argument for innate, language-relevant predispositions that make language learning particularly easy? Also, are the mechanisms used in linguistic processing exclusive to language, or do they involve other, more general capacities? Finally, is language necessarily a more complex achievement than everything else that infants accomplish in their cognitive, visual, and motor development?

## Language and the Species Specificity Argument

Human speech is constructed from combinations of sounds that vary subtly in duration, interval, order, stress, and pitch. Human speech perception is based on the rapid processing of this temporal information. It is the special acoustic features of the input that allow the brain to distinguish speech sounds. But is such categorical processing of vocalizations exclusive to humans? Research shows that nonhuman primates also make and perceive such distinctions in their communicative calls. Japanese macaques, for instance, have been shown to use temporal cues to distinguish various types of calls. Specifically, they have been tested for their sensitivity to subtle differences in the acoustic structure of different calls that are produced under different circumstances and covary within changing contexts. So the calls produced to indicate domination across members of a group differ from those of an isolated macaque that has lost its mother. Detailed analyses of the acoustics of macaque calls show that this species, like humans, has a specialized mechanism that categorizes communicative vocalizations on the basis of the timing characteristics of each call. Similar capacities are likely to exist in other primate species.

The resemblance to human language at this very basic level of auditory processing may not be very convincing. But human words and primate calls share other important features that lend further support to the notion of a communicative continuum. Many primate vocalizations have been shown to be referential. So the calls produced to signify dominance in a group or to mark territory are qualitatively different from those warning of the presence of a pred-ator. But the distinctions go even further. Pitch and duration of calls also mark such things as type, location, and quantity of food; iden-tity of predators; and complex hierarchies of social relationships. The calls of vervet monkeys, for instance, have been shown to differ acoustically depending on whether the predator is a snake, leopard, eagle, baboon, human, and so on. And in response to these calls from a conspecific (a member of their own species), the other vervet monkeys display behavioral reactions that are specific to the partic-ular danger present. For example, if one vervet emits a "snake call," others nearby will immediately look down to the ground. In con-trast, if an "eagle call" is emitted, the vervets will look up at the sky. Research has also demonstrated that these pairings of calls and be-haviors are produced even when vervet calls are played through a tape recorder. This precludes the possibility that the monkeys simply copy the appropriate behavior from the caller.

The communication system of rhesus monkeys may turn out to be even more complex. Subtle differences have been found among calls relating to different types of food. When a rhesus monkey finds a high-quality and highly valued (rare) food, it produces a specific call that is different from the one emitted when a more common food source is found. Rhesus monkeys nearby respond differentially to such calls. One might argue that these different calls are reflex re-sponses to the food itself. But again, research using tape recordings of rhesus monkey calls has demonstrated that different food calls produce different behavioral responses even in the absence of actual food. This suggests that these monkeys have developed internal rep-resentations of the different types of food and have categorized these according to acoustic differences in the associated calls. The behav-ioral responses to food calls also differ as a function of the status of the caller. Rhesus monkeys are able to extract very subtle acoustic distinctions upon hearing a call and form multiple representations of the input, simultaneously storing information about the features of the acoustic signal, the food type, the current context, as well as the caller's identity and emotional state.

The fact that primate calls are both referential and representational points to substantial similarities between the functions of some aspects of human and nonhuman communicative systems. But the continuum between humans and primates extends beyond the systems themselves, to the way the brain processes this type of auditory information. The brains of adult rhesus monkeys show left hemispheric specialization for the processing of conspecific calls, in much the same way that human brains display lateralization by the location of speech processing in the left temporal lobe for right-handed adults. This hemispheric lateralization is not found in infant monkeys, however. So in both the rhesus infant and the human infant, specialization for the processing of communicative vocalizations becomes progressively localized in the left hemisphere of the brain as the infant develops. This suggests at least some evolutionary continuity across certain language-related capacities of humans and nonhuman primates.

Despite the similarities between primate and human systems of communication, there are clearly some fundamental differences. Other species do not make vocalizations for purely interactive ends. Calls are mainly used to bring about a desired behavior or outcome. They are instrumental, but not declarative. A primate, for instance, will not call to signal that the predator has gone, nor on other occasions vocalize about the absence that day of any predators. In contrast, even young toddlers use speech to share information for purely conversational purposes, indicating such things as absence via declarative statements like "allgone Daddy" or "bye-bye car." Other species never seem to refer to the past, the future, or the hypothetical. Their vocalizations are grounded in the context in which they appear. They might produce a call referring to a change in hierarchy brought about by a fight that has just taken place, but the reason for the call itself will be found in the immediate context.

Beyond the referential limitations of nonhuman primate systems, human language stands alone in its complex grammatical structure. No other species strings vocalizations together in ways specifically designed to vary meaning. Monkeys may produce several calls one after another, but there is no internal structure that ties the individual calls together in the same way as words are put together to form phrases, sentences, and narratives. The human child's drive to use language in a structured, grammatical way is unique, as is her capacity to create endless new meanings through a rich vocabulary and the use of morphosyntax.

Primate species in the wild have been found to have a relatively wide "vocabulary" of communicative calls. Chimpanzees, our closest relatives, are reported to produce some thirty-six different calls to signify various meanings. Nonetheless, it is difficult to compare the actual functions of these "vocabularies" with the words of human language. So a different approach to establishing the true extent of similarities between the language capacities of nonhuman primates and humans has been to examine the abilities of captive primates with respect to aspects of human language. This research has made the headlines in recent years, with certain chimpanzees reaching relative stardom and being credited with the ability to "talk" through manual signs or computer keyboards. But as we shall see, these results should be approached with caution.

One of the most well-known studies is the "Nim Chimsky" project (named after the famous Noam Chomsky). Nim, who died recently, was an intelligent chimpanzee brought up like a child in a loving human environment. His caregivers endeavored to teach him American Sign Language. They were specifically interested to see whether Nim could learn a wider vocabulary of signs than calls in the wild, and whether, in this nurturing linguistic environment, he would come to display some basic use of syntax.

After a very lengthy training period, Nim had produced 20,000 utterances. He even seemed to produce a number of multisign combinations. But these results are not as impressive as they might at first appear. Closer analysis of the chimpanzee's productions demonstrated that his vast communicative output was in fact mainly composed of the repetition of ten or so common signs. This limited repertoire was also primarily made up of food-related terms. When signs were strung together, they were simply juxtaposed and not organized in a structured way to form specific variations in meaning. Two-sign utterances might include, for instance, "banana eat" or "eat eat." Longer utterances were simply formed by repeating or adding the most common signs onto the end of a previous utterance. Nim might thus produce a three-sign utterance like "banana banana eat," or a five-sign string like, "banana eat eat Nim banana." Such utterances do not reveal any use of syntax, nor do they demonstrate that the chimpanzee ever really progressed beyond the single-sign stage. These findings held for the entire developmental period, and the adult Nim displayed no further linguistic progress.

The research on Kanzi, a bonobo (pygmy chimpanzee) raised in captivity, provides further insights into the potential language capacities of nonhuman primates. Kanzi is a particularly intelligent chimpanzee trained to use lexigrams (symbols representing words) on a computer keyboard to communicate with his trainers, and also incidentally has come to comprehend the trainer's oral instructions. This approach was designed as an alternative to teaching sign, in order to overcome the possible confounding effect of producing difficult manual signs. Kanzi quickly learned to associate the lexigrams with pictures of objects, with real objects, and with spoken words. He has achieved a considerable "vocabulary" with which he has been able to communicate simple requests to his trainers. Such achievements have been held up as evidence that, for Kanzi, the lexigrams have functioned like arbitrary symbols. It is argued that his lexigrams have entailed complex conceptual representations and have been used as "words" (referring symbolically to categories of objects).

Claims about the symbolic nature of lexigrams need to be treated with some caution. Indeed, reports of chimpanzee language research tend to use terms like "word," "symbol," "language," and "communication" rather loosely and interchangeably. But such terms are not equivalent, nor can they be transparently generalized from human to chimpanzee behavior. No one denies that many nonhuman species have evolved complex systems of communication. But there is still a lack of conclusive evidence that any other species possesses the capacity to acquire a system equivalent to human language. In fact, close reexamination of Kanzi's output reveals that, like Nim, a very high proportion of the lexigrams he uses are food related and are employed predominantly to request some desired object or action.

Unlike the words of human language, Kanzi's "words" do not appear to relate to specific concepts. For example, the lexigram for "strawberry" is used to encompass a variety of situations, objects and events. He might therefore produce this lexigram both when he wants to eat a strawberry and when he wishes to go out to the garden where fruits are grown.

One might be tempted to compare this multiple use of lexigrams to overgeneralizations in children. But there is a crucial difference between these two cases. Unlike the language-learning child who narrows the referential scope of individual words as his vocabulary grows, Kanzi's lexigrams seem to remain very broad in their usage throughout his development. He does not show any spontaneous drive to learn new lexigrams in order to further his communicative abilities.

There are, then, certain vital differences between the ways that trained chimpanzees and young human learners approach language. Nim seemed to use his signs to refer to general themes rather than precise taxonomic categories. It is possible that Kanzi's lexigrams will turn out to be partially taxonomic in nature, but this remains to be shown conclusively. In both cases, the chimpanzees' output has tended to be instrumental, produced to obtain food or praise from the trainer or to instigate a favorite activity like tickling. This implies that the chimpanzees associate their productions mainly with expected outcomes, learning the signs or lexigrams in terms of their pragmatic functions. There is no evidence that they realize that everything has a name and can be referred to with "words."

This limited use of signs or lexigrams stands in stark contrast to the human child's language production, where early words are used as a springboard for increasingly complex uses of language. For the young child, words may initially be used too generally but, unlike the chimpanzee, the referential scope soon narrows. Furthermore, while early on words may be used to fulfill a limited function like requesting, they very quickly become multifunctional for the child and are used declaratively.

So although the achievements of captive-raised chimpanzees are impressive, the "linguistic" abilities of these trained primates are dramatically different from those of young children. For instance, the functions of utterances differ substantially in both cases. Toddlers' uses of language seem to have the principal aim of establishing and maintaining social interaction. Nim's signed utterances, by contrast, generally overlapped with his trainer's signing, in anticipation of food reinforcements. His communicative endeavors completely lacked the turn-taking qualities of human linguistic interaction. Unlike children who show a natural curiosity about language, neither Nim nor Kanzi asked for something new to be named. Nim, for instance, required constant reinforcement so as not to forget newly acquired signs. In both cases, there seemed to be little spontaneous drive to increase vocabulary or to manipulate meaning through the use of increasingly structured strings, as is the case for the human child.

Another area of contention in chimpanzee research is the primate's ability to use syntax. At the earliest stages of human language production, the toddler already displays a great deal of syntactic awareness. Early word combinations are rarely composed of simple word repetitions or the mere juxtaposition of words. Within months of uttering their first words, toddlers begin experimenting with language by combining certain words in specific orders. In contrast to the trained chimpanzee, children enter this stage naturally and, once word combination is under way, they avoid producing strings that noticeably violate the grammar of their language. Cases like those of Nim and Kanzi present a very different picture. While some have argued that the strings produced by nonhuman subjects are clear evidence of a drive toward syntax, closer examination of the data fails to support such a claim. Many of the chimpanzee's strings turn out to be nonsensical, to display no grammatical constraints whatsoever, and to be difficult to interpret beyond the single-sign level. It is tempting to assign intentional complex meaning to a string like "banana eat banana you Nim." But any interpretations we might make of such sign strings remain speculative; they cannot be directly projected onto the nonhuman primate. In other words, just because we are able to find ways of translating such lengthy strings into meaningful utterances does not mean that they reveal a capacity for syntax in the chimpanzee.

Nonhuman primate studies remain a fascinating area of research that will no doubt continue to bring us closer to understanding the evolutionary roots of human language. Kanzi is still developing and may turn out to have more capacity than hitherto suspected. The data yielded so far, however, remain promising but inconclusive. For some of the ways in which vocabulary functions, there does indeed seem to be a continuum across human and other animal "languages." On certain vital levels, however, human language remains unique. In particular, our capacity for grammar does not seem to be found in any other species. We seem to be alone in having developed the capacity for morphosyntax that gives our language its infinite potential.

### Is Human Language Innate?

If we acknowledge that there are commonalities across human and animal communication, but that human language is also unique, then language acquisition must, at some level, be innately guided. As we have seen, it is our use of grammar that sets human language apart from the communicative systems of all other species. But does this necessarily imply that we are born with a fully specified universal grammar? We argue that it is not grammar per se that is evolution's gift to the human species, but rather the capacity for learning grammar.

For those who adhere to nativist approaches, certain human adaptations not seen in other species provide evidence that humans represent a leap in evolution. Unique capacities such as grammar, along with certain fine motor and cognitive differences, are held up as indicating an evolutionary discontinuity between humans and other primate species. Almost all species are, at birth, immediately mobile, relatively independent, and already able to learn to produce their communicative repertoire. For the human neonate, the case is very different. The infant faces a lengthy period of maturation and experience outside of the womb before she is able to move around alone, keep warm, feed herself, control her vocalizations, and handle objects. The human baby remains completely dependent on other humans for her survival and for several months produces few language-related vocalizations.

One reason why humans take much longer than other species to produce their species-specific "calls" is that at birth the vocal tract of the human infant is disproportionately short compared to the rest of the articulatory system. The oral cavity is broader, the larynx is higher, and the tongue is more forward than later in development. This significantly limits the infant's ability to vocalize. It is only at around six months that the vocal tract will become more adult-like and allow the baby to begin babbling language-like sounds. So in humans, the *physical* capacity to produce language is not present at birth. Nonhuman infant primates take a shorter time to produce adult-like calls, but never progress beyond the use of a fairly limited vocabulary or surpass the single-call level. Human infants, in contrast, show sophisticated sensitivity to language structure prior to production and quickly surpass their primate cousins at every level once production begins.

For nativists, such differences indicate that the development of human language is, from the outset, fundamentally different from the communicative development of other species and displays innate qualities unique to man. They argue that the human child's natural and speedy ability to acquire morphosyntax supports the existence of an innate universal grammar. Grammar is considered to be a genetic gift resulting from an evolutionary accident. And the human brain is seen as having adapted differently from other primate brains. For such theorists, the brain is built with prespecified circuits devoted exclusively to the processing of grammar. From this viewpoint, human language cannot be fitted on a continuum with other animal communicative systems, because the animal systems fail to display any trace of grammar.

But there are other ways of approaching the evidence. Non-nativist theories argue that human language can actually be thought of as a new machine built out of old parts. From this point of view, it is claimed that human adaptations do not reflect an evolutionary dissociation between humans and their primate relatives. Compared to other species, all primates have a lengthy period of postnatal development before reaching maturity; the one for humans is just particularly long. A reexamination of certain human capacities previously heralded as unique to our species places doubt on claims about evolutionary discontinuity. New evidence implies that the lengthy postnatal period of learning may actually be adaptive and play a far greater role than hitherto imagined. For instance, the pincer grip—the use of the thumb and index finger to grasp small objects—was once believed to be particular to humans. Other primates were not accredited with having reached this level of manual dexterity. Recent experimental studies of chimpanzee behavior, however, have discovered that this species becomes capable after infancy of a similar sort of grip, using the thumb and middle finger to pick up tiny objects. This technique is learned through trial and error and experience, as in the human case. So, we can see that what was once used as evidence of an evolutionarily unique capacity in humans now supports the notion of an evolutionary continuum.

Human language has been similarly reexamined to determine whether it truly represents a sudden, novel evolutionary adaptation. Human language is "new" in evolutionary terms only in that it makes novel uses of old capacities. Such capacities are described as "old" because they are the result of gradual evolutionary adaptation and have their roots in our common ancestry with other primates. The specialized, localized circuits for language found in the adult human brain are therefore not seen as innate, but as emerging from the brain's interaction with the linguistic environment during development. From this stance, language does indeed *become* a specialized function of the human brain, but it does not start out that way.

Nowadays, even the notion of progressive brain localization for language is being challenged. As we saw in Chapter 7, when a young child undergoes a left hemispherectomy (the area that has been associated with grammar in adulthood), the right hemisphere takes over language acquisition and alone can support normal development. Interestingly, if the damage occurs to regions linked with spatial processing, recovery of function is far less successful. This suggests that there may be a more significant innate component to spatial processing than to language capacities. Close reexamination of brain activity in normal subjects is also casting doubt on the strict localization of language processing even in normal adults. Comparisons across adult brains suggest a great deal of individual variation in terms of where language functions are located. In fact, when neuroscientists produce maps of brain function, the areas they consider to be critical for language rarely overlap. Recent data suggest that linguistic knowledge is much more broadly represented across the human brain—that is, language-processing circuits are far more widely distributed than previously thought.

The new focus on real-time processing of stimuli has shown just how sensitive the human brain is to tiny variations in the timing of speech. We argue that it is precisely this rapid processing ability that is evolution's legacy to the development of human language. Our view is that the infant is not born with prespecified knowledge of grammar. What is innately required for language acquisition to take place are neurocomputational properties particularly well suited to the rapidly spoken or signed sequences that form human languages. Through continued exposure to the phonology, semantics, pragmatics, and morphosyntax of the native tongue, some brain circuits will indeed become specialized for language *over time*. But the adult end state cannot be used as evidence for innate speech or language modules in the infant.

## Language in the Context of General Development

Most people conceive of our species as being at the top of the evolutionary tree. In reality, we are not. The chimpanzee, the whale, and the spider are today just as evolved as we are. We did not descend from the chimpanzee or from any other existing species. The evolutionary lines of current species separated long ago, and we have all progressively found the optimum level of adaptation to our particular physical and social environments in today's world. It is thus impossible to rank human language as "more evolved" than, say, the spider's web or the whale's song.

Language is often thought of as the greatest achievement in a child's life. To many adult onlookers, its progress is more noticeable and seems more impressive than the perfection of capacities like manual dexterity or learning to walk. But there are many other areas of child development that also require lengthy periods of learning and are as complex and impressive as language. The fine-tuning and coordination of vision and motor control that occur during the first three years of life, for example, are often taken for granted. Nevertheless, they represent incredible feats of learning. Being able to use a spoon or chopsticks to feed oneself may seem unimpressive and is rarely marveled at. But it takes well over two years for this seemingly simple skill to be properly acquired. When you take a spoon, scoop food onto it, and bring it to your mouth, your brain has to make precise, rapid, and simultaneous calculations and coordinate a large number of different movements for the procedure to be successfully completed. Distance, size, texture, and consistency of the objects involved must be anticipated. The movements of fingers, hand, arm, mouth, and tongue all have to be controlled. Balance is also involved in keeping the food on the spoon during the journey to the mouth. And all this does not even take into account the chewing and swallowing that takes place once the food has made it into the mouth!

How does this ability gradually develop? Before the infant even begins the weaning process, she has already been practicing controlling her arm movements. From four weeks onward, the baby attempts to swipe at objects within her reach, but she is unable to make a single, calculated trajectory with her arm. Her swiping action is made up of many submovements that will only become progressively more direct, efficient, and coordinated with time and a great deal of practice. The same is true for her grasping abilities, which take a long time to fully develop. Even a child as old as three years finds holding and manipulating a pencil a challenge. Learning about the width and length of the pencil in order to hold the pencil steady, bring it carefully to the paper, and produce a drawing requires much experience. So even basic acts like reaching for a toy, feeding oneself, and holding a pencil all represent major developmental achievements. In the domain of motor control, evolution has not innately given the child predetermined abilities such as reaching or grasping, but instead has prespecified a long postnatal period during which such skills can be acquired. The same is true for the general ability to sit, walk, manipulate tools, run, jump, hum a tune, use numbers, or perform complex spatial tasks. In each case, evolution could have prespecified the components of these skills at birth. But it did not.

In fact, human beings as well as other primates are at birth relatively unspecialized. Infants possess very few ready-to-use intellectual or physical abilities. Other animals tend to need a vastly shorter postnatal period of development to reach maturity. They attain their complex adult state very quickly, but the cost of this is to render the organism relatively inflexible to changes in the environment. By contrast, in the primate case, and particularly in humans, it is the lengthy period of physical and cognitive immaturity that gradually gives rise through learning to the highly complex adult state. As a result, humans can readily adapt to challenging new environments.

We are left with an interesting paradox: for humans, evolutionary specialization manifests itself by a relative *lack* of specialization at birth. If this is the evolutionary solution for many human physical and cognitive skills, in our view it is also the most likely solution for language. We therefore propose approaching language as one of several human abilities requiring protracted experience over a long developmental period, rather than as an entirely special case. If we do so, having reconsidered all the issues discussed in this book, we will soon see that evolution's answer in the human case has *not* been to provide extensive prespecified linguistic knowledge. Rather, evolution has provided humans with a wide variety of learning mechanisms and a very long developmental period in which to learn and shape our brains. This is what makes us special, because it gives us a greater capacity for adapting to, learning from, and ultimately changing our environment.

## The Future

Approaching language from a truly developmental perspective has brought to the fore the need to better understand how the brain progressively structures itself. One area of developmental psycholinguistics that we predict will become increasingly prominent in the twenty-first century is precisely how brain processes change over the gradual course of language development. We know already that infant brains are "busier" than child or adult brains. The auditory cortex forms far more connections in response to sounds in infancy than in later life. In fact, between the ages of four months and one year, there are 150 percent more pathways in this part of the brain than are found in adult auditory cortex. It is only later, after the age of two years, that pruning of redundant connections and strengthening of appropriate pathways lead to adult-like levels of synaptic density. We still need to understand more fully how the brain specializes over time. Our prediction is that the use of longitudinal brain imaging studies will one day yield a detailed picture of what it really means to have language. By placing an ever-greater emphasis on seeing how brain pathways gradually change over time, rather than looking at the adult end state, we will finally be able to chart the full development of language acquisition from fetus to adolescent.

**ONE** WHAT IS LANGUAGE ACQUISITION?

Bruner, J. *Child's Talk: Learning to Use Language.* Norton, 1983.

Chomsky, N. "A review of B. F. Skinner's 'Verbal Behavior,'" in J. A. Fodor and J. J. Katz, eds., *The Structure of Language: Readings in the Philosophy of Language,* 547–578. Prentice Hall, 1964.

Elman, J. L., E. Bates, M. H. Johnson, A. Karmiloff-Smith, D. Parisi, and K. Plunkett. *Rethinking Innateness: A Connectionist Perspective on Development.* MIT Press, 1996.

Karmiloff-Smith, A. *Beyond Modularity: A Developmental Perspective on Cognitive Science.* MIT Press, 1992.

Piaget, J. *The Language and Thought of the Child.* Routledge & Kegan Paul, 1955.

Pinker, S. *The Language Instinct.* Penguin, 1994.

Sinclair, H. "Sensorimotor action patterns as the condition for the acquisition of syntax," in R. Huxley and E. Ingrams, eds., *Language Acquisition: Models and Methods,* 121–136. Academic Press, 1971.

Skinner, B. F. *Verbal Behavior.* Appleton-Century-Crofts, 1957.

Tomasello, M. *The New Psychology of Language: Cognitive and Functional Approaches.* Cambridge University Press, 1998.

**TWO** EXPERIMENTAL PARADIGMS FOR STUDYING LANGUAGE ACQUISITION

Albin, D. D., and C. H. Echols. Stressed and word-final syllables in infant-directed speech. *Infant Behavior and Development* 19 (1996): 401–418.

Aslin, R. N. "Segmentation of fluent speech into words: learning models and the role of maternal input," in B. de Boysson-Bardies, S. de Schonen, P. Jusczyk, P. MacNeilage, and J. Morton, eds., *Developmental*

*Neurocognition: Speech and Face Processing in the First Year,* 305–316. Kluwer, 1992.

Berko-Gleason, J. The child's learning of English morphology. *Word* 14 (1958): 150–177.

Bever, T. G. "The cognitive basis for linguistic structures," in J. R. Hayes, ed., *Cognition and the Development of Language,* 279–352. Wiley, 1970.

Bloom, L. *Language Development from Two to Three.* Cambridge University Press, 1991.

————. *One Word at a Time.* The Hague: Mouton, 1973.

Brown, R. *A First Language: The Early Stages.* Harvard University Press, 1973.

Brown, R., and C. Hanlon. "Derivational complexity and order of acquisition in child speech," in J. R. Hayes, ed., *Cognition and the Development of Language,* 11–54. Wiley, 1970.

Byrne, B., and E. Davidson. On putting the horse before the cart: exploring conceptual bases of word order via acquisition of a miniature artificial language. *Journal of Memory and Language* 24 (1985): 377–389.

Dale, S., E. Bates, S. J. Reznik, and C. Morisset. The validity of a parent report instrument of child language at 20 months. *Journal of Child Language* 16 (1989): 239–250.

Eimas, P. D., and J. L. Miller. Organisation in the perception of segmental and suprasegmental information by infants. *Infant Behavior and Development* 4 (1981): 395–399.

Ervin-Tripp, S., and C. Mitchell-Kernan, eds., *Child Discourse.* Academic Press, 1977.

Fagan, J. F. Memory in the infant. *Journal of Experimental Child Psychology* 9 (1970): 217–226.

Fenson, L., P. Dale, S. Reznik, D. Thal, E. Bates, J. Hartung, S. Pethick, and J. S. Reilly. *The MacArthur Communicative Development Inventories: User's Guide and Technical Manual.* Singular Publishing Group, 1993.

Fernald, A. Four-month-old infants prefer to listen to motherese. *Infant Behavior and Development* 8 (1985): 181–195.

Fraser, C., U. Bellugi, and R. Brown. Control of grammar in imitation, comprehension and production. *Journal of Verbal Learning and Verbal Behavior* 2 (1963): 121–135.

Gerken, L. A., B. Laudau, and R. E. Remez. Function morphemes in young children's speech perception and production. *Developmental Psychology* 27 (1990): 204–216.

Golinkoff, R. M., K. Hirsh-Pasek, K. M. Cauley, and L. Gordon. The eyes have it: lexical and syntactic comprehension in a new paradigm. *Journal of Child Language* 14 (1987): 23–46.

Hepper, P. G., D. Scott, and S. Shahidullah. Newborn and fetal response to maternal voice. *Journal of Reproduction and Infant Development* 11 (1993): 147–153.

Hesketh, S., A. Christophe, and G. Dehaene Lambertz. Non-nutritive sucking and sentence processing. *Infant Behavior and Development* 20 (1997): 263–269.

Hirsh-Pasek, K., and R. M. Golinkoff. *The Origins of Grammar: Evidence from Early Language Comprehension,* esp. chapter 5. MIT Press, 1996.

Hollich, G. J., K. Hirsh-Pasek, and R. M. Golinkoff. Breaking the language barrier: an emergent coalition model for the origins of word learning. *Monograph of the Society for Research in Child Development* (2000).

Johnson, M. H. *Developmental Cognitive Neuroscience: An Introduction.* London: Blackwell, 1997.

Jusczyk, P. W., A. D. Friederici, J. M. I. Wessels, V. Y. Svenkerud, and A. M. Jusczyk. Infants' sensitivity to the sound patterns of native language words. *Journal of Memory and Language* 32 (1993): 402–420.

Karmiloff-Smith, A. Language and cognitive processes from a developmental perspective. *Language and Cognitive Processes* 1 (1985): 60–85.

Kutas, M., and S. A. Hillyard. "Event-related potentials in cognitive science," in M. S. Gazzaniga, ed., *Handbook of Cognitive Neuroscience,* 387–410. Plenum Publishing Corporation, 1984.

Lecanuet, J. P., W. P. Fifer, N. A. Krasnegor, and W. P. Smotherman, eds., *Fetal Development: A Psychobiological Perspective.* Lawrence Erlbaum Associates, 1995.

Lempert, H. Animacy constraints on preschool children's acquisition of syntax. *Child Development* 60 (1989): 237–245.

MacWhinney, B., and C. Snow. The Child Language Data Exchange System (CHILDES). *Journal of Child Language* 12 (1985): 271–295. CHILDES web sites: http://childes.psy.cmu.edu/ (United States); http://atila-www.uia.ac.be/childes (Europe); and http://jchat.sccs.chukyo-u.ac.jp (Japan).

Mandler, J. M., and N. S. Johnson. Remembrance of things parsed: story structure and recall. *Cognitive Psychology* 9 (1977): 111–151.

McDonald, J. L., J. K. Bock, and M. H. Kelly. Word and world order: semantic, phonological and metrical determinants of serial position. *Cognitive Psychology* 25 (1993): 188–230.

Mehler, J., J. Bertoncini, M. Barriere, and D. Jassik-Gerschenfeld. Infant recognition of mother's voice. *Perception* 7 (1978): 491–497.

Molfese, D. L. "Event related potentials and language precesses," in A. W. K. Gaillard and W. Ritter, eds., *Tutorials in ERP Research: Endogenous Components,* 345–368. North Holland Publishing, 1983.

Nazzi, T., D. G. Kemler Nelson, P. W. Jusczyk, and A. M. Jusczyk. Six-month-olds' detection of clauses in continuous speech: effects of prosodic well-formedness. *Infancy* 1 (2000): 123–147.

Neville, H. J. "Neurobiology of cognitive and language processing: effects of early experience," in K. Gibson and A. C. Petersen, eds., *Brain Maturation and Behavioral Development: Biosocial Dimensions: Cognitive Development: Comparative and cross-cultural dimensions*, 355–380. Aldine Grutyer Press, 1991.

Preez, P. du. Units of information in the acquisition of language. *Language and Speech* 17 (1974): 369–376.

Skinner, B. F. *Verbal Behavior*. Appleton-Century-Crofts, 1957.

Slobin, D. I., and C. A. Welsh. "Elicited imitation as a research tool in developmental psycholinguistics," in C. A. Rerguson and D. I. Slobin, eds., *Studies of Child Language Development*, 485–496. Holt, Rhinehart & Winston, 1973.

Smyth, R. Conceptual perspective-taking and children's interpretation of pronouns in reported speech. *Journal of Child Language* 22 (1995): 171–187.

Stein, N. L., and E. R. Albro. The emergence of narrative understanding: evidence for rapid learning in personally relevant contexts. *Issues in Education* 2 (1996): 83–98.

Tyler, L. K. *Spoken Language Comprehension: An Experimental Approach to Normal and Disordered Processing*. MIT Press, 1992.

Ullman, M. T. Acceptability ratings of regular and irregular past tense forms: evidence for a dual-system model of language from word frequency and phonological neighborhood effects. *Language and Cognitive Processes* 14 (1999): 47–67.

**THREE** SPEECH PERCEPTION IN AND OUT OF THE WOMB

Aslin, R. N., J. R. Saffran, and E. L. Newport. Computation of conditional probability statistics by 8-month-old infants. *Psychological Science* 9 (1998): 321–324.

Bijeljac-Babic, R., J. Bertoncini, and J. Mehler. How do 4-day-old infants categorize multisyllabic utterances? *Developmental Psychology* 29, no. 4 (1993): 711–721.

Bosch, L., and N. Sebastián-Gallés. Native-language recognition abilities in 4-month-old infants from monolingual and bilingual environments. *Cognition* 65 (1997): 33–69.

Bruner, J. S. From communication to language: a psychological perspective. *Cognition* 3 (1975): 255–287.

Christophe, A., and J. Morton. Is Dutch native English? *Developmental Science* 1 (1998): 215–220.

DeCasper, A. J., and W. P. Fifer. Of human bonding: newborns prefer their mothers' voices. *Science* 208 (1980): 1174–1176.

Eimas, P. D., and J. L. Miller. Organization in the perception of speech by young infants. *Psychological Science* 3 (1992): 340–345.

Goodsitt, J. V., J. L. Morgan, and P. K. Kuhl. Perceptual strategies in prelingual speech segmentation. *Journal of Child Language* 20 (1993): 229–252.

Hepper, P. G., D. Scott, and S. Shahidullah. Newborn and fetal response to maternal voice. *Journal of Reproduction and Infant Development* 11 (1993): 147–153.

Jusczyk, P. W., A. D. Friederici, J. M. I. Wessels, V. Y. Svenkerud, and A. M. Jusczyk. Infants' sensitivity to the sound patterns of native language words. *Journal of Memory and Language* 32 (1993): 402–420.

Kuhl, P. K. "Perception, cognition, and the ontogenetic and phylogenetic emergence of human speech," in S. Brauth, W. Hall, and R. Dooling, eds., *Plasticity of Development*, 73–106. MIT Press, 1991.

Mehler, J., P. Jusczyk, G. Lambertz, N. Halsted, J. Bertoncini, and C. Amiel-Tison. A precursor of language acquisition in young infants. *Cognition* 29 (1988): 143–178.

Moon, C., R. Panneton Cooper, and W. P. Fifer. Two-day-olds prefer their native language. *Infant Behavior and Development* 16 (1993): 495–500.

Morgan, J. L., and J. R. Saffran. Emerging integration of sequential and suprasegmental information in preverbal speech segmentation. *Child Development* 66 (1995): 911–936.

Nazzi, T., J. Bertoncini, and J. Mehler. Language discrimination by newborns: towards an understanding of the role of rhythm. *Journal of Experimental Psychology: Human Perception and Performance* 24 (1998): 756–766.

Schatz, M. Children's comprehension of question-directives. *Journal of Child Language* 5 (1978): 39–46.

Schieffelin, B. B. A developmental study of pragmatic appropriateness of word order and case marking in Kaluli. *Behavioral Development Monograph*, 1981.

Shahidullah, S., and P. G. Hepper. The developmental origins of fetal responsiveness to an acoustic stimulus. *Journal of Reproduction and Infant Psychology* 11 (1993): 135–142.

Spence, M. J., and M. S. Freeman. Newborn infants prefer the maternal low-pass filtered voice, but not the maternal whispered voice. *Infant Behavior and Development* 19 (1996): 199–212.

Werker, J. F., and J. E. Pegg. "Infant speech perception and phonological acquisition," in C. Ferguson, L. Menn, and C. Stoel-Gammon, eds.,

*Phonological Development: Models, Research, Implications.* York Press, 1992.

FOUR   LEARNING ABOUT THE MEANING OF WORDS

Baldwin, D. A. Early referential understanding: infants' ability to recognize referential acts for what they are. *Developmental Psychology* 29 (1993): 832–843.

Barrett, M. "Early lexical development," in P. Fletcher and B. MacWhinney, eds., *The Handbook of Child Language,* 362–392. Blackwell, 1995.

Berthoud-Papandropoulou, I. "An experimental study of children's ideas about language," in A. Sinclair, R. J. Jarvella, and W. J. M. Levelt, eds., *The Child's Conception of Language,* 55–64. Springer-Verlag, 1978.

Bialystok, E. "Metalinguistic awareness: the development of children's representations of language," in C. Pratt and A. F. Garton, eds., *Systems of Representation in Children: Development and Use,* 211–234. John Wiley & Sons, 1993.

Bloom, P., and L. Markson. Intention and analogy in children's naming of pictorial representations. *Psychological Science* 9 (1998): 200–204.

Bornstein, M. H., M. O. Haynes, and K. M. Painter. Sources of child vocabulary competence: a multivariate model. *Journal of Child Language* 25 (1998): 367–393.

Bowerman, M., and S. C. Levinson, eds. *Language Acquisition and Conceptual Development.* Cambridge University Press (2000).

Bruner, J. *Child's Talk: Learning to Use Language.* Norton, 1983.

Carey, S. "The child as word learner," in M. Halle, J. Bresnan, and G. A. Miller, eds., *Linguistic Theory and Psychological Reality,* 264–293. MIT Press, 1978.

Carey, S., and E. Bartlett. Acquiring a single new word. *Proceedings of the Stanford Child Language Conference* 15 (1978): 17–29.

Clark, E. *The Lexicon in Acquisition.* Cambridge University Press, 1993.

Corrigan, R. Cognitive correlates in language: differential criteria yield differential results. *Child Development* 50 (1979): 617–631.

Crystal, D. *The English Language.* Penguin, 1988.

———. *Language Play.* Penguin, 1998.

Dromi, E. *Early Lexical Development.* Cambridge University Press, 1987.

Fenson, L., P. Dale, S. Reznik, D. Thal, E. Bates, J. Hartung, S. Pethick, and J. S. Reilly. *The MacArthur Communicative Development Inventories: User's Guide and Technical Manual.* Singular Publishing Group, 1993.

Ferguson, C. A. Baby talk in six languages. *American Anthropologist* 66 (1964): 103–113.

Fletcher, P., and B. MacWhinney, eds. *The Handbook of Child Language.* Blackwell, 1995.

Golinkoff, R. M., C. B. Mervis, and K. Hirsh-Pasek. Early object labels: the case for a developmental lexical principles framework. *Journal of Child Language* 21 (1994): 125–155.

Gopnik, A., and A. N. Meltzoff. Semantic and cognitive development in 15- to 21-month-old children. *Journal of Child Language* 11 (1984): 495–513.

Hardy-Brown, K, and R. Plomin. Infant communicative development: evidence from adoptive and biological families for genetic and environmental influences on rate differences. *Developmental Psychology* 21 (1985): 378–385.

Heath, S. B. Oral and literate traditions among black Americans living in poverty. *American Psychologist* 44 (1989): 367–373.

Hollich, G. J., K. Hirsh-Pasek, and R. M. Golinkoff. Breaking the language barrier: an emergent coalition model for the origins of word learning. *Monograph of the Society for Research in Child Development* (2000).

Howard, G. *The Good English Guide: English Useage in the 1990s.* Macmillan, 1993.

Karmiloff-Smith, A., J. Grant, M-C. Jones, K. Sims, and P. Cuckle. Rethinking metalinguistic awareness: representing and accessing what counts as a word. *Cognition* 58 (1996): 197–219.

Katz, N., E. Baker, and J. Macnamara. What's in a name? A study of how children learn common and proper names. *Child Development* 45 (1974): 469–473.

Keil, F. C. Constraints on knowledge and cognitive development. *Psychological Review* 88 (1981): 197–227.

Keil, F. C., and N. Batterman. A characteristic-to-defining shift in the development of word meaning. *Journal of Verbal Learning and Verbal Behavior* 23 (1984): 221–236.

MacNamara, J. The cognitive basis of language learning in children. *Psychological Review* 79 (1972): 1–13.

Marchman, V., and E. Bates. Continuity in lexical and morphological development: a test of the critical mass hypothesis. *Journal of Child Language* 21 (1994): 339–366.

Markman, E. M. *Categorization and Naming in Children.* MIT Press, 1989.

McShane, J. *Cognitive Development: An Information Processing Approach.* Blackwell, 1991.

Menyuk, P., J. Liebergott, M. Schultz, M. Chesnick, and L. Ferrier. Patterns of early lexical and cognitive development in premature and full term infants. *Journal of Speech and Hearing Research* 34 (1991): 88–94.

Mervis, C. B., and J. Bertrand. "Acquisition of early object labels: the roles of operating principles and input," in A. P. Kaiser and D. B. Gray, eds., *Enhancing Children's Communication: Research Foundations for Intervention*, 287–316. Paul H. Brookes Publishing, 1993.

Messer, D. J. *The Development of Communication from Social Interaction to Language*. New York: Wiley, 1994.

Naigles, L., and E. Hoff-Ginsberg. Why are some verbs learned before other verbs? Effects on input frequency and structure on children's early verb use. *Journal of Child Language* 25 (1998): 95–120.

Nelson, K. "The dual category problem in the acquisition of action words," in M. Tomasello and W. E. Merriman, eds., *Beyond Names for Things: Young Children's Acquisition of Verbs*, 223–250. Lawrence Erlbaum Associates, 1995.

————. *Language in Cognitive Development: The Emergence of the Mediated Mind*. Cambridge University Press, 1996.

Nippold, M. *Later Language Development*, 2d ed. Pro-Ed, 1998.

Ochs, E., and B. Schieffelin. "The impact of language socialization on grammatical development," in P. Fletcher and B. MacWhinney, eds., *The Handbook of Child Language*, 73–94. Blackwell, 1995.

Oller, K., and R. Eilers. The role of audition in infant babbling. *Child Development* 59 (1988): 441–449.

Plomin, R. Genetic change and continuity from fourteen to twenty months: The MacArthur Longitudinal Twin Study. *Child Development* 64, no. 5 (1993) 1354–1376.

Plunkett, K. "Connectionist approaches to language acquisition," in P. Fletcher and B. MacWhinney, eds., *The Handbook of Child Language*, 36–72. Blackwell, 1995.

Romaine, S. *The Language of Children and Adolescents: The Acquisition of Communicative Competence*. Blackwell, 1984.

Saffran, J. R., E. L. Newport, and R. N. Aslin. Word segmentation: the role of distributional cues. *Journal of Memory and Language* 35 (1996): 606–621.

Saussure, F. de. *Cours de Linguistique Général*. France: Payot, 1916.

Schatz, M. *A Toddler's Life: Becoming a Person*. Oxford University Press, 1994.

Schieffelin, B. B. "Do different worlds mean different words? An example from Papua New Guinea," in S. U. Philipps, S. Steele, et al., *Language, Gender, and Sex in Comparative Perspective: Studies in the Social and Cultural Foundations of Language*, 249–260. Cambridge University Press, 1987.

Schieffelin, B. B., and E. Ochs. *Language Socialization across Cultures*. Cambridge University Press, 1986.

Schwartz, R., and L. B. Leonard. Do children pick and choose? An examination of phonological selection and avoidance in early lexical acquisition. *Journal of Child Language* 9 (1982): 319–336.

Slobin, D. I. "Crosslinguistic evidence for the language-making capacity," in D. I. Slobin, ed., *The Crosslinguistic Study of Language Acquisition*, vol. 2: *Theoretical Issues*, 1157–1256. Lawrence Erlbaum Associates, 1985.

Slobin, D. I., J. Gerhardt, A. Kyratzis, and I. Guo-Jiansheng, eds. *Social Interaction, Social Context, and Language: Essays in Honor of Susan Ervin-Tripp*. Lawrence Erlbaum Associates, 1996.

Snow, C. E. "The conversational context of language acquisition," in R. Campbell and P. Smith, eds., *Recent Advances in the Psychology of Language: Language Development and Mother-Child Interaction*, vol. 4A, 253–270. Plenum Press, 1978.

Swingley, D., J. P. Pinto, and A. Fernald. Continuous processing in word recognition at 24 months. *Cognition* 71 (1999): 73–108.

Tyler, L. K., and W. D. Marslen-Wilson. Children's processing of spoken language. *Journal of Verbal Learning and Verbal Behavior* 20 (1981): 400–416.

Waxman, S. R., and T. D. Kosowski. Nouns mark category relations: toddlers' and preschoolers' word-learning biases. *Child Development* 61 (1990): 1461–1473.

## FIVE  BECOMING A GRAMMATICAL BEING

Akhtar, N., and M. Tomasello. Young children's productivity with word order and verb morphology. *Developmental Psychology* 33 (1997): 952–965.

Atkinson, M. *Children's Syntax: An Introduction to Principles and Parameters Theory*. Blackwell, 1992.

Bates, E., P. S. Dale, and D. Thal. "Individual differences and their implications for theories of language development," in P. Fletcher and B. MacWhinney, eds., *The Handbook of Child Language*, 96–151. Blackwell, 1995.

Bates, E., and B. MacWhinney. "Functionalism and the competition model," in B. MacWhinney and E. Bates, eds., *The Crosslinguistic Study of Sentence Processing*, 3–76. Cambridge University Press, 1989.

Berthoud-Papandropoulou, I. "An experimental study of children's ideas about language," in A. Sinclair, R. J. Jarvella, and W. J. M. Levelt, eds., *The Child's Conception of Language*, 55–64. Springer-Verlag, 1978.

Bever, T. G. "The cognitive basis for linguistic structures," in J. R. Hayes, ed., *Cognition and the Development of Language*, 279–352. Wiley, 1970.

Bloom, L. *Language Development: Form and Function in Emerging Grammars.* MIT Press, 1970.

Bloom, P. Controversies in language acquisition: word learning and the part of speech. *Perceptual and Cognitive Development* 1 (1996): 151–184.

——. Syntactic distinction in child language. *Journal of Child Language* 17 (1990): 343–356.

Braine, M. D. S. Children's first word combinations. *Monographs of the Society for Research in Child Development* 41, ser. 164 (1976).

Brown, R. *A First Language: The Early Stages.* Harvard University Press, 1973.

Bruner, J. From communication to language: a psychological perspective. *Cognition* 3 (1975): 255–287.

Chomsky, N. *Knowledge of Language.* Praeger, 1985.

——. *Lectures on Government and Binding.* Foris, 1981.

——. *The Minimalist Program.* MIT Press, 1995.

——. "A review of B. F. Skinner's 'Verbal Behavior,'" in J. A. Fodor and J. J. Katz, eds., *The Structure of Language: Readings in the Philosophy of Language,* 547–578. Prentice Hall, 1964.

Cook, V. J. *Chomsky's Universal Grammar: An Introduction.* Blackwell, 1989.

Crain, S., and D. Lillo-Martin. *An Introduction to Linguistic Theory and Language Acquisition.* Blackwell, 1999.

De Villiers, J. G., and P. A. De Villiers. "The acquisition of English dative and passive," in D. I. Slobin, ed., *The Crosslinguistic Study of Language Acquisition,* vol. 1, 27–140. Lawrence Erlbaum Associates, 1985.

Elman, J. L., E. Bates, M. H. Johnson, A. Karmiloff-Smith, D. Parisi, and K. Plunkett. *Rethinking Innateness: A Connectionist Perspective on Development.* MIT Press, 1996.

Farrar, M. J. Discourse and the acquisition of grammatical morphemes. *Journal of Child Language* 17 (1990): 607–624.

Fernald, A., and R. McRoberts. "Prosodic bootstrapping: a critical analysis of the argument and the evidence," in J. L. Morgan and K. Demuth, eds., *Signal to Syntax: Bootstrapping from Speech to Grammar in Early Acquisition,* 365–388. Lawrence Erlbaum Associates, 1996.

Gallaway, C., and B. Richards, eds. *Input and Interaction in Language Acquisition.* Cambridge University Press, 1994.

Gerken, L. A. Young children's representation of prosodic phonology: evidence from English-speaker's weak syllable omissions. *Journal of Memory and Language* 1 (1994): 19–38.

Gerken, L. A., B. Landau, and R. E. Remez. Function morphemes in young children's speech perception and production. *Developmental Psychology* 27 (1990): 204–216.

Gleitman, L. R. The structural sources of verb meanings. *Language Acquisition* 1 (1990): 3–55.

Gopnik, A., and A. N. Meltzoff. Relations between semantic and cognitive development in the one-word stage: The specificity hypothesis. *Child Development* 57 (1986): 1040–1053.

Hirsh-Pasek, K., and R. M. Golinkoff. *The Origins of Grammar: Evidence from Early Language Comprehension.* MIT Press, 1996.

Hoff-Ginsberg, E. Function and structure in maternal speech: their relation to the child's development of syntax. *Developmental Psychology* 22 (1986): 155–163.

———. Maternal speech and the child's development of syntax: a further look. *Journal of Child Language* 17 (1990): 85–99.

Hoff-Ginsberg, E., and M. Schatz. Linguistic input and the child's acquisition of language. *Psychological Bulletin* 92 (1982): 3–26.

Hyams, N. M. *Language Acquisition and the Theory of Parameters.* Reidel, 1986.

Jusczyk, P. W., K. Hirsh-Pasek, D. G. Kemler-Nelson, K. Kennedy, A. Woodward, and J. Piwoz. Perception of acoustic correlates of major phrasal boundaries by young infants. *Cognitive Psychology* 24 (1992): 252–293.

Karmiloff-Smith, A. *Beyond Modularity: A Developmental Perspective on Cognitive Science.* MIT Press, 1992.

———. *A Functional Approach to Child Language.* Cambridge University Press, 1979.

Kemler Nelson, D. G., K. Hirsh-Pasek, P. W. Jusczyk, and K. Wright Cassidy. How the prosodic cues in motherese might assist language learning. *Journal of Child Language* 16 (1989): 53–68.

Kemler Nelson, D. G., P. W. Jusczyk, D. R. Mandel, J. Myers, A. Turk, and L. Gerken. The head-turn preference procedure for testing auditory perception. *Infant Behavior and Development* 18 (1995): 111–116.

Landau, B., and L. Gleitman. *Language and experience: Evidence from the blind child.* Harvard University Press, 1985.

Lieven, E. V. M. "Crosslinguistic and crosscultural aspects of language addressed to children," in C. Gallaway and B. Richards, eds., *Input and Interaction in Language Acquisition,* 56–73. Cambridge University Press, 1994.

Lieven, E. V. M., J. M. Pine, and G. Baldwin. Positional learning and early grammatical development. *Journal of Child Language* 24 (1997): 187–219.

MacNamara, J., and G. E. Reyes, eds. *The Logical Foundations of Cognition.* Oxford University Press, 1994.

MacWhinney, B., E. Bates, and R. Kliegl. Cue validity and sentence interpretation in English, German and Italian. *Journal of Verbal Learning and Verbal Behavior* 23 (1984): 127–150.

Mandel, D. R., P. W. Jusczyk, and D. G. Kemler Nelson. Does sentential prosody help infants organize and remember speech information? *Cognition* 53 (1994): 155–180.

Mandel, D. R., D. G. Kemler Nelson, and P. W. Jusczyk. Infants remember the order of words in a spoken sentence. *Cognitive Development* 11 (1996): 181–196.

Mandler, J. M. How to build a baby II: Conceptual primitives. *Psychological Review* 99, no. 4 (1992): 587–604.

Marchman, V. Constraints on plasticity in a connectionist model of the English past tense. *Journal of Cognitive Neuroscience* 5, no. 2 (1993): 215–234.

Marcus, G. F. Negative evidence in language acquisition. *Cognition* 46 (1993): 53–85.

Marcus, G. F., M. Ullman, S. Pinker, M. Hollander, T. J. Rosen, and F. Xu. Overregularization in language acquisition. *Monographs of the Society for Research in Child Development* 57, no. 228 (1992).

Marcus, G. F., S. Vijayan, S. B. Rao, and P. M. Vishton. Rule learning by seven-month-old infants. *Science* 283 (1999): 77–80.

Meisel, J. M. "Parameters in acquisition," in P. Fletcher and B. MacWhinney, eds., *The Handbook of Child Language*. Blackwell, 1995.

Messer, D. J. *The Development of Communication from Social Interaction to Language*. New York: Wiley, 1994.

Morgan, J. L., and K. Demuth, eds. *Signal to Syntax: Bootstrapping from Speech to Grammar in Early Acquisition*. Lawrence Erlbaum Associates, 1996.

Nelson, K. Individual differences in language development. *Developmental Psychology* 17 (1981): 170–187.

———. Some attributes of adjectives used by young children. *Cognition* 4 (1976): 13–30.

Ochs, E., and B. Schieffelin. "The impact of language socialization on grammatical development," in P. Fletcher and B. MacWhinney, eds., *The Handbook of Child Language*, 73–94. Blackwell, 1995.

Peters, A. "Language segmentation: operating principles for the perception and analysis of language," in D. I. Slobin, ed., *The Crosslinguistic Study of Language Acquisition*, vol. 2: *Theoretical Issues*. Lawrence Erlbaum Associates, 1985.

Pettito, L. A. On the evidence for linguistic abilities in signing apes. *Brain and Language* 8 (1979): 162–183.

Piaget, J. *The Language and Thought of the Child*. Routledge & Kegan Paul, 1955.

Pine, J. Reanalysing rote-learned phrases: individual differences in the transition to multi-word speech. *Journal of Child Language* 20 (1993): 551–571.

Pinker, S. "The bootstrapping problem in language acquisition," in M. MacWhinney, ed., *Mechanisms of Language Acquisition,* 399–442. Lawrence Erlbaum Associates, 1987.

———. *The Language Instinct.* Penguin, 1994.

———. *Language Learnability and Language Development.* Harvard University Press, 1984.

Plunkett, K. "Connectionist approaches to language acquisition," in P. Fletcher and B. MacWhinney, eds., *The Handbook of Child Language,* 36–72. Blackwell, 1995.

Richards, B. J. *Language Development and Individual Differences: A Study of Auxiliary Verb Learning.* Cambridge University Press, 1990.

Richards, B. J., and P. Robinson. Environmental correlates of child copula verb growth. *Journal of Child Language* 20 (1993): 243–362.

Schieffelin, B. B. A developmental study of pragmatic appropriateness of word order and case marking in Kaluli. *Behavioral Development Monograph,* 1981.

Sinclair, H. "Sensorimotor action patterns as the condition for the acquisition of syntax," in R. Huxley and E. Ingrams, eds., *Language Acquisition: Models and Methods,* 121–135. Academic Press, 1971.

Slobin, D. I. "Cognitive prerequisites for the development of grammar," in C. A. Rerguson and D. I. Slobin, eds., *Studies of Child Language Development,* 175–276. Holt, Rhinehart & Winston, 1973.

———, ed. *The Crosslinguistic Study of Language Acquisition,* vol. 2: *Theoretical Issues.* Lawrence Erlbaum Associates, 1985.

Snow, C. E. "Beginning from baby talk: twenty years of research on input in interaction," in C. Gallaway and B. Richards, eds., *Input and Interaction in Language Acquisition,* 3–12. Cambridge University Press, 1994.

———. "Mothers' speech research: from input to acquisition," in C. E. Snow and C. A. Ferguson, eds., *Talking to Children: Language Input and Acquisition,* 31–50. Cambridge University Press, 1977.

Snow, C. E., and C. A. Ferguson, eds., *Talking to Children: Language Input and Acquisition.* Cambridge University Press, 1977.

Thomas, M. S. C., and A. Karmiloff-Smith. Modelling language acquisition in atypical phenotypes. Submitted.

Tomasello, M. Do young children have adult syntactic competence? *Cognition* 74 (2000): 209–253.

———. *First Verbs: A Case Study of Early Grammatical Development.* Cambridge University Press, 1992.

————. Language is not an instinct. *Cognitive Development* 10 (1995): 131–156.

————. The return of constructions. *Journal of Child Language* 25 (1998): 431–442.

Uriagereka, J. *Rhyme and Reason: An Introduction to Minimalist Syntax.* MIT Press, 1998.

Valian, V. Syntactic categories in the speech of young children. *Developmental Psychology* 22 (1986): 562–579.

**SIX  BEYOND THE SENTENCE**

Bamberg, M. *The Acquisition of Narratives: Learning to Use Language.* Mouton de Gruyter, 1987.

————, ed. *Narrative Development: Six Approaches.* Lawrence Erlbaum Associates, 1997.

Berman, R. A., and D. I. Slobin. *Relating Events in Narrative: A Crosslinguistic Developmental Study.* Lawrence Erlbaum Associates, 1994.

Bruner, J. *Child's Talk: Learning to Use Language.* Norton, 1983.

Dunbar, R. I. M. Coevolution of neocortical size, group size and language in humans. *Behavioral and Brain Sciences* 16 (1993): 681–735.

Gallaway, C., and B. Richards, eds. *Input and Interaction in Language Acquisition.* Cambridge University Press, 1994.

Gernsbacher, M., and T. Givon, eds. *Coherence in Conversational Interaction.* J. Benjamins, 1995.

Halliday, M. A. K. *Learning How to Mean.* Arnold, 1975.

Johnson, N. S., and J. M. Mandler. A tale of two structures: underlying and surface forms in stories. *Poetics* 9 (1980): 51–86.

Karmiloff-Smith, A. Language and cognitive processes from a developmental perspective. *Language and Cognitive Processes* 1 (1985): 60–85.

Kuczaj, S. A., ed. *Discourse Development.* Springer-Verlag, 1984.

Lieven, E. V. M. "Turn taking and pragmatics: two issues in early child language," in R. N. Campbell and P. T. Smith, eds., *Recent Advances in the Psychology of Language: Language Development and Mother-Child Interaction,* vol. 4B, 215–236. Plenum Press, 1978.

Siegal, M. *Knowing Children: Experiments in Conversation and Cognition.* Lawrence Erlbaum Associates, 1990.

Stein, N. L. "Building complexity and coherence: children's use of goal-structured knowledge in telling stories," in M. G. W. Bamberg, ed., *Narrative Development: Six Approaches,* 5–44. Lawrence Erlbaum Associates, 1997.

————. "The development of children's storytelling skill," in M. Franklin and S. Barten, eds., *Child Language: A Reader,* 282–279. Oxford University Press, 1988.

### SEVEN   ATYPICAL LANGUAGE DEVELOPMENT

Bates, E., and D. Thal. "Associations and dissociations in child language development," in J. Miller, ed., *Research on Child Language Disorders: A Decade of Progress,* 145–168. Pro-Ed, 1991.

Bates, E., D. Thal, B. L. Finlay, and B. Clancy. Early language development and its neural correlates. In F. Boller and J. Grafman (ser. eds.) and I. Rapin and S. Segalowitz (vol. eds.), *Handbook of Neuropsychology,* vol. 7: *Child Neurology,* 2d ed. Elsevier (in press).

Bates, E., D. Thal, D. Trauner, L. Fenson, D. Aram, J. Eisele, and R. Nass. From first words to grammar in children with focal brain injury. In D. Thal and J. Reilly, eds., *Developmental Neuropsychology* 13, no. 3 (Special issue on origins of communication disorders) (1997): 275–343.

Bellugi, U., P. P. Wang, and T. Jernigan. "Williams Syndrome: an unusual neuropsychological profile," in S. H. Broman and J. Grafman, eds., *Atypical Cognitive Deficit in Developmental Disorders: Implications for Brain Function,* 23–56. Lawrence Erlbaum Associates, 1994.

Bishop, D. V. M. *Uncommon Understanding: Development and Disorders of Language Comprehension in Children.* Psychology Press, 1997.

Conti-Ramsden, G. "Language interaction with atypical language learners," in C. Gallaway and B. Richards, eds., *Input and Interaction in Language Acquisition,* 185–190. Cambridge University Press, 1994.

Fowler, A. E. "Language in mental retardation: associations with and dissections from general cognition," in J. A. Burack, R. M. Hodapp, and E. Zigler, *Handbook of Mental Retardation and Development,* 290–333. Cambridge University Press, 1998.

Goldin-Meadow, S., and H. Feldman. The development of language-like communication without a language model. *Science* 197 (1977): 401–403.

Gopnik, M. Feature-blind grammar and dysphasia. *Nature* 344 (1990): 715–717.

Grant, J., A. Karmiloff-Smith, S. E. Gathercole, S. Paterson, P. Howlin, M. Davies, and O. Udwin. Phonological short-term memory and its relationship to language in Williams Syndrome. *Journal of Cognitive Neuropsychiatry* 2, no. 2 (1997): 81–99.

Harris, M. *Language Experience and Early Language Development.* Lawrence Erlbaum Associates, 1992.

Jernigan, T. L., U. Bellugi, E. Sowell, S. Doherty, and J. R. Hesselink. Cerebral morphologic distinctions between Williams and Down syndromes. *Archives of Neurology* 50 (1993): 186–191.

Johnson, M. H. *Developmental Cognitive Neuroscience: An Introduction.* Blackwell, 1997.

Karmiloff-Smith, A. Development itself is the key to understanding developmental disorders. *Trends in Cognitive Sciences* 2 no. 10 (1998): 389–398.

Karmiloff-Smith, A., J. Grant, I. Berthoud, M. Davies, P. Howlin, and O. Udwin. Language and Williams syndrome: how intact is "intact"? *Child Development* 68 (1997): 246–262.

Landau, B., and L. R. Gleitman. *Language and Experience: Evidence from the Blind Child.* Harvard University Press, 1985.

Leonard, L. B. *Children with Specific Language Impairment.* MIT Press, 1998.

Leppänen, P. H. T., and H. Lyytinen. Auditory event-related potentials in the study of developmental language-related disorders. *Audiology & Neuro-Otology* 2 (1997): 308–340.

Locke, J. L. *The Child's Path to Spoken Language.* Harvard University Press, 1993.

McDonald, J. L. Language acquisition: the acquisition of linguistic structure in normal and special populations. *Annual Review of Psychology* 48 (1997): 215–241.

Mervis, C. B., C. A. Morris, J. Bertrand, and B. F. Robinson. "Williams syndrome: findings from an integrated program of research," in H. Tager-Flusberg, ed., *Neurodevelopmental Disorders,* 65–110. MIT Press, 1999.

Neville, H. J., D. L. Mills, and U. Bellugi. "Effects of altered auditory sensitivity and age of language acquisition on the development of language-relevant neural systems: preliminary studies of Williams syndrome," in S. Broman and J. Grafman, eds., *Atypical Cognitive Deficits in Developmental Disorders: Implications for Brain Function,* 67–83. Lawrence Erlbaum Associates, 1994.

Newmeyer, F. J. Genetic dysphasia and linguistic theory. *Journal of Neurolinguistics* 10 (1997): 47–73.

Newport, E. L., and R. P. Meier. "The acquisition of American Sign Language," in D. I. Slobin, ed., *The Crosslinguistic Study of Language Acquisition,* vol. 1, 881–938. Lawrence Erlbaum Associates, 1985.

Oliver, A., M. H. Johnson, A. Karmiloff-Smith, and B. Pennington. Deviations in the emergence of representations: a neuroconstructivist framework for analysing developmental disorders. *Developmental Science* 3 (2000): 1–23.

Paterson, S. J., J. H. Brown, M. K. Gsodl, M. H. Johnson, and A. Karmiloff-

Smith. Cognitive modularity and genetic disorders. *Science* 286, 5448 (1999): 2355–2358.

Pennington B. F., and M. Walsh. "Neuropsychology and developmental psychopathology," in D. Cicchetti and D. J. Cohen, eds., *Developmental Psychopathology*, vol. 1: *Theory and Methods*, 254–290. New York: Wiley, 1995.

Pettito, L. A. On the autonomy of language and gesture: evidence from the acquisition of personal pronouns in American Sign Language. *Cognition* 27 (1987): 1–52.

Pinker, S. *The Language Instinct*. Penguin, 1994.

Plante, E. "Phenotypic variability in brain-behavior studies of specific language impairment," in M. Rice, ed., *Toward a Genetics of Language*, 317–335. Lawrence Erlbaum Associates, 1996.

Rice, M., ed. *Toward a Genetics of Language*. Lawrence Erlbaum Associates, 1996.

Rossen, M. E., S. Klima, U. Bellugi, A. Bihrle, and W. Jones. "Interaction between language and cognition: evidence from Williams syndrome," in J. H. Beitchman, N. J. Cohen, M. M. Konstantareas, and R. Tannock, eds., *Language, Learning, and Behavior Disorders: Developmental, Biological, and Clinical Perspectives*, 367–392. New York: Cambridge University Press, 1996.

Senghas, A., M. Coppola, E. L. Newport, and T. Supalla, "Argument structure in Nicaraguan Sign Language: the emergence of grammatical devices," in E. Hughes, M. Hughes, and A. Greenhill, eds., *Proceedings of the Twenty-first Annual Boston University Conference on Language Development*, vol. 2, 550–561. Cascadilla Press, 1997.

Singer Harris, N. G., U Bellugi, E. Bates, W. Jones, and M. Rossen. Contrasting profiles of language development in children with Williams and Down syndromes. *Developmental Neuropsychology* 13 (1997): 345–370.

Stevens, T., and A. Karmiloff-Smith. Word learning in a special population: do individuals with Williams syndrome obey lexical constraints? *Journal of Child Language* 24 (1997): 737–765.

Suppala, T. "Serial verbs of motion in American Sign Language," in S. D. Fischer and Patricia Siple, eds., *Theoretical Issues in Sign Language Research*, vol. 1: *Linguistics*, 127–152. The University of Chicago Press, 1990.

Tager-Flusberg, H., ed. *Neurodevelopmental Disorders*. MIT Press, 1999.

Tallal, P. Perceptual and linguistic factors in the language impairment of developmental dysphasics: an experimental investigation with the Token Test. *Cortex* 1 (1975): 196–205.

Tallal, P., M. Merzenich, S. Miller, and W. Jenkins. Language learning impairments: integrating basic science, technology and remediation. *Experimental Brain Research* 123 (1998): 210–219.

Thomas, M. S. C. Connectionist models of atypical development and individual differences. In R. J. Sternberg, J. Lautrey, and T. Lubart, eds., *Models of Intelligence for the Next Millenium*. American Psychological Association (in press).

Thomas, M. S. C., J. Grant, M. Gsodl, E. Laing, Z. Barham, L. Lakusta, L. K. Tyler, S. Grice, S. Paterson, and A. Karmiloff-Smith. Can atypical phenotypes be used to fractionate the language system? The case of Williams syndrome. *Language and Cognitive Processes* (in press).

Tyler, L. K., A. Karmiloff-Smith, J. K. Voice, T. Stevens, J. Grant, O. Udwin, M. Davies, and P. Howlin. Do individuals with Williams syndrome have bizarre semantics? Evidence for lexical organization using an online task. *Cortex* 33 (1997): 515–527.

Van der Lely, H. K. J., and M. T. Ullman. Past tense morphology in specifically language-impaired and normally developing children (in press).

**EIGHT**  RETHINKING THE NATURE-NURTURE DEBATE

Bates, E., D. Thal, and J. Janowsky. "Early language development and its neural correlates," in I. Rapin and S. Segalowitz, eds., *Handbook of Neuropsychology*, vol. 7: *Child Neuropsychology*, 69–110. Elsevier, 1992.

Bickerton, D. The language bioprogram hypothesis. *Behavioral and Brain Sciences* 7 (1984): 173–221.

Bjorklund, D. F., and R. G. Schwartz. "The adaptive nature of developmental immaturity: implications for language acquisition and language disabilities," in M. D. Smith and J. S. Damico, *Childhood Language Disorders*, 17–40. Thieme Medical Publishers, 1996.

Butterworth, G. E., and S. Itakura. Development of precision grips in chimpanzees. *Developmental Science* 1 (1998): 39–43.

Gomez, J. C. *The Developing Primate Mind: The Evolution of Cognitive Development*. Developing Child Series, Harvard University Press, forthcoming.

Hauser, M. D. *The Evolution of Communication*. MIT Press, 1996.

Karmiloff, K., and A. Karmiloff-Smith. *Everything Your Baby Would Ask . . . if Only He or She Could Talk*. New York: Golden Books, 1999.

Karmiloff-Smith, A. Development itself is the key to understanding developmental disorders. *Trends in Cognitive Sciences* 2, no. 10 (1998): 389–398.

Kuhl, P. K. "Perception, cognition, and the ontogenetic and phylogenetic emergence of human speech," in S. Brauth, W. Hall, and R. Dooling, eds., *Plasticity of Development*, 73–106. MIT Press, 1991.

Lightfoot, D. The child's trigger experience—Degree 0 learnability. *Behavioral and Brain Sciences* 12 (1995): 498–508.

Locke, J. L., K. E. Berken, L. McMinn-Larson, and D. Wein. Emergent control of manual and vocal-motor activity in relation to the development of speech. *Brain and Language* 51 (1995): 498–508.

Pettito, L. A. "On the ontogenetic requirements for early language acquisition," in B. de Boysson-Bardies, S. de Schonen, P. Jusczyk, P. McNeilage, and J. Morton, eds., *Developmental Neurocognition: Speech and Face Processing in the First Year of Life*, 365–383. Kluwer Academic, 1993.

Savage-Rumbaugh, S. K. McDonald, R. Sevcik, W. Hopkins, and E. Rupert. Spontaneous symbol acquisition and communicative use by pygmy chimpanzees. *Journal of Experimental Psychology: General* 115 (1986): 211–235.

Seidenberg, M. S. "Evidence from great apes concerning the biological bases of language," in W. Demopoulos and A. Marras, eds., *Language Learning and Concept Acquisition: Foundational Issues*, 29–53. Ablex, 1986.

Tomasello, M. *The Cultural Origins of Human Cognition*. Harvard University Press, 1999.